MUSIC, SOCIETY, AGENCY

MUSIC, SOCIETY, AGENCY

Edited by
NANCY NOVEMBER

BOSTON
2023

Library of Congress Cataloging-in-Publication Data

Names: November, Nancy, editor.
Title: Music, society, agency / edited by Nancy November.
Description: Boston : Academic Studies Press, 2023. | Series: Studies in
   the History and Sociology of Music | Includes bibliographical references
   and index.
Identifiers: LCCN 2023041419 (print) | LCCN 2023041420 (ebook) |
   ISBN 9798887193946 (hardback) | ISBN 9798887193953 (adobe pdf) |
   ISBN 9798887193960 (epub)
Subjects: LCSH: Music—Social aspects. | Agent (Philosophy) |
   Music—Performance—Social aspects.
Classification: LCC ML3916 .M87825 2023 (print) | LCC ML3916 (ebook) |
   DDC 306.4/842—dc23/eng/20230922
LC record available at https://lccn.loc.gov/2023041419
LC ebook record available at https://lccn.loc.gov/2023041420

ISBN 9798887193946 (hardback)
ISBN 9798887193953 (adobe pdf)
ISBN 9798887193960 (epub)

Copyright © 2023 Academic Studies Press
All rights reserved

Book design by Tatiana Vernikov
Cover design by Ivan Grave
On the cover: Takū's clan elders and purotu performance specialists (1970s).
   Photographer unknown

Published by Academic Studies Press
1577 Beacon Street
Brookline, MA 02446, USA
press@academicstudiespress.com
www.academicstudiespress.com

Contents

Introduction ... 7
    Nancy November

Part One: Cultural and Cross-Cultural Agencies

The Year the Music Died: Agency in the Context ... 14
of Demise on Takū, Papua New Guinea
    Richard Moyle

His Majesty's Theatre: A Hub of Musical ... 35
and Theatrical Entertainment in Colonial Dunedin
    Sandra Crawshaw

"In the Tiki Tiki Tiki Tiki Tiki Room": ... 55
Musicalizing the South Pacific in Disney's Theme Parks
    Gregory Camp

Part Two: Vocal Music's Agencies

Figaro Transmuted through the Agency of Neapolitan Social ... 74
and Political Creatives: Niccolò Piccinni's *La serva onorata*
    Lawrence Mays

Josephinism and Leopold Koželuh's Masonic Cantata ... 113
Joseph der Menschheit Segen
    Allan Badley

Agency, Politics, and Opera Arrangements ... 136
in Fanny von Arnstein's Salons
    Nancy November

Part Three: Performance and Agency

Reflections on Aladdin's Lamp: Creative Practice Research   156
    in-and-through Historically Informed Performance
> *Imogen Morris*

When Your Heart is Set on Both Broadway and the Met: 174
    An Exploration of Vocal Technique in Contemporary Musical Theatre
> *Christopher McRae*

Part Four: Composition and Agency

Ratner's Topoi and the Cultural Middlebrow   200
    in Britten's First Suite for Cello
> *Eliana Dunford*

Provincializing Practice: Agency and Positionality   222
    in Cross-Cultural Music in Aotearoa New Zealand
> *Celeste Oram*

Contributors   247

Index   250

Introduction

Musicologists have increasingly used a wide-angled lens to study of music in society and explore how it is intertwined with issues of politics, gender, religion, race, psychology, memory, and space. Recent studies of music in connection with society take in a variety of musical phenomena from diverse periods and genres—medieval, classical, opera, rock, and so on. This book not only asks how music and society are, and have been, intertwined and mutually influential, but also examines the agents behind these connections: who determines musical cultures in society? Which social groups are represented in particular musical contexts? Which social groups are silenced or less well represented in music's histories, and why? This volume arose from a conference of the same title, a meeting of the New Zealand Musicological Society, which was held in Auckland, New Zealand in July 2020. Thus there is a strong emphasis on the Pacific. Its four parts explore, in order, cultural and cross-cultural agencies, agencies within vocal music, performance and agency, and agency regarding composition.

Part one, concerning cultural and cross-cultural agencies, is devoted to the Pacific. The first chapter, "The Year the Music Died," documents agency in the context of the diminution over two generations of almost an entire musical culture among the atoll community on Takū in Papua New Guinea. The author, Richard Moyle, has been involved with the community since 1994. In that time Takū has changed from a vibrant island community of 600 people, who sing and dance both contemporary and ancient creations for on average twenty hours each week, to a remnant of 150 residents, occasionally performing mostly imported material. Moyle charts the change from hundreds of locally composed songs boasting of fishing success to a small repertoire of love songs in another language; from long songs acknowledging the presence of ancestors and their help in everyday activities to short dance songs, highly repetitive in both lyrics and movements; from graveside songs forewarning spirits of the imminent arrival of a dead resident in the afterworld to songs asking an ancient foreign deity to comfort the living. He considers how aesthetics and networks of social relationships help define how Takū shape and sustain musical standards, and how they categorize themselves in various sacred and secular circumstances, in and outside the island's ritual arena. Such agency gradually brought about changes in the performing arts and society itself.

Using contemporary newspapers and ephemera collections, Sandra Crawshaw explores the agents responsible for building up His Majesty's Theatre in Dunedin, New Zealand, as a major cultural institution in the early part of the twentieth century and "one of the finest and best-appointed theatres in the colonies." Until John Mansfield Thomson's *The Oxford History of New Zealand Music* was published in 1991, very little had been written about the early days of New Zealand's musical culture. With an "overseas is better" attitude, New Zealanders' agency within music history was often overlooked. In recent years, research has revealed that the cultural and musical life in New Zealand from colonial times onwards was a lot richer and more varied than was previously believed. Many recent studies have focused upon institutions such as New Zealand's national and regional orchestras, chamber music societies, and choral and opera activities, telling fascinating stories of their struggles to become established. His Majesty's Theatre had its beginnings in the agricultural sector, starting life in 1896 as the Agricultural Hall. Funded privately by a group of businessmen and gentlemen farmers, who then took a gamble on the vision of entrepreneur J. C. Williamson, the hall was lavishly refurbished and renamed in 1902. Williamson's wealth and innate business sense gave him influence over what New Zealand audiences came to see, and the new, up-to-date His Majesty's Theatre extended his reach.

The theme of who gets to speak on behalf of a culture is taken up in Gregory Camp's "'In the Tiki Tiki Tiki Tiki Tiki Room: Musicalizing the South Pacific in Disney's Theme Parks." The Walt Disney Company has frequently used the South Pacific as a setting for its various films, television shows, and theme parks. Its use of music in these texts marks the company's attitude (and the attitude they construct for their global audiences) towards the region. Camp examines Disney's construction of South Pacific music in its theme parks as a reflection of the societies in which they operate. In the 1950s and '60s Disney capitalized on the Tiki craze of the time by designing Disneyland's Adventureland largely around American ideas of the "exotic" South Pacific and its music, with attractions ranging from the mostly fictitious version of Pacific music heard in the Enchanted Tiki Room to the somewhat more authentic constructions in the Tahitian Terrace restaurant's floor show (and, later, the similar luau show at Walt Disney World's Polynesian Village Resort). While in more recent Disney films such as *Lilo & Stitch* (2002) and *Moana* (2016) the company has attempted to convey a Pacific soundscape grounded in local musics, giving agency to the people whose stories are told, the theme parks have largely retained their midcentury exoticism. This disconnect between the parks and the films shows this massive multinational corporation caught between nostalgia for '50s pop culture and a desire for authenticity, trying to speak and sing both to and for people in multiple societies around the world.

Part 2 shifts attention from the Pacific to Europe and from the twentieth century to the late eighteenth and early nineteenth centuries. In "Figaro Transmuted through the Agency of Neapolitan Creatives: Niccolò Piccinni's *La serva onorata*," Lawrence Mays discusses how Giambattista Lorenzi and composer Niccolò Piccinni exerted agency. The libretto for *La serva onorata*, premiered in Naples in 1792, is a substantially reworked version of Lorenzo Da Ponte's *Le nozze di Figaro*, which premiered in Vienna in 1786. The Neapolitan king and queen had much contact with Da Ponte in Vienna, and it is likely that they offered his libretto to a local theatre. Lorenzi's engagement to recast the imported text was consistent with the preference of impresarios to employ librettists who knew Neapolitan taste, customs, and dialect. Influences on the authors' creative choices included the expectations of theatre management, performers, and audiences. Although Lorenzi's libretto draws heavily on Da Ponte's, with many points of concurrence and some nearly identical wording, new elements are added and the overall tone is more farcical and at times vulgar, consistent with local preference. Piccinni demonstrates his ability to meld eclectic influences within a circumscribed environment. Mays explores how the librettist and composer, both in the final phases of successful careers, translated a known opera for a particular theatrical milieu. Its enthusiastic reception in Naples was a testament to their artistic choices under various constraints and influences.

Allan Badley takes the setting to Vienna with his "Leopold Koželuh's Masonic Cantata *Joseph der Menschheit Segen* and Josephinism," which discusses how freemasonry affected agency. On 1 September 1783, Koželuh's *Joseph der Menschheit Segen* was performed in Vienna for the first and possibly only time in a ceremony of thanksgiving organized by the Zu den drei Adlern, Zur gekrönten Hoffnung, and Zur Beständigkeit lodges. The early 1780s was a golden age for freemasonry in Vienna. Initially Emperor Joseph II approved of the many practical ways in which the craft involved itself in the education and welfare of the poor. But by 1785 he had become sufficiently alarmed by the rapid growth of freemasonry throughout the Habsburg lands to publish a patent that demanded its radical reorganization; this led to a sharp decline in lodge membership during the late 1780s and increasing suspicion of the movement in general after the outbreak of the French Revolution. This chapter considers *Joseph der Menschheit*

Segen in the context of Habsburg imperial politics of the 1780s and their impact on society, and also examines the incorporation of masonic symbolism in both Leopold Föderl's libretto and Koželuh's score. The composer's arrangement of the work for voices and fortepiano, published in Vienna by Torricella in December 1784, took the work to a wider public, and its handsomely engraved title page includes many masonic symbols that even non-masons would have recognized. To what extent Koželuh endorsed the sentiments expressed in the work is unknown, but the care with which he treated certain aspects of masonic symbolism suggests that he was sincere in his commitment to the craft, and belief in its value as an agent of societal change.

Arrangements of musical works offer a fascinating field for exploring matters of agency within musical culture. Nancy November's chapter "Agency, Politics, and Opera Arrangements in Fanny Arnstein's Salons" stays within the context of Vienna but now in the early nineteenth century, when arrangements of public music flourished in great variety in that city. She asks: what does this culture of musical arrangements tell us about shifting musical and social values and agency in this period, especially as they concern women? Focusing on Fanny von Arnstein in particular, she considers how arrangements offered amateurs agency in terms of education, entertainment, and sociability in the home, and a bridge to public music-making. This was particularly valuable to female amateurs, who otherwise had little say or share in the public spheres of composition, criticism, and orchestral performance. Even when it seemed to offer sheer entertainment or straightforward escapism, private sphere music-making also helped to define musicians' sense of freedom—a freedom of choice regarding what they heard, where they heard it, and how. Here we can already speak of a cultivation of agency, understood as simple autonomy; but arrangements could also assist those who otherwise had no "voice" in the public sphere with talking politics. The chapter zooms in on a salon hosted by Arnstein in which the programming choices, as well as the performance of arrangements, spoke subtly against the politics of Emperor Francis I, implying a perception of him a tyrannical dictator.

Part 3 moves to the topic of performance and agency. Anner Bylsma described the interpretative process used in Historically Informed Performance (HIP) as "Aladdin rubbing his lamp": serendipitous discovery with little to do with historical correctness. In "Reflections on Aladdin's Lamp: Creative Practice Research in-and-through Historically Informed Performance," Imogen Morris explores this process further, with the goal of developing a theoretical framework for conducting Creative Practice Research (CPR) in-and-through HIP. In such research, the agency of the performer-researcher is vital to the research process, allowing the creative practice and insights of the HIP musician—previously considered too subjective to constitute scholarly knowledge—to be recognized and used as valid sources of evidence. She explores the ways performers assimilate historical information into their playing and overcome gaps in scholarly knowledge. The findings reveal that the performer's experience, expertise, and intuition are integral to transforming historical evidence into a convincing performance that moves the emotions of a modern-day audience. This conclusion leads to a concept of "artistic values" in this context: principles that guide how a performer interprets, filters, and even manipulates historical information in their decision-making process.

Artistic decision-making is the subject of Christopher McRae's "When Your Heart is Set on Both Broadway and the Met: An Exploration of Vocal Technique in Contemporary Musical Theater"—this time with regard to contemporary vocal music. Singers today are expected to be able to perform a wide range of repertoire. This is especially true of musical theatre singers, where the array of potential vocal approaches to the repertoire is vast and a singer's vocal choices become a crucial part of performance. The malleability required to widen these choices, along with vocal health and longevity, is important for sustaining a career in musical theatre. Since the integration of the microphone into musical theatre, singers' agency has greatly increased, with a wider palette of viable vocal styles to choose from, using both classical and contemporary paradigms of singing. Current literature on vocal technique tends to focus on only one of these vocal paradigms at a time; few studies explore the crossover of the two. This chapter examines how crossover of vocal choices is achieved and to what the effect. Analyzing the work of notable sopranos Kristin Chenoweth, Audra McDonald, and Kelli O'Hara, all of whom integrate classical vocal choices into contemporary singing, McRae explore the efficacy of stylistic crossover.

Part 4 addresses the agency of composers. While the broad appeal of Benjamin Britten's music did wonders for his popularity with the listening public, his eclectic fusion of "high" modernist elements and more familiar "populist" elements made his work an easy target for the twentieth century's aesthetic purists. Eliana Dunford considers his uneasy agency in "Ratner's Topoi and the Cultural Middlebrow in Britten's First Suite for Cello." For Theodor Adorno, Britten was emblematic of a generation of composers who had "adjusted to mass culture by means of calculated feeble-mindedness," thus surrendering their compositional agency. Commentators such as Clement Greenberg derided Britten's works as counterfeits (albeit highly skillful) of authentic modernist writing. Dunford argues that rather than representing a duplicitous betrayal of modernism's ideals, Britten's synthesis of "high" and "low" elements is a reflection of a growing "middlebrow" culture in postwar Britain.

The context returns to New Zealand in Celeste Oram's "Provincializing Practice: Agency and Positionality in Cross-Cultural Music in Aotearoa New Zealand." Oram surveys and expands some critical tools that contribute to discourse on the fast-growing genre of art music in New Zealand involving classically trained musicians performing together with taonga pūoro (traditional Māori musical instruments) musicians. While Oram's own creative work in this genre has necessitated learning about taonga pūoro, it has equally compelled her to deepen her critical engagement with the Eurological cultures whose influence she regularly negotiates as a composer. Her method departs from recent musicology's focus on high-profile cross-cultural works, looking instead to ecologies of practice. In particular, she argues that, especially in cross-cultural settings, such moments of practice are inevitably compromised and contradictory. So the value of critical reflection on one's own practice is not in defending or exonerating one's creative decisions, but rather in accounting frankly for one's complex positionality as a postcolonial agent.

Nancy November

Part One

Cultural and Cross-Cultural Agencies

The Year the Music Died: Agency in the Context of Demise on Takū, Papua New Guinea

Richard Moyle

In the context of music, agency can influence the mundane and the extraordinary, the secular and the sacred, as individuals and institutions shape their identities while acting within determined social and cultural frameworks. In ethnomusicology, agency can, for example, impact a single dance genre over a broad geographical area,[1] be a political tool within a study of musical beauty or shape the aesthetics of lyric expressivity,[2] and survey an entire nation.[3] Thomas Turino reflects on the agency of individuals[4] and Jeff Todd Titon, providing a broad summary of the term, parses the data by placing it under the heading "the ethnomusicology of,"[5] much in the way that Merriam introduced the phrase "the anthropology of" half a century earlier in order to characterize a particular research process in his own studies of "music in culture."[6]

---

1   Michael Iyanaga, "Why Saints Love Samba: A Historical Perspective on Black Agency and the Rearticulation of Catholicism in Bahia, Brazil," *Black Music Research Journal* 35 (2015): 119–147.

2   Barry Shank, "The Political Agency of Musical Beauty," *American Quarterly* 63 (2011): 831–855; Robert Kauffman, "Lyric's Expression: Musicality, Conceptuality, Critical Agency," *Cultural Critique* 60 (2005): 197–216.

3   Bode Omojola, *Yorùbá Music in the Twentieth Century: Identity, Agency, and Performance Practice* (Rochester: University of Rochester Press, 2014).

4   Thomas Turino, *Music as Social Life: The Politics of Participation* (Chicago: University of Chicago Press, 2006).

5   Jeff Todd Titon, "Music, the Public Interest, and the Practice of Ethnomusicology," *Ethnomusicology* 36 (1992): 315–322.

6   Alan P. Merriam, *The Anthropology of Music* (Evanston: Northwestern University Press, 1964); idem, *Ethnomusicology of the Flathead Indians* (New York: Wenner-Green Foundation for Anthropological Research, 1967).

Using Alfred Gell's definition of agency[7]—a point where the potentially infinite chain of causality is broken and a "beginning" is attributed to a certain entity—it is possible to posit the obverse: just as any change has a forward-looking "first" (or presence), it also has a backward-looking "last" (or absence). It is probably true that, as a matter of course, most ethnomusicological studies mention or analyze the growth and/or decline of specific genres within a culture; and, indeed, the notion of musical life as a static and finite entity "out there" to be "discovered" has been largely overtaken by the view that musical output is a malleable, adaptive entity reflecting the social and cultural agencies that create and sustain it. In Titon's words, it is "shifting, situational and humanly."[8]

Of course, the impact of influential individuals is inversely proportional to the numbers of people under study, and population size also affects the feasibility of attributing performative "firsts" and "lasts" based on direct observation or indirect confirmation. Regardless of the constraints of time and resources, and the size of "the field," as ethnomusicologists we are sometimes faced with the temptation to extrapolate. From our direct experiences and observations, we may ascribe to people un-met and locations un-visited the same musical preferences and practices, attitudes and actions found elsewhere in the community, region, or country as those comprising our empirical data set. It is rare indeed to have extended access to an entire community that is distinguished linguistically and culturally and separated geographically and identifiable musically from its neighbors—a community large enough to be genealogically sustainable, but small enough to be directly observable much of the time; a community agreeable enough not just to tolerate an endlessly inquisitive outsider for month after month, year after year for almost two generations, but also to actively support, in both principle and practice, a research programmed resulting in four books at their own specific request.[9] This chapter examines musical agency at work in such a community—Takū, in Papua New Guinea—which has a population size that accommodates generalizations, particularly first times and last times, because they are directly observable.

---

7   Alfred Gell, *Art and Agency: An Anthropological Theory* (Oxford: Clarendon Press, 1998), 63.
8   Titon, "Music, the Public Interest, and the Practice of Ethnomusicology," 319.
9   See for example, Richard M. Moyle, *Nā Kkai—Takū Musical Fables* (Boroko: Institute for Papua New Guinea Studies, 2004); idem, *Songs from The Second Float / A Musical Ethnography of Takū Atoll, Papua New Guinea*, Pacific Islands Monograph Series 21 (Honolulu: University of Hawaii Press, Center for Pacific Island Studies, 2007); idem, *A Dictionary of Takuu* (Canberra: Pacific Linguistics, 2011); and idem, *Takū Ritual and Belief. Polynesian Religion in Practice* (Adelaide: Crawford House Publishing, 2018).

Elsewhere, I have detailed Takū's checkered history and a population varying wildly within the last two hundred years—from as few as eleven to as many as eight hundred.[10] I have also documented the extraordinary musical output of the adult population, during my fieldwork years, of approximately one hundred and fifty;[11] and how I stopped recording after one thousand songs and shifted towards learning and participating—moving from a passive audience member to an (albeit hesitant) performer, a change that was encouraged and supported.

On any musical occasion, individual Takū may choose to perform or abstain, and thus occupy the category of performer or audience. However, this rather crude division fails to take into account the influence of identity and personality, and creates potential conflicts of interest that arise from numerous coexisting interpersonal relationships and the wishes and expectations of parties in those relationships. Not all performers, for example, may participate happily, willingly, or satisfactorily,[12] and not all audience members are necessarily comfortable being simply passive observers. Putting aside the semantic difficulties of examining performance without an audience, and vice versa, all the personnel present are there as a result of a multiplicity of self-identities and agencies. The situation extends both backward and forward in time, affecting prior acts of creation and learning, as well as future acts of reception and recollection. Much of what occurs, and when and with whom, depends on social linkages.

After compiling and revising genealogies over several years, it became clear to me that most Takū were connected to as many as 30% of the entire community by a number of relationship webs, which, while maintained, were weighted at different times according to different obligations and expectations. Such connections occurred:

- Directly and frequently, with consanguineal kin supplying labour and consumables (fish, garden produce).
- Indirectly but frequently, with affinal kin supplying consumables (fish, garden produce).
- Directly but occasionally, with a single younger community member in a relationship of lifelong guardianship (supplying food, clothing, cash).

---

10 See Moyle, *Songs from The Second Float* and *Takū Ritual and Belief*.
11 I spent most summers on the Polynesian-speaking island (whose language is also called Takū) between 1994 and 2010, when regular shipping stopped, and have maintained contact through social media for the past twelve years.
12 A situation Turino calls "participatory consent" in *Music as Social Life*, 77.

- Directly and frequently with one's fellow clan members, supplying labor and expertise.
- Directly but infrequently with one's clan elder, supplying labor at rituals.
- Directly but infrequently with one's grand-patrilineal kin, to decide the exchange of goods following a death or a bride-wealth presentation.
- Directly but infrequently with one's bilateral kin at a bride-wealth presentation or during the five-day tukumai (grief removal) ritual.[13]

Through such context-dependent means, Takū represent themselves to others both inside and outside their immediate circles of membership.

Only in song lyrics does a Takū resident publicly proclaim himself (the situation is confined to adult males) as an independent individual: for example, in lyrics such as "I returned with my catch of two hundred" and "Sini used the ocean as his garden." And only in song conveyed by a medium does the spirit of a dead individual resident identify themself by name: for example, "Hotu walked alone into the bush in the sacred wind, dancing at dawn" and "[A]s the school

FIGURE 1. Takū's assembled community during day two of a tukumai ritual.
Photograph: Richard Moyle

---

13   See Moyle, "Te Tukumai—Ending the Grief," Vimeo Video, 17:37, June 10, 2015, https://vimeo.com/130386785.

of tuna arrived beyond the channel, Haite's spirit accompanied it."[14] Such self-identifications reflect, in part, Takū aesthetic principles.

The Takū sense of musical aesthetics varies according to song genre, date of composition, and composer. In former times, spirit-originating dance songs, for example, were intended for performance over more than one generation. Moreover, the composer's association (through affiliation) with one of the community's five clans made such songs into precise statements of individual and clan identity required when performing a tukumai ritual for a recently deceased fellow clansperson.[15] Most of these songs—which are still performed—are of the *sau* women's dance genre. Two afternoons of the ritual are devoted to such performances, where personal interpretation is not a local concept: emphasis is on faithfulness to the musical artefact: it must be correct in melody and lyrics, all uttered in unison, and accurate in the synchrony of its dance movements (or roundly criticized if these are absent). An additional reason for close attention to perfection of detail is the unseen, but believed, presence at the performance venue of ancestor spirits; while they are attracted by the sights and sounds, they are also able to inflict punishment on an errant singer or dancer. Indeed, for this reason dancers wear protective amulets. Each song, and each section within each song, has a unique melody.

In contrast, songs composed by the living emphasize—within local conventions—lyric and melodic originality. Most compositions of this kind are *tuki* songs—songs that praise a dead individual and are first performed at the tukumai ritual several months after the death. Until the 1990s, each of the five clans had a patrilineally defined *purotu*—male performance specialist—responsible for both leading the performance of items already in the repertoire and creating new ones on demand. Until the decline of the genre itself two decades later, the deceased's clan and the wider community expected each new tuki to be original, again with an established framework of structure and singing style. Of course, such an arrangement depends on an intergenerational supply of creative sons, and the apparent rigidity of this arrangement proved a weakness as the numbers of purotu declined from five in the 1970s to just one in the 1990s. Understandably, when I visited in the 1990s, the 1970s were regarded by many adults as a kind of golden age for the performing arts.

---

14   See Moyle, *Songs from The Second Float*, chapter 5.
15   Richard M. Moyle, "Keeping It in the family: Ancestral Talkback on Takū," in *Spirit Possession and Communication in Religious and Cultural Contexts*, ed. Caroline Blyth (Oxford: Routledge, 2020), 119–134.

Figure 2. Women dancing a *sau*.
Photograph: Richard Moyle

Tuki song lyrics are intended *ki ahu te tautai* (to praise the master-fisherman) for his exploits in catching *ika tau* (prestige fish), such as pelagic shark, oilfish, and tuna, which in turn depend on the availability of nine-meter ocean-going canoes. Canoe carvers and users combine their skills and experience to provide the island's staple diet of fish, and both categories of men are recognized in tuki songs and routinely praised to the point where history morphs into acceptably loving exaggeration.[16] In the absence of any purotu specialist since 1993, tuki melodies and lyrical phrases became formulaic compositions delegated to less creative clan members. Further reflecting the aesthetic preference for musical novelty, a singing group will attract private criticism if it merely composes new lyrics for an already existing melody.

The island's population peaked in the 1990s during a ten-year civil war when several hundred Takū were forced to return from working on Bougainville Island. All the available housing was filled by almost seven hundred people, but the sea was bountiful enough to feed everyone. Canoe-building intensified, and the two building yards echoed daily with the sound of adzes as drift logs were

---

16 Richard M. Moyle, "Celebrating and Enhancing a Virtual Past through Singing: The Polynesian Community on Takū," in *Performing History: Approaches to History across Musicology*, ed. Nancy November (Boston: Academic Studies Press, 2020), 101–114.

made into hulls and older craft and their gear were repaired. But there were no more remittances from family members working on Bougainville, and local supplies of imported cloth, food, and fishing gear soon ran out.

From around 1996, former Bougainville workers left the island with their families to seek work elsewhere in Papua New Guinea—and few ever returned. Some of those who left were proficient in the large-scale dances each clan owned; others were in line to inherit the dances. Around two hundred people went to find work elsewhere in the country before the new millennium. These developments, as well as the absence of regular shipping in the previous ten years and consequent lack of European food, fishing gear, medicine, and clothing, prompted some expatriate Takū to charter small cargo boats and take away entire families. Most resettled two hundred kilometers away in ad hoc communities near Buka, North Bougainville, where they remain, in less than ideal living conditions.

It has been possible to observe a steady stream of last performances of large-scale dances, which are distinctive in that the formations constitute straight lines and adhere to the following strict protocols: hereditary personal ownership, hereditary dance line leaders, and performances lasting more than twenty minutes. Although these ancient dances were brought to the island and taught by ancestral spirits, and although their performance was maintained to ensure those spirits remained happy and well disposed, all of them were discontinued on the then-owner's death because the rightful next owners—whose presiding presence was a necessary condition—were either untrained or permanently off-island.

Performance of women's *sau* dances, in particular, which are spirit-composed and communicated via a medium, depended on the supportive presence of a small group of elderly women singers, since younger women showed little enthusiasm for participation and no tuition was offered. As progressively fewer knowledgeable women remained on the island, *sau* performance was shortened to a few sections known to the remaining singers, and, as numbers of singers continued to drop, confined to fewer and fewer individual dances.

The tukumai ritual incorporated more than thirty hours of singing and dancing, but by 2006 there were simply not enough people to sustain this duration; and the numbers of new songs composed for the dead declined, while reliance

Figure 3. Senior women singing to accompany a sau dance.
Photograph: Richard Moyle

on the use of existing melodies and stock poetic phrases increased. All of these events are best represented in a timeline:[17]

Year	Event	Population
Fifteenth century (twenty generations of people and three generations of spirits)	The atoll was raised from the ocean and colonized by ancestor spirits; intermarriage with humans produced the first human generations.	c. 20
1616	First European sighting (by Abel Tasman).	unknown

---

17 Details of the events in the table are summarized in Moyle, *Songs from The Second Float*, chapter 1.

1795	(Re)discovery of island by James Mortlock, who named it after himself.	unknown
1843	A reported clash with an American ship harvesting sea cucumbers killed one crew and three Takū. The event was captured in a dance song still popular one hundred and fifty years later.	unknown
1850–60	Foreign ships avoid the island after false rumors of cannibalism.	unknown
1870s	The *ariki* (paramount chief) had no children, so he nominated his adopted son (he had survived drifting from distant Nukumanu Island) as the next titleholder. It is widely believed that that ariki possessed a limited knowledge of Takū ritual procedures and that some lapsed as a result.	n/a
1880s	Smallpox was accidently introduced and the population reduced to a mere twelve.	12
1886	The island was unwittingly sold to a foreigner, Emma Forsayth; foreign plantation workers were introduced; and the indigenous population forcibly relocated to longhouses on a small islet for forty-five years. Some rituals ceased.	unknown
1928	Nukutoa Island on the atoll was bought by an expatriate copra trader, and the population relocated there under conditions favorable to cultural practices and rapid population growth.	110
1928–1961	The sources for an extensive set of population figures appear in Moyle, *Songs from the Second Float / A Musical Ethnography of Takū Atoll, Papua New Guinea*, 19.	110–385

Then followed a further unprecedented event, occurring within living memory and having equally major ramifications:

1963	The first known death off-island of an ariki (from smallpox, on Bougainville Island), creating dread and fear and leading to a temporary breakdown of social order until a regent was appointed.	385

Takū's music genres were not developed for purely musical reasons, but from combinations of social and/or cultural desires: emotional release, the praise of individual achievement in an otherwise egalitarian society, the need to appease ancestors, the wish to assuage among the living fear of the unknown. Such forms of agency can create their own forms of vulnerability. In Takū's case, the lasting uncertainty following the ariki's death had knock-on effects:

1963	The last *tānaki* séance. (A medium would sing a dance song given to them by a recently deceased ancestor, which attendant clan members memorized for performance from a single hearing.) The acting ariki stopped the practice, fearing his ignorance of the protocols would bring widespread harm.	
1963	Last purification ritual for a new mother. This, too, was stopped by the acting ariki out of fear.	
1964	Last formal daylong walking tour around the reefs of the atoll to entertain a principal mourner after a local death. The practice was replaced by a brief walk around the village periphery.	
1973	The death of Sāre Manauī, a prominent composer and performance specialist whose compositions remained popular into the twenty-first century.	
1993	The death of the last purotu clan performance specialist.	
1994–2010	My own fieldwork period.	600–400
1994	Fifteen oceangoing canoes, some with sails, were in constant use. Ten or more songs praising pelagic fishing were composed each year.	

1994	Last performance of the *paki* dance. Because of insufficient time to teach the large numbers of younger men wanting to dance it for the first time, the performance was judged to be of an unsatisfactory standard (and, indeed, stopped completely at one point as the dancers, who were singing, and the accompanying instrumentalists could not hear each other). Fear of supernatural consequences was widespread but misplaced.	
1997	The last performance of *nā sore Tuiatua* song series, a single forty-minute performance of songs honoring a recently deceased descendant of the owner, not heard on the island for more than a generation.	
1997	The last occasion when a clan elder performed invocations as a log was dragged from the sea by one of the canoe-building yards. Subsequent elders were not taught the ritual by their fathers.	
2000	The last oceangoing canoe sail was found to have rotted and was not replaced; thenceforth, all pelagic fishing used outboard motors. New praise songs stopped referring to travel under sail.	
2002	Death of Nūnua Posongat, the community's most knowledgeable man in matters of singing and dancing. (See Moyle 2002.)	491
2004	Creation of the last *mē hau* woven garment, made by men but worn by women. The practice was replaced by imported cotton made into skirts by women (See Moyle 2017).	400
2004	Last performance of the large-scale *hoe Mōmoa* women's dance; the elderly owner died soon afterwards without teaching a successor.	
2004	Thirty-five canoes built following the arrival of an exceptional number of drift logs; many were poorly constructed and soon abandoned.	
2007	Only four or five oceangoing canoes still seaworthy, as a result of skilled carvers and their families emigrating.	

2012	The death of the ariki Avo Sini and appointment of Pāsia Mōmoa as successor. The death was unexpected and appointment unplanned. Pāsia soon left the island for extended medical treatment in Australia.	
2015	Death of the ariki Pāsia off-island. Tukuteata Kaiposu appointed as successor.	
2016	Death of Tūhea, a highly knowledgeable and influential woman, wife of Nūnua.	200
2018	Only two large canoes remain seaworthy; none has been carved for a decade. It was no longer possible to praise oceangoing canoe successes in any newly composed tuki.	
2019	For lack of competent singers in each clan, the last song performance to take place beside a corpse.	
2019	The last new tuki is composed and performed at a tukumai.	
2020	The last tukumai ritual is held. The five-day ritual is normally attended by all able-bodied adults. Unmarried young men and women do not usually attend the month-long rehearsals of the new songs that will be sung there or the twelve-hour continuous singing and dancing that begins the event. Similarly, young adults do not normally attend or participate in the marathon parties where dozens of songs and dances are performed.

This year was evidently the last time any activity occurred on the marae. Thereafter, commemorative proceedings were held in the relevant clan elder's house and involved spirit mediums exclusively. | |
| 2021 | Only one man on the island can currently perform funerary songs; he chooses to sing them solely for his own clan. His only living age-peer, who happens to be the ariki, is now showing signs of dementia and takes no active part in group activities. | 150 |

| 2021 | Dance performances off-island continue at parties and cultural displays, using the existing repertoire of songs; no new compositions are presented. | |
| 2021 | The death of the last man able to sing funerary songs. | 150 |

FIGURE 4. The last mē hau women's garment made on the island (2004).
Photograph: Richard Moyle

As indicated above, the most frequently sung song category until two years ago was the tuki song praising fishermen,[18] composed in the months after a local death. In 1997, following an unprecedented twelve deaths on the island that year, forty new tuki were composed and sung. By 2016, however, most of the generation of men and women on Takū who knew the repertoire and sang tuki frequently had emigrated. No tuki appear to have been composed in the last

---

18   I recorded more than three hundred in the active repertoire from this genre, the one containing the greatest number of individual compositions.

five years. In the 1990s, more than ten sau dances were in the active repertoire; but from 2005 to 2010, only two were sung, and none in its entirety. The writing was on the sand. No sau have been performed for at least five years. Other performances have continued, however, with a shift away from longer to shorter dances, and from ancient creations to those from the golden age.

There is great irony here. Until a decade ago, the occasion of a death used to spark the single greatest number of new compositions and the longest duration of communal singing— some thirty hours over five days. Yet the death of key individuals in the island's recent history has brought about a steady decline in composition, performer numbers, and performances. Speaking of Takū's spirit population, a man once told me that "Lātou ku sē lavā te oti" (they can never die). That may be true in a metaphysical sense, but the truth is that they have become neglected and are largely irrelevant to life off-island.

If there is a single identifiable point in time when a decline began, it is 1963, when the ariki died off-island. In a society like Takū, which places great weight on precedent, any unprecedented action is believed likely to have significant personal, harmful consequences. The scale of the consequences aligns with the status of the individual concerned. In this case, the succession of Takū's highest-ranking individual was jeopardized—the successor is supposed to gain his supernatural authority by crawling over the corpse of the incumbent—and makeshift arrangements continued for several years. Community anxiety was reflected in the sudden decline in the number of rituals and various performance genres.

The demise of the position of purotu performance specialist (there is one for each of the five clans) is largely attributable to genealogical gaps, since the position was held patrilineally and not all titleholders had a son. Nūnua Posongat and his wife Tūhea had a phenomenal combined knowledge of their clan's song repertoire, equivalent to that of a purotu, although they were not specialists officially for genealogical reasons. They functioned informally in the capacity of purotu until they died, and were not replaced.

Women's and men's ancient dances are owned individually, and intergenerational transmission obviously relies on children of the appropriate gender and disposition. The dancers' clan identities have, however, remained static; and overall numbers have declined as fewer younger individuals are interested in participation.

Creators of tuki songs have widely varying compositional and poetic skills. Clichéd melodies and stock lyrics are the hallmark of inferior songs, which are then privately criticized and are unlikely to enjoy repeat performances. Such

FIGURE 5a. Women dancing a manakoho in 1997.
Photograph: Richard Moyle

FIGURE 5b. The same dance in 2006.
Photograph: Richard Moyle

songs were on the increase during my latter years on the island, suggesting a drop-off in the number of proficient resident composers. The two song genres performed beside a corpse, and by only a handful of senior residents, became specialized out of existence as a few key older residents emigrated to Buka.

Is this process reversible? Can the traditions and rituals continue off-island, where 90% of Takū speakers now live? Here are some matters to consider:

1. There are evidently no resident composers on the island for the songs created and sung following a local death.
2. By convention, the performance of older songs and dances is restricted to the marae ritual arena, and then only with the presiding and protective presence of the ariki. The sole off-island public performance was in 1974 when Queen Elizabeth II visited Bougainville.
3. The tukumai ritual includes activities inside the clan elder's house and under the protective care of ancestral spirits believed to have resided there. No such protection extends off-island.
4. Many Christian denominations actively discourage belief in ancestral spirits and actively encourage use of their own marriage and burial rites, as well as exercise control over daily activities. Evangelical churches abound off-island, competing even among themselves for expatriate converts.

FIGURE 6. A protection ritual for male clan members taking place inside an elder's house following a shark attack.
Photograph: Richard Moyle

Modification of any of these practices would of necessity impinge on the community-wide authority of the ariki—itself an unprecedented act and, therefore, unlikely—and would also effectively negate the tenets of traditional religious practice and belief.

Takū's small community size and well-defined geographical boundaries permit the examination of the assumptions of unified, homogeneous identity underpinning much ethnomusicological study, as well as confirmation of the evidence of agency in both individual and communal activities. The Takū ideology of personal identity posits agency as something fixed, but capable of elevation, both short-term in a secular context (through outstanding success in fishing or canoe racing) and long-term in a ritual context (through succession to a title as clan head or assistant). Social elevation in the context of the performing arts spans both these contexts: on the one hand, some individuals are known community-wide for their creative and performance skills in particular song genres, while others inherit executant ownership of a particular dance genre and lead performance of that one form in a long programme on the community's ritual arena. Both these sets of activities have been progressively impacted by population decline.

Residents' descriptions of most institutional positions stress heredity and gender as primary qualifications. Although genealogies confirm that such an

FIGURE 7a. Takū's clan elders and purotu performance specialists (1970s).
Sāre Manauī is seated front left.
Photographer unknown

arrangement has existed for more than a century, the results of pragmatic alternatives are also evident. The exigencies of long-term residence on a small and remote atoll call for prompt alternatives and backups to ensure cultural continuity when an incumbent is unwell or temporarily away. Obviously, overall population numbers determine the size of the pool of potential appointees, and the recent rapid decline of the performance culture detailed in this chapter is directly linked to population decline.

In contrast with other appointments and an overarching social framework of egalitarianism, however, three classes of resident earn their social elevation through outstanding personal achievement: in canoe building, pelagic fishing, and the creation of songs and dances. All are now effectively defunct. The demise of canoe-builders led to the end of pelagic fishing, and the position of clan performance specialist met its end because of the lack of creative skills in any potential successor rather than an unwillingness to take up the role. The possession of such skills by a married couple not genealogically qualified for formal appointment resulted in a bending of the rules for twenty-five years, and ceased only with the couple's own deaths. While acknowledging and exploiting their

FIGURE 7b. Clan elders on the marae in 1999, without any purotu.
Photograph: Richard Moyle

skills during that period, the community declined to give them the title of performance specialist. What looks like a contravention of the norm is viewed from within more as a sustained exigency. The various forms of agency and willingness reflective of group and individual views and actions, have been primary movers in the overall drift.

In the 1990s, the 1970s were remembered wistfully as a golden age, when the prolific and charismatic performance specialist Sāre Manauī was active. In 2021, according to expatriate Takū on Facebook, the recordings I made in the 1990s—that is, of present-day elderly Takū—portrayed the "real" golden age. In both the 1990s and 2020s, the "nostalgia zone" was a period two generations earlier. The reception of the hundreds of photos and hours of videos I have posted on Facebook, YouTube, and Vimeo confirm this, and requests for specific audio recordings and ethnographic information are ongoing.

In speech and in song lyrics during my fieldwork period, Takū consistently referred to their island as "te henua nei" (this island), and for the last thirty years it has been simply called Takū by expatriates. But now, Facebook posters nostalgically call it "my island home," even when they live far away or have never even seen it. A degree of social distance has accompanied geographical separation.

Such attitudes suggest at least the possibility that Takū will become more of an expatriate holiday destination than a resettlement location—a point to recharge cultural interest and familiarity and to reaffirm cultural identity. The economic realities facing a family that wishes to improve its prospects and the dependence of families on material goods in an increasingly capitalist economy have so far prevented significant numbers of people returning to the atoll; only individuals have settled there.

Additionally, the skills required for effective fishing, gardening, and housebuilding—as well as the body of executant ritual knowledge needed to maintain Takū's religious activities—have been retained by only a few able-bodied expatriates. It seems likely that any substantial and permanent resettlement on the island would require significant lifestyle changes, as multiple agencies impinge on the old social, religious, and cultural order. I witnessed a measurable decline in intergenerational participation in song and dance performances, and any further changes may also be age-related.

Theoretically, it is possible for Takū expatriates to return to the island and attempt to revive traditional singing and dancing practices. Takū fought back from near extinction in the 1880s after the epidemic and their numbers are better now than then; but so far there is no evidence from Facebook posts or in private emails of any agency fueling a desire to return permanently. It is clear that to sustain the music and religious traditions in their earlier forms will require an irreducible core of individuals who are not only culturally knowledgeable but also genealogically accredited and in residence on the island. It is also apparent that such a core no longer exists on Takū or off-island. That said, two local men bought passenger boats in mid-2021 and at the time of writing there is an approximately monthly service out of Buka. An optimist might feel encouraged. And the arrival in Bougainville of Covid-19 in 2021 may encourage some people to return to the island for reasons of personal safety. Time will tell, of course, but time appears to be running out.

Bibliography

Friederici, Georg. *Wissenschaftliche Ergebnisse einer amtlichen Forschungsreise nach dem Bismarck-Archipel im Jahre 1908*. Vol. 2. Berlin: E. S. Mittler & Son, 1912.

Gell, Alfred. *Art and Agency: An Anthropological Theory*. Oxford: Clarendon Press, 1998.

Iyanaga, Michael. "Why Saints Love Samba: A Historical Perspective on Black Agency and the Rearticulation of Catholicism in Bahia, Brazil." *Black Music Research Journal* 35 (2015): 119–147.

Kaufman, Robert. "Lyric's Expression: Musicality, Conceptuality, Critical Agency." *Cultural Critique* 60 (2005): 197–216.

Merriam, Alan P. *The Anthropology of Music*. Evanston: Northwestern University Press, 1964.

———. *Ethnomusicology of the Flathead Indians*. New York: Wenner-Green Foundation for Anthropological Research, 1967.

Moyle, Richard M. Obituary of Nunua Posongat. *SEM Newsletter* 36 (2002): 20–21.

———. *Nā Kkai: Takū's Musical Fables*. Boroko: Institute for Papua New Guinea Studies, 2004.

———. *Songs from the Second Float / A Musical Ethnography of Takū Atoll, Papua New Guinea*. Pacific Islands Monograph Series 21. Honolulu: Center for Pacific Island Studies, University of Hawaii Press, 2007.

———. *A Dictionary of Takuu*. Canberra: Pacific Linguistics, 2011.

———. *Takū Ritual and Belief. Polynesian Religion in Practice*. Adelaide, Crawford House Publishing, 2018.

———. "Te Tukumai—Ending the Grief." Vimeo Video, 17:37. June 10, 2015. https://vimeo.com/130386785.

———. "Celebrating and Enhancing a Virtual Past through Singing: The Polynesian Community on Takū." In *Performing History: Approaches to History Across Musicology,* edited by Nancy November, 101–114. Boston: Academic Studies Press, 2020.

———. "Keeping It in the Family: Ancestral Talkback on Takū." In *Spirit Possession and Communication in Religious and Cultural Contexts*, edited by Caroline Blyth, 119–134. Oxford: Routledge, 2020.

Omojola, Bode. *Yorùbá Music in the Twentieth Century: Identity, Agency, and Performance Practice*. Rochester: University of Rochester Press, 2014.

Shank, Barry. "The Political Agency of Musical Beauty." *American Quarterly* 63 (2011): 831–855.

Titon, Jeff Todd. "Music, the Public Interest, and the Practice of Ethnomusicology." *Ethnomusicology* 36 (1992): 315–322.

Turino, Thomas. *Music as Social Life: The Politics of Participation*. Chicago: University of Chicago Press, 2006.

Stock, Jonathan P. J. "Towards an Ethnomusicology of the Individual, or Biographical Writing in Ethnomusicology." *The World of Music* 43 (2001): 5–19.

His Majesty's Theatre: A Hub of Musical and Theatrical Entertainment in Colonial Dunedin

Sandra Crawshaw

Twenty-first-century New Zealand is home to a rich and diverse music scene. The pop musicians Lorde, Kimbra, and Neil Finn, for example, have enjoyed enormous success; and the country's classical music has come of age too. The New Zealand Symphony Orchestra is world class, the National Youth Choir won the "Choir of the World" title at the International Eisteddfod in Llangollen, Wales in 1999, and there are professional regional orchestras that perform regularly. In addition, concert artists such as Michael Houston, Amalia Hall, and Stephen DePledge, are acclaimed throughout the world.

Things have certainly changed for the better. Standards have risen, learning has come from mistakes, and public attitudes have become more positive towards the entertainment industry. In 1970s and 1980s New Zealand, the perception among emerging classical musicians was that everything abroad was superior. To become a serious artist, one had to study in Europe or the United States. New Zealand's classical music scene simply did not measure up, and some even considered the country a cultural desert. There was scant evidence to the contrary. For New Zealanders, the country's history was one of agriculture, politics, war, and sport. Art had played little part. It seems that this sense of inferiority was reinforced, in no small part, by Czech immigrant Fred Turnovsky, who arrived in New Zealand as a refugee in January 1940. He became a significant patron of the arts, and, to his credit, played a large role in establishing Chamber Music New Zealand. This institution has brought many artists to New Zealand, and its Schools Chamber Music Competition, unique to this country, has fostered many outstanding young musicians. Yet Turnovsky often spoke with great disdain about the state of the arts in New Zealand. For example, in his autobiography he observed that the "attitude of New Zealanders to the public presentation of arts was conditioned by the philistinism of an earlier colonial period which stood in the way of change."[1] Studying the history of music at tertiary level in the 1980s, I considered his observation of New Zealand society's lack of artistic sophistication to be well founded, given there was little or no mention of anything pertaining to the country's music in textbooks. Nothing I found in the literature contradicted Turnovsky's assertion of a colonial history of philistinism.

Musicologists now argue that culture and the arts in early New Zealand were more aligned with the rest of the world than previously believed, and that society in general was much more globally connected than many histories suggest. By 1876, trans-Tasman cables were in place and telegraph communications between Australia, New Zealand, and Britain were possible. By the latter half of the nineteenth century, global cargo and passenger shipping routes were also well established. New Zealand's own Union Company had commenced business in Dunedin in 1875, with numerous vessels providing access to many parts of the world.[2] For example, in 1902, the London-based opera singer Nellie Melba made an extended tour of Australia and New Zealand, her travels closely reported by the newspapers of the time. From London, she voyaged to New York on Cunard's luxurious *RMS Compania*; she then boarded the *Miowera* in Vancouver, reaching Brisbane, Australia, via Suva, Fiji. After several months touring Australia she boarded the Union Company's *SS Moeraki* in Hobart, arriving a week later in Bluff, New Zealand.

In 1944, Maurice Hurst wrote a brief chronological history of entertainment in New Zealand, in which he acknowledged the theatrical entrepreneurs of the time, including J. C. Williamson. A manager of great wealth and instinct, Williamson engaged the best overseas talent for his many touring companies. As a result, Australian and New Zealand audiences could see the latest Puccini opera or Broadway or West End play, sometimes only a year or so after its writing. In 1945, Margaret Campbell's *Music in Dunedin* offered a concise chronological history of music in Otago from 1848. She referred occasionally to international visitors and provided valuable accounts of the local musicians, teachers, and community organizations that laid the foundations for a developing musical

---

1   Fred Turnovsky, *Turnovsky: Fifty Years in New Zealand* (Wellington: Allen & Unwin, 1990), 151.
2   N. H. Brewer, *A Century of Style: Great Ships of the Union Line. 1875–1976* (Wellington: A. H. & A. W. Reed Ltd., 1982), vii–viii.

culture in the city. It was not until 1991 that John Mansfield Thomson produced the first comprehensive account of New Zealand music, *The Oxford History of New Zealand Music*. Tracing musical events from early Māori and settler beginnings, Thomson also detailed the many outstanding musicians who visited New Zealand in the early part of the twentieth century, such as Fritz Kreisler, Ignacy Paderewski, and Melba, to name just a few. New Zealanders were also lauded overseas, including singer Princess Te Rangi Pai, conductor Warwick Braithwaite, and pianist Vera Moore. Nowadays, many histories of musical organizations, such as choral societies and orchestras, are appearing, and colorful stories about their origins are being told.

The city of Dunedin, in the lower South Island, was generally not particularly well represented in early histories; other centers were considered more vibrant. Perhaps because of its Scottish Presbyterian roots, the city had a reputation as straitlaced and thrifty, and the literature perpetuated this image. The popular press, such as the *NZ Truth* newspaper, frequently referred to "Dour Dunedin."[3] Yet the city was often the first major New Zealand city to welcome the many celebrity artists, including Melba, and their companies on tour. The port of Bluff, at the southern extreme of the South Island, was the main port of call for passenger steamers to and from Melbourne (via Hobart). Disembarking passengers would immediately board the train to Dunedin. Unfortunately, the town of Invercargill, just north of Bluff, missed out on many of the international artists and companies who visited, as its only suitable venue, the Theatre Royale, had been sold in January 1903 and turned into a furniture shop.[4]

Researching the performers and companies that visited Dunedin, I noticed that a particular theatre stood out. Once a vital entertainment hub, the building still exists, albeit in a derelict state. According to Martin Phillips of the Chills,[5] its last incarnation, before it was abandoned, was as Sammy's Nightclub, the home of the famed '70s and '80s Dunedin Sound. In a radio broadcast, he said, "I think it used to be called His Majesty's or something."[6] He was correct.

---

3   For example: "Soulless Sweaters. A Den in Dour Dunedin," *NZ Truth*, June 6, 1908, 5.
4   Invercargill acquired city status in 1930.
5   The Chills are a Dunedin rock band formed in 1980 with hit songs such as "Pink Frost" and "Submarine Bells."
6   "Martin Phillips of the Chills Shows Ds Dunedin's Historic Venues," RNZ, October 14, 2017, https://rnz.co.nz/national/programmes/nat-music/audio/2018617859/the-birthplaces-of-the-dunedin-sound.

Early newspapers are perhaps the most important source of information. As a primary means of communication, the role of the colonial newspaper was to inform, educate, and entertain the general public. The Otago region was very well served with local publications as far back as the 1850s. The city of Dunedin had two dailies, the *Evening Star* and the *Otago Daily Times*, and a weekly newspaper, the *Otago Witness*. They covered in detail local and international news and events, the meetings of societies, gossip and opinions, and published reviews and critiques (no holds barred).

The Agricultural Hall

FIGURE 1. Agricultural Hall, Dunedin. Te Papa, Wellington.

Aptly for New Zealand, the theatre had its beginnings in the rural sector, starting life as the Agricultural Hall. The gold rush in the 1870s made Dunedin the most prominent and wealthiest city in New Zealand, but it quickly lost this status as the gold petered out. The city's economic development had to rely more on agricultural and pastoral income. After several unsuccessful attempts, the Otago

Agricultural and Pastoral Association was finally established in December 1876. This organization was to support the farming community throughout Otago, a primary objective being to organize the annual winter shows. The events promoted stock, produce, and agricultural equipment, and often also included exhibits from other sectors such as brewing, manufacturing, and imported goods. Over a decade, these shows grew in size and popularity, eventually outgrowing their usual venue, the Garrison Hall.

On June 24, 1895, the *Otago Daily Times* printed a copy of a letter from a special committee of the Otago A. and P. Society (later called the Agricultural Hall Company) addressed to the New Zealand premier Richard Seddon.[7] It detailed a proposal to build an agricultural hall to be used for the annual Winter Show, other exhibitions, and by the community. The society claimed that a larger and better venue for the agricultural displays was required. Having itemized the costs, Dunedin asked the government to match its own contribution. The government refused, so it was decided to raise funds by other means. Records indicate that debentures were offered; and by March 1896, the Otago Agricultural Hall Company had raised six thousand pounds, divided into shares of one pound each. Shareholders included prominent citizens of Dunedin, such as Thomas Fergus, Thomas Brydone, Robert Campbell, and James Hazlett; and businesses such as Dalgety & Co. Ltd., Speights & Co., and Donaghy and Co.—all still in operation today—were also listed in the holdings.[8]

Almost immediately, Dunedin architect James Hislop was appointed to oversee plans and construction. Hislop, the son of Scottish settlers, was well known and respected in the city as the architect responsible for many private dwellings of prominent citizens. His reputation was cemented when he was appointed the architect for the Exhibition Buildings erected for the New Zealand Exhibition of 1889.[9] After the new Agricultural Hall's foundation stone was laid in June 1896, building progressed rapidly. The venue was completed a year later, in time for the Winter Show. It could seat close to one thousand people. As it was Queen Victoria's Diamond Jubilee, the first such event held for a British monarch, and celebrations were planned across the country, June 1897 was the perfect time to open the hall.

---

7   "Proposed Agricultural Hall," *Otago Daily Times*, June 24, 1896, 4. As a rule, newspaper references from this period are all anonymous.
8   Otago Agricultural Hall Company, Archives New Zealand, Te Rua Mahara o te Kāwanatanga, North Dunedin.
9   "Exhibition Buildings," *Evening Star*, January 30, 1889, 2.

On a fine day on June 21, the Kaikorai Band played outside the Crawford Street entrances as an excited audience entered the new building.[10] After many lengthy speeches, the acting premier and minister of land and agriculture, the Hon. John McKenzie, declared the hall open and the inaugural concert was presented by the Dunedin Orchestral Society and the Dunedin Liedertafel.[11] The next day, June 22, the celebrations of the Diamond Jubilee began. Thousands of people had poured into the city to enjoy the parades and spectacular light displays. And the day after that, the Winter Show opened in the new hall, and proved the largest and most successful to date.

Providing a music venue was not among the original intentions of the directors of the Agricultural Hall Company, but the hall proved to be most adaptable for concerts, with a large capacity and surprisingly good acoustics. It was quickly hired by various community groups. A Masonic service commemorating the Queen's Diamond Jubilee, for example, with a full orchestra and two-hundred-strong choir, was attended by nearly three thousand people.[12] In the same year, the hall hosted several concerts by various Dunedin musical groups, in between events such as the Dog and Poultry Show (with musical entertainment provided by the North East Valley Band), the annual Horticultural Show and the wool sales. One large spectacle was a combined Floral Fete and Bicycle Gymkhana, which included large flower

FIGURE 2. Programme cover for the opening of the Agricultural Hall. Hocken Library.

---

10 "The Agricultural Buildings," *Evening Star*, June 22, 1897, 2. The Kaikorai Brass Band was formed sometime in 1881, according to an advertisement for a Grand Ball to fundraise for it in the *Evening Star*, September 21, 1881.

11 The Dunedin Liedertafel, now known as the Royal Dunedin Male Choir, was formed in October 1882. An Orchestral Society, in some guise, had existed in Dunedin since 1875.

12 "Masonic Service," *Otago Witness*, July 8, 1897, 21.

displays, children dancing, and a specially choreographed demonstration featuring ladies dressed in white riding bicycles decorated with flowers and accompanied by music.

The Jubilee Anniversary of Otago fell in 1898, and plans were set in motion for a Grand Industrial Exhibition to mark the occasion. This was again underwritten by the Agricultural Hall Company directors. The hall was altered to improve the acoustics and accommodate upwards of four hundred musicians and choristers and new buildings were erected. Opening on March 22, the exhibition continued for several months. The new buildings included a large annex for the industrial displays and various stage shows and concerts were scheduled. These included a spectacular dance display depicting the history of Otago, choreographed by Italian choreographer Signor Alfredo Borzoni. New technology was also shown (kinematics, for example) and contests were held for choirs, instrumentalists, and brass bands.

There was also a special Exhibition Orchestra which played at various events. It presented a sacred concert of solo and orchestral items. The orchestra opened with a Mozart overture, but had to omit the final programmed item because the audience had vanished. It transpired that there was an open door at the back of the auditorium leading to displays in the annex, with a constant stream of people moving in and out. The disturbance, as reported in the *Otago Daily Times*, was such that one of the singers "struggled on despairingly with his song, much of which was, in consequence of the noise, inaudible."[13] Newspaper advertisements for concerts would subsequently state that the connecting doors would no longer open between items.

The capacity of the hall was tested, particularly at an English drama (with requisite musical accompaniment), staged by playwright Barrie Marschel.[14] The *Evening Star* reported that on one evening a large attendance was expected, but not the seven thousand people who tried to get in. Some people, the paper reported, were still being turned away when "the fiddlers had their elbows jammed with the bows in position but no room to draw a stroke, and a party of small boys who had invaded the stage fell through a portion of the side drape."[15]

The final concerts for the exhibition were given by Amy Sherwin and her Concert Company, the first international company to appear at the hall.

---

13 "The Jubilee Exhibition," *Otago Daily Times*, April 9, 1898, 6.
14 Barrie Marschel also wrote and staged one of the first New Zealand dramas, *Humarire Taniwha*, in the Agricultural Hall in January 1897.
15 "Exhibition Notes," *Evening Star*, May 9, 1898, 2.

Sherwin, an acclaimed Australian soprano known as the "Tasmanian Nightingale," had met with considerable success abroad. Three concerts were given, with a grand piano and organ provided for the occasion by Messrs. C. Begg and Co.

The Royal Treatment

According to Maurice Hurst, the final years of the nineteenth century were "an interesting time for New Zealand theatre-goers, and the tide of visiting companies and stage stars [grew] steadily."[16] He referred to 1901–1910 as the "Golden Era." There were visits by several world famous artists, including Melba, Mark Hambourg, and Clara Butt, while "a continuous procession of successful dramatic and operatic companies kept the sphere of entertainment bright and busy."[17]

In May 1902, acclaimed Australian soprano Amy Castles and her company, brought to New Zealand by the entrepreneur J. C. Williamson, performed in the Agricultural Hall. This was the first of just six appearances in New Zealand. As the hall could accommodate at least two thousand people, a concert was scheduled for Dunedin. Both Wellington and Auckland had two concerts each because their theatres could accommodate about fifteen hundred at most.[18] The concert was a great success, with close to three thousand people present, according to the *Otago Witness*. Castles even wrote a testimonial extolling the quality of the acoustics in the Hall and its suitability for concerts. One month later, Bert Royle, a representative of J. C. Williamson, recommended that the Agricultural Hall Company refurbish the hall and turn it into a state-of-the-art theatre, to which they agreed.

Renovations were carried out under the supervision of J. Turner, another representative from J. C. Williamson's organization; and the building, renamed His Majesty's Theatre, was opened on December 3, 1902. Significant changes to the stage and wings had considerably enlarged their working size. The latest in

---

16 Maurice Hurst, *Music and the Stage in New Zealand: A Century of Entertainment 1840–1943* (Wellington: Charles Begg & Co. Ltd., 1944), 33.
17 Ibid., 41.
18 Wellington's Opera House, built in 1886, had seating for approximately 1370, according to an article detailing the opening—"The Opening of the New Opera House," *Evening Post*, November 18, 1886, 2; the Opera House in Auckland, built in 1881, had a capacity of 1500, with extra seats added for Castles' visit.

FIGURE 3. The Proscenium of His Majesty's Theatre. Hocken Library.

staging technology was also installed, enhancing the hall's suitability for visiting theatrical companies. The original gallery was removed and replaced by a dress circle, and incandescent lamps were fitted throughout. The seating was now more luxurious and the stage was framed by a decorative plaster proscenium which still exists today.

According to reviews, opening night was attended by a packed, cheering audience. They were brought to their feet with a rousing version of the national anthem; and, as the *Otago Daily Times* reported, "To commemorate the occasion a flashlight photograph of the theatre and audience was taken before the commencement of the programme."[19] All were eventually seated to enjoy J. C. Williamson's Musical Comedy Company perform *A Runaway Girl*. The company put on three other musical comedies during the fortnight-long season, which closed on December 18. Williamson, by way of his agent Pete Hughes, thoroughly endorsed the refurbishment in a letter to the Agricultural Hall Company, later published in the *Otago Witness*:

---

19 "His Majesty's Theatre," *Otago Daily Times*, December 4, 1902, 5

> I do not think you could find a better stage in the whole of the Australian colonies. It has every requirement possible, and the light which your fine electric plant gives is second to none.... The acoustic properties are all that could be desired, as you are able to hear distinctly every word that is spoken from the stage in all parts of the house.... In conclusion, I must, therefore, congratulate your directors in having what I consider one of the finest and best-appointed theatres in the colonies.[20]

The Dunedin Choral Society was the first local music group to perform at His Majesty's. Handel's *Messiah*, conducted by James Coombes, was given on Christmas Eve. The auditorium was so crowded that people had to be turned away. The *Evening Star* review stated that the chorus made a good impression—and not just because of the good acoustics. The tenors and basses were particularly good, despite there being many more women: "The singers numbered seventy-one ladies and thirty-six gentlemen ... the outnumbering ladies did not have to reduce their volume very much in order to make proper balance of the parts."[21]

According to Hurst, 1903 was a year of exceptional events, with luminaries such as Melba, Mark Hambourg, and Antonia Dolores visiting New Zealand. With a theatre such as His Majesty's, Dunedin could now host international celebrities easily. The arrival of Nellie Melba, fresh from a tour of Australia that began in September 1902, was highly anticipated. She had come from London at the behest of Australian-based theatre producer George Musgrove. It had been reported that J. C. Williamson had balked at her fees and turned her down.[22] The newspapers followed her Australian tour very closely, reporting on her travels, concerts, and soirées—even the fashions and jewelry she wore. She was met by a crowd at the Dunedin railway station and whisked off to a mayoral welcome. Tickets to her concert were very expensive for the time. There were two prices: one guinea and half a guinea (approximately two hundred and one hundred NZ dollars today). Still, people travelled from distant parts of Otago just to hear Melba sing. The *Cromwell Argus* reported that a double buggy of ladies and gentlemen left Cromwell for Dunedin to hear the "Divine Melba." Some even travelled from as far as Ōtautau in Southland.[23] Despite the cost, His Majesty's Theatre was filled and the reviews in the newspapers afterwards were lavish in

---

20 "Theatrical and Musical Notes," *Otago Witness*, January 21, 1903, 56.
21 "The Choral Society," *Evening Star*, December 26, 1902, 3.
22 "Local and General," *Otago Witness*, October 2, 1901, 26.
23 "Dunedin Gossip," *Cromwell Argus*, February 24, 1903, 5. The town of Cromwell is 220 kilometers from Dunedin; Ōtautau is 237 kilometers.

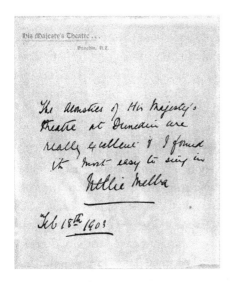

FIGURE 4. Testimonial written by Nellie Melba. Hocken Library.

their praise. Melba was apparently satisfied with the theatre, leaving behind a written testimonial commending its acoustics.

The singer then travelled on to Christchurch, where she also encountered enthusiastic crowds. The *Star*'s music critic, most likely Charles Baeyertz, was not so impressed: "she is not by any means the greatest artist who has sung in the colonies." He also slated members of her company:

> Mr Frederick Griffiths, the flautist of the company, played a "grey" and exceedingly uninteresting Hungarian Fantasy. He is probably the least attractive flautist of any pretensions who has ever been heard in Christchurch.[24]

Otherwise, Melba enjoyed a rapturous reception wherever she appeared in the country.

Dunedin was relatively well served by performance spaces. The Alhambra Theatre, owned by Fullers, had an ever-changing vaudeville program. Events at the Garrison Hall, the Choral Hall, and the Princess Theatre were well patronized, but their small scale limited what they could stage. Newly refurbished and thoroughly modernized, His Majesty's Theatre was now attracting entertainments on a par with almost anything in Australasia.

Soprano Antonia Dolores was another renowned vocalist to visit New Zealand in 1903. Dolores was well known and popular with audiences, having visited the country on several previous occasions and given five recitals in Dunedin's Garrison Hall in April 1902. After a two-year tour of Australia and New

---

24 "The Melba Concert," *Star*, February 21, 1903, 7.

Zealand, her concert on April 8 1903 was to be her last before returning to the United States and Europe. Unusually, she was accompanied only by her pianist Clarance Newell, rather than by a concert company. The reviews were effusive and the theatre was completely full. The *Evening Star* described the decorated stage and the comfort of the audience, many of whom had travelled from country districts. Special mention was also given to the program: "the turning of the programme into a book of words that gave the translation as well as the original verse proved to be an appreciated innovation, enabling the listeners to follow the singing and also to test the artiste's enunciation and expression."[25] The audience was rapturous, and Dolores received many bouquets of flowers and even a basket of grapes at the conclusion of the evening. Rumors of an extra appearance were confirmed when a sacred concert was announced for Good Friday (April 10) featuring Dolores, Newell, and baritone John Prouse, who was brought from Wellington especially for the occasion.[26]

Russian pianist Hambourg, one of the great pianists of the time, was also touring Australasia in 1903. He arrived in New Zealand in June. According to Margaret Campbell, touring solo pianists were less common than vocal soloists and violinists.[27] The local newspapers took it upon themselves to educate the public as to the stature of Hambourg by printing articles and reviews from overseas concerts—particularly his appearances in Australia—and generally providing advance publicity. Days before his first concert, an essay in the *Evening Star* discussed his position amongst the master pianists like Paderewski and Busoni.

Touring with a concert party including his brother Boris Hambourg, a virtuoso cellist, and Australian flautist John Lemmoné, Hambourg performed four concerts in His Majesty's Theatre in June. He then returned in August, giving three farewell concerts. In his seven concerts, Hambourg mostly performed repertoire from the Romantic period, with many standard works by Chopin, Liszt, and Rubenstein, along with several Beethoven sonatas. He also played sonatas for cello and piano with his brother, such as those of Grieg and Mendelssohn. Audiences were large and appreciative, and because the programs were

---

25 "Mdlle Dolores," *Evening Star*, April 9, 1903, 6.

26 John Prouse was a popular New Zealand bass-baritone who performed internationally. He was also New Zealand's first commercially recorded artist.

27 Margaret Campbell, *Music in Dunedin: An Historical Account of Dunedin's Musicians and Musical Societies from the Founding of the Province in 1848* (Dunedin: Charles Begg & Co. Ltd., 1945), 76.

FIGURE 5. Mark Hambourg, Boris Hambourg. National Portrait Gallery, London.

different each evening, many people came to hear him more than once. Boris later married Dunedin pianist Maria Bauchop.

Australian contralto Ada Crossley was another much-admired singer to visit Dunedin. Brought from London by J. C. Williamson, Crossley's tour of Australia was much reported on by Otago newspapers. Journalists discussed her concerts and published interviews and other items of interest. New Zealand audiences appeared to share with Australia a delight in an antipodean artist doing well abroad. Her concert party included Austrian violinist Jacques Jacob and twenty-one-year-old Percy Grainger. Her two concerts in Dunedin attracted record numbers of advance bookings.[28] The demand for seats was so great that four hundred extra chairs lined the back of the stage of His Majesty's. Attendance at the second concert was estimated at close to 2800.[29] The two concerts featured many popular composers of the time, including Cécile Chaminade, Edward German, Blumenthal, and Arthur Sullivan. Jacob performed works by Edvard Grieg, Pablo Sarasate, Camille Saint-Saëns, and Max Bruch, and Grainger performed the Bach-Tausig arrangement of the Toccata and Fugue in D Minor, along with several Chopin encores.

His Majesty's Theatre was not just reserved for international acts, of course. It was also used for annual local events. For instance, the Dunedin Competitions Society (inaugurated in 1902) hired the theatre from 1903 onwards for their annual festival. Interest in the festival grew year by year, as did the number of categories offered. It was at these competitions that the public would first encounter pianist Vera Moore, a competitor from the age of seven, and future conductor Warwick Braithwaite, also a talented young pianist. In 1904, the Dunedin

---

28 "Ada Crossley Concerts: Greta Rush for Seats," *Otago Daily Times*, November 16, 1903, 6.
29 "Miss Ada Crossley," *Evening Star*, November 21, 1903, 8.

Choral Society took advantage of British singer Watkin Mills's visit in early September and staged a Choral Festival. Both Handel's *Messiah* and Haydn's *Creation* were performed on either side of a recital given by Mills. Talented local soprano Amy Murphy was one of the soloists, along with Auckland tenor Walter Whyte. Attendances were large, but not to capacity, apparently due to very wet weather, which also affected other events in the city. It was reported that rain had been falling continuously for nearly five days.[30]

The greatly anticipated arrival of Polish pianist Paderewski came just over a week after the departure of Mills. Starting his tour in Auckland on August 31, Paderewski travelled down the country by train, accompanied by an entourage including his wife and pet parrot. Two recitals were given at His Majesty's Theatre to large audiences. The *Otago Daily Times* review of his second concert was very detailed and brimming with superlatives. The hall was described as full apart from a small section of the dress circle, blamed on the wintry weather, which caused "not a few to lose perhaps the opportunity of a lifetime." The program was challenging, including Bach's Chromatic Fantasy and Fugue in D Minor, Schumann's *Carnivale*, and Beethoven's "Moonlight" Sonata. Paderewski also performed works by Liszt, Chopin, and his own *Cracovienne*. The reviewer spoke to Paderewski afterwards and asked his opinion of New Zealand audiences. He replied: "They are not perhaps so enthusiastic as those in England or in Germany, but no doubt that is a matter of temperament."[31]

Change of Hands

In July 1907 a small paragraph in the *Otago Daily Times* announced the pending purchase of His Majesty's Theatre by John Fuller and Sons, and the transaction was completed later that year. The purchase price was reported as fifteen thousand pounds. It was, according to the *Evening Star*, "the largest deal in theatre property, besides being the largest cash transaction for same, that New Zealand has witnessed."[32]

The Fuller name, famous throughout New Zealand and Australia, was synonymous with popular entertainment, particularly vaudeville. From small beginnings in the 1890s, John Fuller Sr., together with his sons Benjamin, John Jr.,

---

30 "The Weather," *Evening Star*, September 9, 1904, 4.
31 "Paderewski. The Second Recital," *Otago Daily Times*, September 24, 1904, 8.
32 Untitled, *Evening Star*, September 30, 1907, 4.

and Walter, managed an ever-growing theatre empire. The purchase of His Majesty's Theatre meant that John Fuller and Sons owned the three main theatres in Dunedin—the others were the Princess and the Alhambra. His Majesty's Theatre, the Theatre Royal in Wellington, and the Opera House in Christchurch were also under the Fuller umbrella.

By 1908, Dunedin audiences were enjoying a variety of entertainment in the three main theatres. Nightly vaudeville shows were a permanent fixture at the Princess, and the Alhambra often showed moving pictures. During that year, various theatre companies booked His Majesty's Theatre. J. C. Williamson's Dramatic and Musical Companies returned for five separate seasons, offering light opera, comedy acts, and plays that had fairly recently been performed in New York or London.

Initially associated with J. C. Williamson, Tom Pollard was also a prominent theatre director, touring with Pollard's Liliputian Opera Company since the 1890s. Based in New Zealand, Pollard booked His Majesty's for most of May 1908 and brought his Juvenile Opera Company (formed in 1907). A company's regular season could last up to a fortnight and involve two or more productions. With its performers ranging in age from six to sixteen, Pollard's Juvenile Opera Company performed three light operas and two evenings of vaudeville over three weeks.

According to Margaret Campbell, the outstanding visit of 1908 was that of Clara Butt and Kennerly Rumford.[33] Brought to New Zealand by entrepreneurs J. & N. Tait, they were met in Dunedin by "some members of the Liedertafel, several members of local musical circles, and a large number of ladies. As the train drew up there was a rush to Madame Clara Butt's carriage, piled with bouquets of flowers which had been presented to her at every station stopped at."[34]

Two concerts were scheduled for Dunedin, and despite tickets being expensive, they sold

FIGURE 6. Clara Butt. National Portrait Gallery, London.

---

33 Campbell, *Music in Dunedin*, 73.
34 "Arrival of Clara Butt," *Otago Daily Times*, February 5, 1908, 2.

well. Reviews in the Dunedin newspapers called her a great artist with a voice of remarkable proportions and agreeable tone quality. As in other cities on the New Zealand tour, extra demand warranted an extra concert, this time in the Garrison Hall. His Majesty's Theatre was unavailable as West's Pictures had just opened.

The tour, with its cheering crowds and capacity audiences, was memorable. Butt's inaugural visit to New Zealand makes the history books not for pleasing audiences, however, but for a notoriously critical review from Charles Baeyertz in his *Triad* magazine:

> Mrs Rumford's diction is extremely sloppy. She lacks refinement, temperament and brains.... If Mrs Rumford is regarded in musical circles as a great singer (in any but a physical sense), English vocal art, or English taste, or both, must be in a parlous state.[35]

In a very brief account of the 1908 tour, Campbell merely noted that the critic of the *Triad* failed to approve of the concerts.[36] John Mansfield Thomson included just a mention of a brisk encounter with Baeyertz, recounting some of the cutting criticism that the *Triad* published: "the joy-filled audience paddled in the shallow waters of English drawing room songs."[37] Joanna Woods wrote more comprehensively of Baeyertz's scathing criticism of what he thought was excessive, undeserved publicity. He did not hold back: "Mrs Rumford owns a big voice, organ-like in quality, but inferiorly played ... she makes mincemeat of a song."[38] As a consequence, not just Butt but also the public were exceedingly insulted by his comments.

New Zealand singers also enjoyed a measure of fame. Popular Dunedin soprano Amy Murphy, engaged by Williamson in 1907, was the prima donna of the Musical Comedy Company for the New Zealand tour in 1908, which played to Dunedin audiences in March. Her sister Dulcie was also in the company. Rosina Buckman was another accomplished New Zealand soprano who would later establish herself in London's Covent Garden. In 1908, she appeared in a special

---

35 This was apparently a direct quote from the *Triad* reprinted in the *Tapanui Times*: "Unfair Criticism," *Clutha Leader*, February 14, 1908, 5.
36 Campbell, *Music in Dunedin*, 73.
37 John Mansfield Thomson, *The Oxford History of New Zealand Music* (Auckland: Oxford University Press, 1991), 136.
38 Joanna Woods, *Facing The Music: Charles Baeyertz and The Triad* (Dunedin, New Zealand: Otago University Press, 1988), 124.

production of Alfred Hill's opera *A Moorish Maid*, performing for four nights in His Majesty's Theatre. The performances were to help raise funds for the Kaikorai Band, which was hoping to compete in the Ballarat Band Contest later that year. Alfred Hill himself came down from Wellington to conduct. A distinctive feature of this production (also performed in 1907) was the "introduction of the Kaikorai Band at the curtain of the first act."[39] The theatre was filled each evening; the ushers had to ask people to sit a little closer to make room. Reviews from the local newspapers were glowing, and Alfred Hill, who was purportedly taking his opera to London, was rightly lauded for his score: "It is at least satisfactory to know that on this occasion the composer has had a little honour in his own country before his clever work secures in the wider field the verdict that its qualities cannot fail to gain."[40]

His Majesty's Theatre continued to offer a wide variety of entertainment, with music to the fore, or at least involved. For example, Rickard's Vaudeville Company included, amongst acrobats and dancers, the Miles-Stavordale Quartet of Musicians. It consisted of banjo players whose instruments were said to imitate the human voice. The Anderson Sheridan Pantomime Company from Australia staged *Cinderella*. This was a lavish production of 108 performers, including skaters, acrobats, a seventy-voice chorus, and orchestra. Cornish tenor Charles Saunders, touring with his wife contralto Clara Robson, gave three recitals at His Majesty's in August 1908. They were accompanied by Dunedin pianist Max Schereck, who himself performed a Chopin Ballade.

In September, a new touring musical attraction performed in the city. Edward Branscombes's Scarlet Troubadours from London, described as a comedy costume company, blended light opera, concert repertoire, and vaudeville. Although relatively unknown, their Dunedin audiences were large and appreciative. The *Otago Daily Times* review provided the best description of the entertainment:

> The Scarlet Troubadours' performance is a notable proof that a variety entertainment can be given quite well by capable performers without in any way descending to coarseness. The company evidently takes its name from the style of costume adopted during the major part of the evening. The male performers wear the dress usually associated with the

---

39 "Amusements," *Evening Star*, May 21, 1908, 6.
40 "Amusements: The Moorish Maid," *Otago Daily Times*, May 28, 1908, 8.

troubadour of a bygone day, scarlet and black being the colours selected, and the ladies are prettily apparelled as peasant girls.[41]

October's biggest event at the theatre was undoubtedly the appearance of contralto Irene Ainsley. This young New Zealand singer was receiving attention normally reserved for divas such as Melba and Butt. Indeed, having heard her sing in 1903, Melba had advised Ainsley to study abroad and she had also helped arrange her debut at Bechstein Hall in London in 1906. The performance led to a summons by the Prince and Princess of Wales to sing before the king at Marlborough House. Her success was reported nationally, her career was assured, and she sang alongside stars like the pianist Ferrucio Busoni and violinist Joseph Szigeti. On tour in New Zealand, her concert company included New Zealand-based Hamilton Hodges, an African American bass baritone, and Mrs. Ernest Queree, a noted accompanist and piano soloist from Auckland.

Ainsley gave two concerts in Dunedin to large audiences. It was agreed that she had a lovely voice and was developing as an artist, but critics from the newspapers pointed out some shortcomings in the young singer (she was twenty-two) and her chosen program. The *Evening Star* review remarked:

> It is perfectly true that many songs intended for soprano or mezzo-soprano are published in lower keys, but that is no justification of the use of these abased editions. They may be supposed to be sold for the use of worn and cracked voices.[42]

The critic may have been Charles Baeyertz, as he had recently judged the Dunedin Competitions Society. However, intelligent advice was also offered. Baeyertz, despite his reputation for directness, was known to support up-and-coming artists:

> Further practice on the concert platform will probably raise Miss Ainsley's value by 100 per cent or more. It may be hoped that she will not only keep more strictly to the contralto domain, but that she will also bring her lower notes, which now constitute a separate section, into better relationship with the middle register. . . . She is a singer of big possibilities.[43]

---

41 "Amusements: The Scarlet Troubadours," *Otago Daily Times*, September 7, 1908, 6.
42 "Amusements: Miss Irene Ainsley," *Evening Star*, October 27, 1908, 6.
43 Ibid.

As established in its first decade, the construction and refurbishment of His Majesty's Theatre, formerly the Agricultural Hall, was a significant addition to the city of Dunedin. Its size and versatility enabled much of the population of Dunedin to experience varied, accessible, and high-quality entertainment, musical and otherwise. With the population at just over forty-seven thousand by 1901, attendance at many events in the city was extraordinary by today's standards. Many historical accounts and biographies document performers, events, audience reception, and social history, but little is written about the venues where all these necessarily take place. Focusing on this one theatre has been revealing. The influence of J. C. Williamson is conspicuous. Though it did not own theatres outright in New Zealand, his organization leased several theatres, including the Opera House in Wellington, and it is evident that Williamson himself had a role in building and maintaining theatres throughout the country. Dunedin would have missed out on the many shows brought to New Zealand by Williamson's companies, among others, if the Agricultural Hall had not been transformed. Having a modern theatre allowed Dunedin to enjoy an extensive range of musical and theatrical entertainment equal to, if not surpassing, the offerings in other cities. And, as well as international touring companies, many local institutions, such as the Operatic Society, two local orchestras, the Choral Society, the Competitions Society, and various theatre groups, took advantage of the space.

Studying the theatre also offers a window into social history. Changes in audience agency, behavior and etiquette are documented and changing tastes examined. This work adds to our growing knowledge about urban life in colonial New Zealand and the leisure pursuits of past generations. It also suggests that "Dour Dunedin" was not as dull and grey as the rest of the country surmised. It was a vibrant and active city, boasting a community that supported and enjoyed a range of musical and artistic endeavors, many of which were held in spacious and well-appointed His Majesty's Theatre.

Bibliography

Newspapers
Clutha Leader (Otago)
Cromwell Argus (Otago)
Evening Post (Wellington)
Evening Star (Otago)
NZ Truth (National)
Otago Daily Times (Otago)
Otago Witness (Otago)
Star (Canterbury)

Books
Brewer, N. H. *A Century of Style: Great Ships of the Union Line 1875–1976*. Wellington: A.H. & A. W. Reed Ltd., 1982.

Campbell, Margaret. *Music in Dunedin: An Historical Account of Dunedin's Musicians and Musical Societies from the Founding of the Province in 1848*. Dunedin: Charles Begg & Co. Ltd., 1945.

Hurst, Maurice. *Music and the Stage in New Zealand: A Century of Entertainment 1840–1943*. Wellington: Charles Begg & Co. Ltd, 1944.

Thomson, John Mansfield. *The Oxford History of New Zealand Music*. Auckland: Oxford University Press, 1991.

Turnovsky, Fred. *Turnovsky: Fifty Years in New Zealand*. Wellington: Allen & Unwin, 1990.

Woods, Joanna. *Facing the Music: Charles Baeyertz and the Triad*. Dunedin: University of Otago Press, 2008.

Online Resource
Radio New Zealand. "Martin Phillips of the Chills shows us Dunedin's Historic Venues." Accessed 20 January, 2022. https://rnz.co.nz/national/programmes/nat-music/audio/2018617859/the-birthplaces-of-the-dunedin-sound

"In the Tiki Tiki Tiki Tiki Tiki Room": Musicalizing the South Pacific in Disney Theme Parks

Gregory Camp

Most visitors to Disney theme parks are guaranteed at some point to have at least one of the many attractions' catchy theme songs running through their brains. Whether this is a pleasurable re-listening or a maddening involuntary repetition depends on the individual's liking for all things Disney, but either way, the songs do their job. Dolls in international costumes sing over and over that "It's a Small World After All," pirates sing "Yo Ho (A Pirate's Life for Me)," and "Grim Grinning Ghosts" greet guests at the Haunted Mansion, pulling park-goers into the world of these attractions. Another such song, perhaps less known but a favorite of die-hard Disney fans, is "The Tiki Tiki Tiki Room" (that's three Tikis in the sheet music title, although in the actual chorus of the song there are five), written in 1963 by Disney house composers Robert B. Sherman and Richard M. Sherman for the Enchanted Tiki Room attraction at Disneyland. This song, which references Polynesian styles in its lyrics and arrangement, is an example of the many musical allusions to geographical regions and historical eras in the Walt Disney Company's film, television, and theme park texts. The company's use of music in these texts is an important marker of its attitude, and the attitude it constructs for its global audiences, towards these regions and times. In the case of the South Pacific styles alluded to in the Tiki Room, this attitude has shifted from the simple excitement of exoticism to something more seemingly authentic.

The South Pacific has featured prominently throughout Disney theme parks' history. In the 1950s and '60s, Disney capitalized on the Tiki fad by designing Disneyland's Adventureland largely around American ideas of the "exotic" South Pacific and its music, with attractions ranging from a mostly fictitious version of Pacific music in the Enchanted Tiki Room to somewhat more authentic music and dance in the Tahitian Terrace restaurant's floor show. These attractions, or variations on their themes, have appeared in Disney parks around the world ever since.[1] While in more recent films such as *Lilo and Stitch* (2002) and *Moana* (2016) Disney has attempted to convey a Pacific soundscape grounded in local musics, giving agency to the people whose stories are told, mid-century exoticism has persisted widely in the theme parks. In some cases, they have leaned even further into nonspecific narratives of place. The history of Disney's musicalization of the South Pacific in its theme parks exemplifies the shifting complexity of regional representation in international consumer entertainment, as audiences bring changing definitions and expectations of authenticity and agency to their experience.

Music in Disney Parks

The Disney theme park experience begins with the opening of Disneyland in 1955. The story of its creation has been frequently told.[2] The short version is that Walt Disney wanted to diversify and expand his studio's output, and he realized after visiting existing amusement parks that there was potential for a more intensely themed park, with intertextual relationships and marketing synergies with the studio's film and television products. While the financial wing of the studio (led by Walt's brother Roy) was skeptical of the venture, within a few years it had paid off and Disneyland remains a cornerstone of the company's success. The park was to provide a variety of immersive experiences, as an ever-changing but finite space where families could feel sheltered from the challenges of the outside world. There would be four "lands," or themed areas, in the park, including Adventureland, my focus here; the others were Frontierland, an idealized version of the American Wild West, Fantasyland, dominated by rides based

---

1   I use "Disney" here to refer to the conglomeration of texts in various genres produced by the Walt Disney Company. Until his death in 1966, Walt Disney himself had an extraordinary amount of control over his studio's product; since his death, his successors have continued to structure the company's activities around his perceived philosophies and aesthetics, leading to a remarkably coherent group of texts. More than any other studio, Disney supports Thomas Schatz's notion of the studio as "auteur" of the films it produces, above any individual director, cinematographer, composer, or other film worker (see Thomas Schatz, *The Genius of the System* [New York: Pantheon, 1988]), and this authorship can easily be expanded to the living texts of the theme parks. For more on the Disney authorship question, see Chris Pallant, *Demystifying Disney* (London: Bloomsbury, 2011).

2   See, for example, Alan Bryman, *Disney and His Worlds* (London: Routledge, 1995) and Richard Snow, *Disney's Land: Walt Disney and the Invention of the Amusement Park That Changed the World* (New York: Scribner, 2019).

on Disney films, and Tomorrowland, where the future (as conceived in the mid-1950s) was entertainingly predicted with space travel and futuristic household appliances. The entry area to the park was Main Street, USA, an idealized American main street featuring Americana-themed shops and restaurants.

The four lands of the park mirrored the genres and settings of the Disney studio's film and television productions, literally so in the anthology series *Disneyland*, which acted as a weekly advertisement for the park and a repository of the studio's back catalogue, each episode aligned to one of the four lands.[3] In the 1950s, the Disney studio was cementing its central place in the American mediascape, and it did so using these four broad categories.[4] Frontierland celebrated the American past (*Davy Crockett* [1955] being the most successful of many Disney westerns and costume pictures); Fantasyland foregrounded fairy tales and whimsy (mostly with an American accent, and was already firmly established by the studio's animated films such as 1937's *Snow White and the Seven Dwarfs*). Tomorrowland projected an ideal American-led future (witness the many science-centered television programs like *Our Friend the Atom* [1957] and *Man in Space* [1955]); and Adventureland showed Americans the rest of the world through American eyes (notably in the True Life Adventures documentary film series).[5] A similar array of lands can be found in the Magic Kingdom at Walt Disney World in Florida (opened in 1971), Tokyo Disneyland (1983), Disneyland Paris (1992), Hong Kong Disneyland (2005), and Shanghai Disneyland (2016). The other Disney parks are also divided into "lands," a convenient way to package products and experiences: EPCOT in Florida is a series of world's fair-style pavilions; Disney's Hollywood Studios in Florida and Walt Disney Studios in Paris consist of movie-style sets; Animal Kingdom in Florida is split into real and imaginary continents; Disney's California Adventure in Anaheim highlights various aspects of California; and Tokyo DisneySea is organized into international ports and islands.

---

3   For a history of Disney television, with detailed episode guides, see Bill Cotter, *The Wonderful World of Disney Television* (New York: Hyperion, 1997).

4   A comprehensive scholarly history of the Disney Studio is at present lacking, but studies that go into various aspects of the studio's products and organization in the 1950s include Richard Schickel, *The Disney Version* (New York: Simon and Schuster, 1968); Cotter, *The Wonderful World of Disney Television*; Leonard Maltin, *The Disney Films* (New York: Disney Editions, 2000); J. P. Telotte, *Disney TV* (Detroit: Wayne State University Press, 2004); and J. P. Telotte, *The Mouse Machine: Disney and Technology* (Chicago: University of Illinois Press, 2008).

5   Telotte, in *Disney TV*, gives an overview of these genres as displayed in the *Disneyland* anthology series.

Since their opening, Disney theme parks have employed music as an integral part of the narratives being portrayed, the music acting like a virtual film score, helping to make the guests (Disney's preferred term for their customers) feel as if they are taking part in the stories being told.[6] In addition to visual theming, the lands use music to heighten their various realities. Main Street, USA and Frontierland musicalize an ideal American past through folk music and popular music from previous centuries; Fantasyland borrows from Disney film scores to construct a live film-like experience; Tomorrowland's supposed music of the future uses present musical styles to imagine future ones; and the Adventurelands around the world foreground musical exoticism in all its problematic guises. The following case studies of the Enchanted Tiki Room, live Polynesian performances, and more recent soundings of Pacific exoticism in the parks will demonstrate how Disney uses fake and real South Pacific music towards its theme parks' narrative goals, and how those goals are met or undermined by the music's authenticity or lack thereof.

The Enchanted Tiki Room

When Adventureland opened in 1955, its main feature was the Jungle Cruise, a boat trip down various rivers of the world surrounded by mechanical animals and transplanted foliage. The goal was to bring guests into the studio's True Life Adventures film series, giving Americans a sense of the plant and animal life of the wide world.[7] The documentary, historical, and scientific aspects of Disneyland in its original conception were quickly minimized in favor of whimsy, especially in Adventureland. In the early 1960s, Disney's Imagineers began to make Adventureland into a more fantastical place, less documentary travelogue and more "fun."[8] Notably, two new musical shows opened: the live Polynesian Revue premiered as the floor show of the new Pacific-themed Tahitian Terrace

---

6   In "Mickey Mouse Muzak: Shaping Experience Musically at Walt Disney World," *Journal of the Society for American Music* 11, no. 1 (2017): 53–69, I theorize more broadly the ways music is used in Disney theme parks.

7   Sam Gennawey, in *The Disneyland Story* (Birmingham, AL: Keen Communications, 2014), explains the history of the development of Adventureland over the years (69–73). For a detailed description of the Walt Disney World version of the land as it was in the mid-'90s, see Stephen M. Fjellman, *Vinyl Leaves: Walt Disney World and America* (Boulder: Westview Press, 1993).

8   For an overview of this history, see Sabrina Mittermeier, *A Cultural History of the Disneyland Theme Parks: Middle Class Kingdoms* (Bristol: Intellect, 2021), 23–31.

restaurant in 1962, and then in 1963 the Enchanted Tiki Room began performances. The Tiki Room features audio-animatronic birds, flowers, and wood carvings which perform a fifteen-minute floor show loosely inspired by the South Pacific. The Tiki Room later opened without major alterations as first-day attractions in Walt Disney World in 1971 and Tokyo Disneyland in 1983. The Disneyland and Disney World versions are currently the same as the 1963 version (albeit shortened to fit more shows into the day), and the attraction is a major site for nostalgia alongside the other 1960s and '70s attractions that generations of park-goers have grown up with, such as the Jungle Cruise, Pirates of the Caribbean, and Haunted Mansion. The Tokyo version (and, for a short time, the Disney World version) was controversially altered from the original; more about that later, but first we need to investigate where the hybrid aesthetics of the Tiki Room came from. Why place at the center of Adventureland a show featuring Pacific-inspired singing birds and flowers?

Polynesian chic, also known as the Tiki craze, emerged in the 1940s and '50s, building on a fad for all things Hawaiian that had begun before World War II. To this fad were added popular culture narrations of the experiences of GIs returning to the US after the war, such as the 1948 musical *South Pacific* and the novel and film *From Here to Eternity* (1951). It took in Hawaiian shirts, wooden carvings, hula dancing, lap guitars, and remnants of Gauguin's Tahitian eroticism, mixed indiscriminately with other "exotic" influences from Africa and Southeast Asia. According to Francesco Adinolfi, "the Pacific represented a vast, unexplored space to be mined. Ex-soldiers dedicated themselves to its commercialization while disavowing their traumatic wartime memories."[9] Pacific exoticism was an attempt to retain (and sometimes fetishize) the positive wartime experiences of Americans abroad while forgetting the negatives. California bars like Trader Vic's and Don the Beachcomber, filled with wood carvings and serving exotic-sounding cocktails, were popular dining and drinking locations. Walt Disney wanted to recreate such experiences in a cleaned-up, usually alcohol-free version for his theme park. Many of these tiki bars featured live performances of "exotic" music, and the Enchanted Tiki Room references these modes of performance. Martin Denny was an influential practitioner of this musical style, notably in his 1957 cover version of "Quiet Village," which had originally appeared on Les Baxter's 1951 album *Ritual of the Savage*, usually regarded as

---

9   Francesco Adinolfi, *Mondo Exotico: Sounds, Visions, Obsessions of the Cocktail Generation* (Durham: Duke University Press, 2008), 4.

the first example of the genre of exotica in pop music.[10] The bird calls and other island noises on Denny's recording, mostly created by the human musicians vocalizing, are clear influences on the Tiki Room's score, and in fact this very song was used as background music in the show's queue.[11]

In the Enchanted Tiki Room, the audience sits in a square room, in four sections of chairs (bleachers in the non-California versions) around a central fountain, surrounded by windows with island backdrops and rain effects to evoke a humid tropical evening. The walls are faux wood and rattan, with extensive Polynesian-style carvings. Above the bleachers are planters packed with hundreds of animatronic birds and flowers, with elaborate lighting that shifts its intensity and focus through the various performances.[12] While the performance space's design is based strongly on the tiki bar aesthetic, the set of songs performed by the birds in the Tiki Room is a bizarre mix of mid-century exotica and early twentieth-century music hall (both English and French varieties). The show is hosted by four parrot compères: the Mexican José, Irish Michael, French Pierre, and German Fritz, adhering to the American stereotypes of these national groups and their accented speech.

The Sherman Brothers' title song "In the Tiki Tiki Tiki Room," which opens the show, is broadly Latin in its rhythms, but uses some Polynesian-style percussion. Typifying Disney theme park themes, short comic verses (each about a different bird) alternate with a catchy, repetitive chorus that encourages singing along. Solo piccolo and muted trumpet lines emphasize the nonspecific tropical feeling. By the 1960s, these instruments and rhythms had become standard markers of pop exoticism in American music, representing the Pacific, East Asia, Africa, or even outer space. This pan-exotic theme song is followed by a whistled version of the Barcarolle from Offenbach's *The Tales of Hoffmann* and then a rendition of the 1932 popular song "Let's All Sing Like the Birdies Sing," sung by the female chorus and imitators of Bing Crosby, Jimmy Durante, and Maurice

---

10　Andrew Wenaus, "Anxiety in Stereo: Les Baxter's *Space Escapade*, Armchair Tourism, Polar Inertia, and Being-in-a-World," *Journal of Popular Music Studies* 26, no. 4 (2014): 484–502. Wenaus notes the commonalities between the exotica style and the "space-age" style that Baxter and Denny also developed after the war, and which was very prominent in Disneyland's Tomorrowland. See also Philip Hayward, ed., *Widening the Horizon: Exoticism in Post-War Popular Music* (New Barnet, Herts: John Libbey, 1999).

11　Adinolfi, *Mondo Exotico*, 59. Disney nearly always uses music in its attractions' queues to condition guests' ears for the attraction to come. See Camp, "Mickey Mouse Muzak," 59.

12　There are 225 birds directed by a fourteen-channel magnetic tape feeding one hundred speakers. Gennawey, *The Disneyland Story*, 183.

Chevalier. The arrangements of all three pieces put them squarely in the 1950s–1960s easy listening style of Mitch Miller and Les Baxter, with woodwind lines circling around the tunes and the occasional jazz chord voicing.

Then things get more Polynesian. We hear the "Hawaiian War Chant," first sung slowly and lyrically by the female birds in close harmony in American-accented Hawaiian, then in a faster version featuring drums, an Yma Sumac impersonator, and a comedy chanter in the style of the well-known Spike Jones novelty recording of the song (1946). This famous *hapa haole* love song has nothing to do with war; that connotation came later with Spike Jones, who sped it up and employed a comic mock-Hawaiian style of chanting.[13] After this song, the tiki gods represented by the wood carvings and totems spread around the space are angered by the noise and create a storm in the theatre, leading to the birds suggesting that it's time to go. After a curtain call, the birds sing the audience out the door with "Heigh Ho" from *Snow White and the Seven Dwarfs*. None of this music, not even the "Hawaiian War Chant" in this particular version, reads as belonging to a specific place; rather, it is generically exotic, enjoyable from home in the US (literally, because the full soundtrack was released on LP shortly after the Tiki Room's opening). But the decor of the space and music's frequent tropes of the exotica genre do lend it an authentically inauthentic South Pacific air.

When we go to the Tiki Room today and hear its 1963 soundtrack, we experience a nostalgic mise-en-abîme, typical of many older Disney texts consumed now. The references to prewar musical styles in the show allowed 1960s adult audiences to feel nostalgic for their own pasts: Crosby, Durante, and Chevalier were not "current" in the '60s but were references from the previous twenty years of popular music, calculated to please the multiple generations Disney has always sought to attract to its products. Audiences in the parks in the 1970s and '80s might have had a similar attitude to the then-recent "exotic" styles of music they heard, reminding them of their own youths. It is unlikely that many present-day audiences have real-life experience of any of the styles referenced (unless of course they are older than most, or if they are musicologists). Their nostalgia is most likely not for the music, but for the attraction itself, one of the things that has seemingly always been part of their time at a Disney park. Evidence for this can be found in the many comments on Disney fan websites like

---

13 See George S. Kanahele and John Berger, *Hawaiian Music and Musicians: An Encyclopedic History* (Honolulu: Mutual Publishing, 2012), 283–285.

allears.net.[14] The words "nostalgia," "classic," and "iconic" appear frequently. In fact, when Disney updated the attraction at Disney World in 1998 to become "Enchanted Tiki Room (Under New Management)" it was regarded by most fans and critics as one of the most disastrous moves the Imagineers had ever made.[15] The negative reception demonstrated to Disney that moving away from nostalgia is risky.

"Enchanted Tiki Room (Under New Management)" uses the conceit that Zazu from *The Lion King* (1994) and Iago from *Aladdin* (1992) undertook the management of the nightclub, taking over from its former hopelessly old-fashioned bird owners. The show began identically to the original version with the four bird hosts waking up the other birds and all singing the title song. Iago quickly interrupts and takes the other birds to task for presenting such an outdated show. He sings a contrafact (new words to an existing melody) of "Friend Like Me" from *Aladdin* to explain the new world of entertainment to the other birds. By using music from *Aladdin*, the Imagineers attempted to bring the show up to date with material familiar to younger audience members. The tiki gods become angry that the show is being changed: the birds sing a version of 1980s calypso hit "Hot Hot Hot," and the tiki goddess of disaster Uh Oa (as in "uh-oh"—get it?) emerges from the center planter and, singing, blasts Iago away. Zazu lets the tiki gods have their say: they become a doo-wop ensemble and sing "In the Still of the Night." This shifts the show into more obvious 1950s nostalgia territory, one for the grandparents, but straight after this the gods make an embarrassing attempt at rap. After some cringey byplay between Iago and Zazu, the hosts, birds, gods, and flowers come together to create a party atmosphere, and all sing Gloria Estefan's "Conga" and then "On Your Feet" to get the audience out of the room. When the Iago animatronic was damaged by fire in 2011, Disney decided not to fix it and instead restored the show to the original 1963 version. "Under New Management" removes the show almost entirely from Pacific exoticism, aside from the very questionable authenticity of the goddess Uh Oa, who is musically coded not as Polynesian but as African American, and

---

14   AllEars.net, Enchanted Tiki Room reviews, accessed April 6, 2022, https://allears.net/reviews/enchanted-tiki-room/.

15   Among many examples of hate-watching from the Disney fan community, see Cole Geryak's report for *Laughing Place*, one of the major Disney fan websites, accessed April 6, 2022, https://www.laughingplace.com/w/featured/2017/12/27/disney-extinct-attractions-enchanted-tiki-room-new-management-now-playing-get-fever/. The article also includes a video of the show.

the architectural setting, which was not changed from the original. Instead, the music leans into multigenerational nostalgia by featuring songs from the 1950s through the 1990s.

Tokyo Disneyland included the Enchanted Tiki Room on its opening day in 1983, showing that this Pacific nostalgia was perceived not only as American. In 1999 it was redesigned as "Get the Fever," a Las Vegas-style jungle show; although the tiki gods were still present, the show was dissociated from the original tiki craze, much as "Under New Management" was in Disney World.[16] The original title song does appear in the show, but in a big band version rather than the Latin-influenced arrangement of the original. In 2008 the Tokyo show was redesigned again as "The Enchanted Tiki Room: Stitch Presents Aloha E Komo Mai," bringing it closer to Polynesia (specifically Hawaii) than any previous version of the attraction by using characters and settings from the 2002 film *Lilo and Stitch*, which was especially popular in Japan.[17] The show begins with the song "Roller Coaster Ride" from the film and, like the original version, also includes the "Hawaiian War Chant," here repositioned in its region of origin. The new show's title song (which comes from the TV *Stitch* series) is sung twice (in Japanese), at the beginning and end of the show. The concepts of aloha and 'ohana (which means family, as the cast of characters constantly remind us) are foregrounded here, as they were in the film, in a move away from unspecific Pacific exoticism into something more culturally informed. The cultural windows here are many: a North American show about Hawaiian culture filtered through a Japanese worldview. These diverse versions of the attraction demonstrate Disney's continuing attempt to provide both nostalgia and originality, and the specific Polynesian-ness of the musical material seems secondary to fulfilling these goals.

Performing Polynesia

The other Polynesian attraction that opened in the early 1960s at Disneyland was the Tahitian Terrace restaurant which featured the Polynesian Revue live

---

16 A video of the show can be found on YouTube at shinji T, "Enchanted Tiki Room 'Get the Fever!,'" YouTube Video, 13:24, July 3 2020, https://www.youtube.com/watch?v=YOWwSbc66EQ&t=520s.

17 A video of this version can be found on YouTube at WDW News Today, "The Enchanted Tiki Room: Stich Presents Aloha e Komo Mai!—Tokyo Disneyland," YouTube video, 12:36, October 10, 2019, https://www.youtube.com/watch?v=oR2mBAuxJJk&t=328s.

show, a concept recreated at the Polynesian Resort at Walt Disney World in the 1970s.[18] Both places featured live performers from the South Pacific region presenting a luau-style cultural show. The earliest versions of the production were presented in a variety show format, with acts like singers, hula dancers, fire walkers, and drumming. Walt Disney himself introduced excerpts the show on the television special *Disneyland after Dark*, which first aired in April of 1962, to inform television viewers about the new nightlife available at Disneyland.[19] The Disneyland version of the show ended in the 1990s, but Polynesian cultural performance has been among the offerings of the Polynesian Village Resort in Disney World for most of its existence. More recent versions include similar variety elements, but in a narrative frame: the most recent Polynesian Village Resort version, *Spirit of Aloha*, was staged as a homecoming celebration for a fictional girl from the islands. Her aunty serves as the MC, and while the primary location seems to be Hawaii, it is mostly set in a nonspecific "Island."[20] Stephen Fjellman notes that the Polynesian show is "authentic tourist dancing rather than authentic dancing or inauthentic tourist dancing."[21] This is indeed the kind of tourist dancing that can be seen around the Pacific islands and elsewhere. While the Disney show has not been studied much by academics, the similar show at the Polynesian Cultural Center (PCC) in Laie, Hawaii, has been. There has historically been some overlap between the performers at Disney World and those at the PCC. The PCC was founded in 1963 as a place where Pacific Island students at nearby Brigham Young University Hawaii could be involved in work-study programs and share their cultures. Much like Disney's Polynesian Resort, the PCC is divided into zones based on the individual island groups, with a large central section that includes a luau stage, where a nightly luau is presented.[22]

---

18 This resort has undergone a number of name changes: it opened in 1971 as the Polynesian Village Resort, from 1985 to 2014 it was shortened to the Polynesian Resort, and the name was lengthened again in 2014 to Polynesian Village Resort and Villas.

19 Cotter, *The Wonderful World of Disney Television*, 103.

20 Disney has announced that *Spirit of Aloha* will not return, having stopped performances due to Covid-19. As of this writing it is uncertain whether a new show will replace it. Lydia Storks, "Spirit of Aloha Permanently Closed in Disney World," AllEarsNet, March 15, 2022, https://allears.net/2022/03/15/spirit-of-aloha-permanently-closed-in-disney-world/. The show can be viewed in many YouTube videos, such as Laughingplace, "Disney's Spirit of Aloha Dinner (Full Show)," YouTube Video, 1:10:22, February 6, 2020, https://www.youtube.com/watch?v=AlnLcvtW09A.

21 *Vinyl Leaves*, 229–230.

22 Christopher B. Balme, "Staging the Pacific: Framing Authenticity in Performances for Tourists at the Polynesian Cultural Center," *Theatre Journal* 50, no. 1 (1998): 53–70.

Disney World's *Spirit of Aloha* luau dinner show features a wide variety of music performed by a live band and a singing and dancing chorus, ranging from traditional Hawaiian hula to Hawaii-set Disney music like "Hawaiian Roller Coaster Ride" from *Lilo and Stitch* (the same song heard in the Tokyo version of the Enchanted Tiki Room). The audience is also brought into the performance space to learn some basic hula steps. While the majority of the music and dance is Hawaiian, some other Polynesian cultures are also introduced, notably a Māori poi dance (with black-lit glow-in-the-dark poi, unlike anything one would see in kapa haka performance in Aotearoa New Zealand). The PCC and Polynesian Resort shows (like the earlier Disney iterations of the show) both climax with Samoan fire-knife dancing. This is an invented tradition, dating from the 1950s, which holds an interesting place in these cultural shows. Anthropologist Jefferey Caneen, studying the PCC, is worth quoting at length:

> When confronted with its technical inauthenticity, Samoan workers at the PCC vehemently maintain that the fire knife dance is "authentic" because 1.) it was created by Samoans, 2.) the knife that is set aflame and used in the dance evolved from a traditional Samoan battle weapon, and 3.) because it is Samoans that continue to change and refine both the knife and the dance. Authenticity for these indigenous people, then, consists not in the faithful representation of historic practices, but in the ethnic identity of those who create, own, and control it. It is authentically Samoan because authentic Samoans say it is. Or in other words, identity rather than authenticity is the primary consideration for these indigenous people.[23]

At the PCC and at Disney World, the current shows present the music and dancing in some kind of cultural framework, rather than as merely a series of "acts." But while the show at the PCC is framed as "authentic," and is viewed after a day full of learning local arts and crafts traditions from Indigenous people, the show at Disney World is framed by rides, shopping, and a wide variety of other music and dance performances. The luau is just another attraction, like the tiki birds, albeit one seemingly more grounded in authenticity.

Discussing the place of Indigenous American culture in Disney parks, cultural historian Victoria Pettersen Lantz argues that "through the level of distance and temporality (the length of time guests spend with representations of the

---

23   Jefferey M. Caneen, "Tourism and Cultural Identity: The Case of the Polynesian Cultural Center," *Athens Journal of Tourism* 1, no. 2 (2014): 101–120, 113.

Native Body), Disney crafts a staged indexical absence of First Nation peoples."[24] She comments that "as Walt Disney World grew in scope and the aims of parks expanded to include cultural exchanges, Disney began to fold references and imagery of First Nation people back into the parks, but in no way that offered a concrete, interactive experience that immersed tourists in Native American cultures."[25] Much, but not quite all, of this insight extends to native Hawaiians and other Polynesian peoples. Guests interact with people from Polynesia at the eponymous resort, being invited to share traditions of song, dance, and food; and even though much of the material was written by non-Polynesians for a Florida theme park, the bodies seen and voices heard performing are Polynesian. Similarly, guests can have less formal interactions with people from the countries represented in World Showcase at EPCOT, or from Africa or Asia in the Animal Kingdom park, but not since Disneyland's first decades have First Nations people been present in the same way, unless playing fictionalized characters like the Disney version of Pocahontas or as distant animatronic figures. And while First Nations music is almost entirely absent from the parks, the Westernized version of Polynesian music discussed here (as well as other non-North American musics) is often audible.[26] Like Pocahontas, Moana is another costumed character guests can encounter frequently along with the music she sings from the film named for her, but paradoxically, the (falsified) historical character Pocahontas seems less "authentic" than the entirely fictional Moana.

Perhaps because the South Pacific, like the territories represented at EPCOT and Animal Kingdom, is not quite so close to "home" (the middle-class Main Street-centered frontier-thesis version of the American continent that Disney foregrounds), the parks' creators have felt more comfortable including some version of its Indigenous voices. Unfortunately, however, the Disney parks of late have retreated to '60s-style exoticism in their musical representation of the South Pacific.

---

24 Victoria Pettersen Lantz, "What's Missing in Frontierland? American Indian Culture and Indexical Absence at Walt Disney World," in *Performance and the Disney Theme Park Experience*, ed. Jennifer A. Kokai and Tom Robson (Cham: Palgrave Macmillan, 2019), 46.

25 Lantz, "What's Missing in Frontierland?," 48.

26 One exception was the dedication of new totems at EPCOT's Canada pavilion in 2017, when the Git-Hoan Dancers, of Pacific Northwest roots, performed in the park for three days (ibid, 56).

Since the '60s

Echoes of the tiki craze have returned over the last few decades in pop culture. Aside from the Enchanted Tiki Room, exotica seems to have reappeared only rarely in Disney parks before the new millennium. Disney has recently directly engaged with tiki nostalgia at the Disneyland Hotel in California, where Trader Sam's Enchanted Tiki Bar opened in 2011. It obviously references the 1950s and '60s, when Disneyland first opened. The music loop played in the bar consists of original 1950s exotica from the likes of Martin Denny, '60s surf rock, and more recent nostalgic exotica played by tribute bands like the Tikiyaki Orchestra.[27] This recent music combines many of the mid-century trends, including space-age, bachelor pad lounge music, and surf rock with the already hybrid exotica style, creating a generic sense of "the '60s" rather than anything culturally specific. Portions of the Enchanted Tiki Room soundtrack are heard as well, Disney's own attraction being part of the nostalgia-fest.

Disney has attempted to address concerns about the inauthenticity inherent in exoticism, notably on the big screen, but few such attempts are reflected consistently in the theme parks. Back in the 1960s, *Swiss Family Robinson* (1960) and *In Search of the Castaways* (1962) offered Disneyfied, inauthentic colonial histories of the South Pacific region. In the early 2000s Disney capitalized on growing interest in Hawaii with a number of Disney Channel films like *Rip Girls* (2000) and *Johnny Tsunami* (1999), and most notably the theatrical animated film *Lilo and Stitch*. These Hawaiian films had some Indigenous musical features, but then in 2016 Disney released *Moana*, with many production crew members from the South Pacific region. In *Moana*, the filmmakers made a well-advertised attempt to tell a Pacific story using Pacific voices. Two of the studio's most recent animated films, *Frozen 2* (2019) and *Raya and the Last Dragon* (2021), employed teams of cultural experts so that indigenous Sámi culture and southeast Asian cultures respectively were portrayed authentically in those films. Such markers of authenticity did not please all audiences from various regions, indicating the difficulty facing a massive multinational but United States-based corporation trying to speak and sing both to and for people around the world.[28]

---

27 A YouTube search will bring up the background music loops of these and more Disney spaces. For example, see MrThemeParkAudios, "Music From Disneyland—Trader Sam's Enchanted Tiki Bar," YouTube Video, 2:05:59, July 13, 2014, https://www.youtube.com/watch?v=PPRGcoTvnQg.

28 In "Disney's *Moana*, the Colonial Screenplay, and Indigenous Labor Extraction in Hollywood Fantasy Films," *Narrative Culture* 6, no. 2 (2019): 188–215, Ida Yoshinaga takes Disney

Moana's soundtrack, though, could be interpreted as raising these postcolonialist concerns to a lesser extent. Sonically, the film in its production process and its final product perhaps succeeded in giving more agency to Polynesian people. For English-speaking audiences, Moana sounds like Auli'i Cravalho, a native Hawaiian actress, and many other members of the voice cast are also of Hawaiian or other Pacific Island ancestry. On the soundtrack we hear Opetaia Foa'i and his group Te Vaka performing music co-written by them, alongside a Pacific choir directed by Igelese Ete, often singing text in Pacific languages (notably Samoan and Tokelauan).[29] Most significantly, *Moana* was fully dubbed into Hawaiian, Te Reo Māori, and Tahitian and distributed to local schools in Hawaii, New Zealand, and French Polynesia.[30] Moana herself is portrayed in the international theme parks along with other Disney princesses, and her music accompanies her appearances in character cavalcades and parades in the parks. Disney is also planning a new *Moana*-inspired attraction at EPCOT called "Journey of Water." While details are being kept under wraps until it opens sometime in the mid-2020s, it will allow guests to "interact with magical, living water in a beautiful and inspiring setting," and music from the film is very likely to accompany this interaction.[31]

That the new Moana attraction and the old Tiki Room attraction exist in the same world is indicative of the balance the studio tries to achieve between

---

to task for setting up a culturally informed setting in the first act of *Moana* but then de-evolving it into Hollywood tropes in its second act. She details the long filmmaking process, where white American male filmmakers were tasked with coming up with a story about a Polynesian girl. While Pacific Islanders were hired to work on the film, their work was contracted and short-term rather than integral to the Disney company. This was true of the music team as well.

29 Madeline Chapman, "Moana composer Opetaia Foa'i on the Story behind the Best Soundtrack since the Lion King," Spinoff, February 15, 2017, https://thespinoff.co.nz/music/15-02-2017/this-is-our-movie-opetaia-foai-on-keeping-moana-authentic-through-music.

30 Whether this was an earnest attempt to give speakers of those languages a recent text to enjoy or a cynical grab at a new market must be left to the reader to decide, but the reception of the Te Reo version was mostly positive among the Māori community and Te Reo dubs of other Disney films are planned. See "Moana Reo Māori Arrives on Disney+ Three Years after Release," Stuff, June 28, 2020, https://www.stuff.co.nz/entertainment/tv-radio/121968586/moana-reo-mori-arrives-on-disney-three-years-after-release. On the complexities of dubbing the voices in *Moana*, see Colleen Montgomery, "From Moana to Vaiana: Voicing the French and Tahitian Dubbed Versions of Disney's *Moana*," American Music 39, no. 2 (2021): 237–251.

31 Kelly Coffey, "'Moana'-Inspired Attraction at EPCOT Begins Taking Shape," Insidethemagic.net, December 4, 2021, https://insidethemagic.net/2021/12/moana-attraction-epcot-construction-progress-kc1/.

sensitive representation of various agents through new texts on the one hand, and the nostalgia appeal of old texts on the other. The major musical challenge for Disney is to represent various groups authentically while taking audiences on the nostalgia trip they are expecting. The complex of nostalgia tropes alluding to the 1950s and '60s (which continues to sell tickets) includes the inauthentic musical portrayals discussed above, exoticism as it was constructed in earlier decades. It is in the parks that this complex negotiation is most marked; after all, one has to take a *physical* trip to experience them. One of Disney's recent narrative initiatives in their parks is the Society of Explorers and Adventurers (SEA), around which a growing number of attractions and soon films, television programs, and books, are based.[32] The SEA, and specifically the music that accompanies the attractions themed to the fictional society, demonstrates an often uncomfortable pull between colonial nostalgia and postcolonial reparation.

The SEA is a fictional society of mostly Western explorers from the early twentieth century who had various relationships with the non-Western lands they were exploring. At Tokyo DisneySea, the park most tied into the SEA, the Tower of Terror is supposedly a hotel built by explorer Harrison Hightower III, who hoarded artefacts from all around the world there instead of displaying them in museums. One of the idols he stole was cursed, causing elevators to drop. Mystic Manor, an attraction at Hong Kong Disneyland, is a ride through SEA member Henry Mystic's collection of artefacts, which come alive when his pet monkey Albert accidentally opens an enchanted music box. It includes a Tribal Arts Room, in which is stored an indiscriminate combination of African and Pacific artefacts. Markers of exotica abound in the music of these attractions as well as in their visual design: the Mystic Manor score was composed by noted film composer Danny Elfman, and the music in the Tribal Arts Room includes the same old elements of South Pacific exoticism as the Tiki Room. Chanting, drums, and syncopations (unrelated to any specific regional tradition) pervade the soundtrack. Like that of most Disney dark rides, the music is based on a single theme heard in a series of sophisticated arrangements that flow into one another as the guests are taken through the attraction. This was an invitation to Elfman to compose a theme that could go through various iterations, a form that of course has a very long history. These themes-and-variations recall the

---

32 The Disney Wiki, a popular fan site, has correlated all of the confirmed and supposed references to the SEA in the Disney parks canon: "Society of Explorers and Adventurers," accessed April 11, 2022, https://disney.fandom.com/wiki/Society_of_Explorers_and_Adventurers.

many eighteenth-century sonatas or symphonic works that include a "Turkish" movement, the period's favored set of exotic tropes similarly domesticated into Western musical structures.[33]

While the message of these rides is to deplore colonial plunder, this whole complex of stories buys into the colonial romance of exploration. That the explorers have stolen artefacts is represented as something bad, but the true origin of the artefacts and their cultural contexts are left unexplored. Instead of being made to feel uncomfortable by the indiscriminate collection of fake artefacts in Mystic's Tribal Arts Room, guests of the manor are thrilled by the exotic music accompanying poor Albert as he tries to undo the curse he accidentally set off. In another missed opportunity, this club of great navigators and explorers only includes Europeans and Americans, ignoring the long and complex history of Pacific and Asian navigation (especially striking since the parks that feature the SEA most prominently are the Asian ones).

We all know that Disney is problematic, and that it has been since Walt Disney founded the company in the 1920s. Each attempt by the studio to be culturally informed seems to be countered by some backwards-looking move. Music, which plays an important role in all Disney's work, represents in microcosm shifting attitudes towards the Pacific. That the music in the parks has stayed largely within the standard tropes of exoticism even while Disney's recent films have been more progressive shows this massive multinational corporation caught between nostalgia for mid-century popular culture and a desire for cultural authenticity. How the company continues to navigate these challenging waters of agency and representation is illustrative of various broader cultural trends.

---

33 Mary Hunter's description of the broad connotations of the *alla turca* style in the Enlightenment could apply just as well to 1960s exotica's use of Polynesian or African musical tropes: "Not only does the musical content of the *alla turca* style represent a straightforwardly 'Orientalist' attitude to Turkish music, but the way this topos was used also exemplifies a classically Orientalizing blurring of boundaries among different sorts of Others." See "The *Alla Turca* Style in the late Eighteenth Century: Race and Gender in the Symphony and the Seraglio," in *The Exotic in Western Music*, ed. Jonathan Bellman (Boston: Northeastern University Press, 1998), 52–53.

Bibliography

Adinolfi, Francesco. *Mondo Exotico: Sounds, Visions, Obsessions of the Cocktail Generation.* Durham: Duke University Press, 2008.

AllEars.net. Enchanted Tiki Room reviews. Accessed April 6, 2022. https://allears.net/reviews/enchanted-tiki-room/.

Balme, Christopher B. "Staging the Pacific: Framing Authenticity in Performances for Tourists at the Polynesian Cultural Center." *Theatre Journal* 50, no. 1 (1998): 53–70.

Bryman, Alan. *Disney and His Worlds.* London: Routledge, 1995.

Camp, Gregory. "Mickey Mouse Muzak: Shaping Experience Musically at Walt Disney World." *Journal of the Society for American Music* 11, no. 1 (2017): 53–69.

Caneen, Jefferey M. "Tourism and Cultural Identity: The Case of the Polynesian Cultural Center." *Athens Journal of Tourism* 1, no. 2 (2014): 101–120.

Chapman, Madeline. "Moana Composer Opetaia Foa'i on the Story behind the Best Soundtrack since the Lion King." *Spinoff*, February 15, 2017. https://thespinoff.co.nz/music/15-02-2017/this-is-our-movie-opetaia-foai-on-keeping-moana-authentic-through-music.

Coffey, Kelly. "'Moana'-Inspired Attraction at EPCOT Begins Taking Shape." Insidethemagic.net, December 4, 2021. https://insidethemagic.net/2021/12/moana-attraction-epcot-construction-progress-kc1/.

Cotter, Bill. *The Wonderful World of Disney Television.* New York: Hyperion, 1997.

Disney Wiki. "Society of Explorers and Adventurers." Accessed April 11, 2022. https://disney.fandom.com/wiki/Society_of_Explorers_and_Adventurers.

Fjellman, Stephen M. *Vinyl Leaves: Walt Disney World and America.* Boulder: Westview Press, 1993.

Gennawey, Sam. *The Disneyland Story.* Birmingham, AL: Keen Communications, 2014.

Geyrak, Cole. "Disney Extinct Attractions: The Enchanted Tiki Room (Under New Management and Now Playing Get the Fever!). *Laughing Place*. Accessed April 6, 2022. https://www.laughingplace.com/w/featured/2017/12/27/disney-extinct-attractions-enchanted-tiki-room-new-management-now-playing-get-fever/.

Hayward, Philip, ed. *Widening the Horizon: Exoticism in Post-War Popular Music.* New Barnet, Herts: John Libbey, 1999.

Hunter, Mary. "The *Alla Turca* Style in the late Eighteenth Century: Race and Gender in the Symphony and the Seraglio." In *The Exotic in Western Music*, edited by Jonathan Bellman, 43–73. Boston: Northeastern University Press, 1998.

Kanahele, George S., and John Berger. *Hawaiian Music and Musicians: An Encyclopedic History.* Honolulu: Mutual Publishing, 2012.

Lantz, Victoria Pettersen. "What's Missing in Frontierland? American Indian Culture and Indexical Absence at Walt Disney World." In *Performance and the Disney Theme*

Park Experience, edited by Jennifer A. Kokai and Tom Robson, 43–63. Cham: Palgrave Macmillan, 2019.

Laughingplace. "Disney's Spirit of Aloha Dinner (Full Show)." YouTube Video, 1:10:22. February 6, 2020. https://www.youtube.com/watch?v=AlnLcvtW09A.

Maltin, Leonard. *The Disney Films*. New York: Disney Editions, 2000.

Mittermeier, Sabrina. *A Cultural History of the Disneyland Theme Parks: Middle Class Kingdoms*. Bristol: Intellect, 2021.

"Moana Reo Māori arrives on Disney+ three years after release." Stuff, June 28, 2020. https://www.stuff.co.nz/entertainment/tv-radio/121968586/moana-reo-mori-arrives-on-disney-three-years-after-release.

MrThemeParkAudios. "Music From Disneyland—Trader Sam's Enchanted Tiki Bar." YouTube Video, 2:05:59. Accessed April 14, 2022. https://www.youtube.com/watch?v=PPRGcoTvnQg.

Montgomery, Colleen. "From Moana to Vaiana: Voicing the French and Tahitian Dubbed Versions of Disney's *Moana*." *American Music* 39, no. 2 (2021): 237–251.

Pallant, Chris. *Demystifying Disney: A History of Disney Feature Animation*. London: Bloomsbury, 2011.

Schatz, Thomas. *The Genius of the System*. New York: Pantheon, 1988.

Schickel, Richard. *The Disney Version*. New York: Simon and Schuster, 1968.

shinji T. "Enchanted Tiki Room 'Get the Fever!'" YouTube Video, 13:29. Accessed April 14, 2022. https://www.youtube.com/watch?v=YOWwSbc66EQ&t=520s.

Snow, Richard. *Disney's Land: Walt Disney and the Invention of the Amusement Park That Changed the World*. New York: Scribner, 2019.

Storks, Lydia. "Spirit of Aloha Permanently Closed in Disney World." AllEarsNet, 15 March 2022. https://allears.net/2022/03/15/spirit-of-aloha-permanently-closed-in-disney-world/.

Telotte, J. P. *Disney TV*. Detroit: Wayne State University Press, 2004.

———. *The Mouse Machine: Disney and Technology*. Chicago: University of Illinois Press, 2008.

WDW News Today. "The Enchanted Tiki Room: Stich Presents Aloha e Komo Mai!—Tokyo Disneyland." YouTube Video, 12:36. October 10, 20. https://www.youtube.com/watch?v=oR2mBAuxJJk&t=328s.

Wenaus, Andrew. "Anxiety in Stereo: Les Baxter's *Space Escapade*, Armchair Tourism, Polar Inertia, and Being-in-a-World." *Journal of Popular Music Studies* 26, no. 4 (2014): 484–502.

Yoshinaga, Ida. "Disney's *Moana*, the Colonial Screenplay, and Indigenous Labor Extraction in Hollywood Fantasy Films." *Narrative Culture* 6, no. 2 (2019): 188–215.

Part Two

Vocal Music's Agencies

Figaro Transmuted through the Agency of Neapolitan Social and Political Creatives: Niccolò Piccinni's *La serva onorata*

Lawrence Mays

Sabato sera andò per la prima volta in scena nel Teatro de' Fiorentini l'opera buffa intitolata La serva onorata, musica del celebre maestro di cappella sig Piccinni. Un immenso popolo concorse a godere di questo spettacolo, quale venne anche onorato dell'amabile presenza del graziosissimo nostro sovrano.[1]

(On Saturday evening the opera buffa entitled *La serva onorata*, with music by the celebrated composer signor Piccinni, appeared on stage for the first time at the Teatro dei Fiorentini. An immense crowd gathered to enjoy this show, which was also honored by the affable presence of our most gracious sovereign.)[2]

La serva onorata—a comic opera in two acts with libretto by Giovanni Battista Lorenzi and music by Niccolò Piccinni—premiered at the Teatro dei Fiorentini in Naples in 1792. Its libretto is a substantially reworked version of Lorenzo Da Ponte's *Le nozze di Figaro* as set by Mozart in 1786.[3] As the quoted extract from an article in a local newspaper notes, there was a large audience at the premiere and King Ferdinand IV of Naples attended. According to Piccinni's biographer

---

1 *Notizie del Mondo* [edition of Naples], September 8, 1792, 189.
2 Translations are by the author.
3 Giovanni Battista Lorenzi, *La serva onorata. Dramma giocoso per musica da rappresentarsi nel Teatro de' Fiorentini per seconda opera del corrente anno 1792.*

Pierre-Louis Ginguené, the opera was a great success.[4] This chapter will examine the influences leading to the transformation of an opera that had enjoyed considerable success in Vienna into a work that was enthusiastically received in Naples. It will describe the kinds of agency exercised by librettist, composer, theater management and performers in response to these influences.[5]

Political Influences on the Opera's Genesis

Although it was not unusual for royals to attend opera performances, the king's presence suggests that, as a result of their exposure to Viennese cultural influences, sovereigns played a role in the genesis of the work. Cultural connections between Vienna and Naples were extensive in the late eighteenth century. They were facilitated by the presence in Naples of Maria Carolina, daughter of Maria Theresia of Austria, who had married the Bourbon king Ferdinand IV in 1768. There was much exchange of music between the cities. A good example is Norbert Hadrava's support for several initiatives to disseminate awareness of "German" music.[6] Other possible vectors for the libretto include prominent singers who performed in both centers—such as Celeste and Anna Coltellini, Stefano Mandini and Vincenzo Calvesi—and the king and the queen themselves.

The royal couple's long visit to Vienna in 1790–91 might, for example, have facilitated the exchange of scores and libretti between the cities. The Neapolitan sovereigns heard excerpts of Mozart's opera there at various times, and they attended a full performance in October 1790. In Vienna they had some association with Da Ponte, who held the position of poet at the court theater from 1783 to 1791. He wrote libretti for two dramatic works performed in 1791 in their honor: *I voti della nazione Napoletana* and *Flora e Minerva*, set to music by

---

4 Pierre-Louis Ginguené, *Notice Sur La Vie et Les Ouvrages de Nicolas Piccinni* (Paris: Veuve Panckoucke, 1800), 83. There appears to be no other source to indicate the opera's fate or degree of appreciation, nor is there any evidence that it was subsequently reprised in Naples or elsewhere.

5 I wish to acknowledge the assistance and advice of Lucio Tufano, with whom I am co-editing a critical edition of this opera for A-R Editions. See: Lucio Tufano and Lawrence Mays, eds., *Niccolò Piccinni, La Serva Onorata* (Middleton, Wisconsin: A-R Editions, forthcoming).

6 Hadrava introduced the Neapolitan public to the orchestral works of Haydn and Dittersdorf and the melodramas of Benda. He also undertook circulation of Neapolitan opera scores to Vienna. See: Giuliana Gialdroni, "La Musica a Napoli Alla Fine Del XVIII Secolo Nelle Lettere Di Norbert Hadrava," *Fonti Musicali Italiane* 1 (1996): 75–143. See also: Anthony R. DelDonna, *Instrumental Music in Late Eighteenth-Century Naples: Politics, Patronage and Artistic Culture* (Cambridge: Cambridge University Press, 2020), 105–116.

Francesco Piticchio and Joseph Weigl respectively. Maria Carolina was known to like music, and it is possible that when she was in the Habsburg capital Da Ponte may have taken the opportunity to offer her his text for use in Naples.[7] His libretto of *Le nozze di Figaro* had been given a new music setting—Maria Carolina's brother Archduke Ferdinand of Austria-Este had commissioned Angelo Tarchi for this undertaking, and it was performed in Monza in 1787. However, Lorenzi apparently based his text on Da Ponte's original libretto, which was published in Vienna in 1786, rather than subsequent revisions.[8] There is no evidence that the sovereigns had any direct influence on Lorenzi in his revision.

Social Influences: Adapting Figaro to the Neapolitan *Vis Comica*

Comic opera libretti by non-Neapolitans were rarely used in their original form in Naples.[9] Published libretti of Venetian operas performed in the city, for example, often indicated that the works were "adjusted to suit the tastes of the audiences of the city." Such adjustments included the addition or substitution of arias, the revision by Neapolitan composers of comic scenes, and the inclusion of local dialect.[10] A case in point is Carlo Goldoni's *Il mondo della luna*, which was written in 1750 and set by Baldassare Galuppi. It was substantially modified by Lorenzi and renamed *La luna abitata*. Set by Paisiello, it was performed at the Teatro Nuovo in Naples in 1768. The revision included characters who spoke in Neapolitan dialect. Paisiello set a further revision of Goldoni's text by an unknown Neapolitan librettist, renamed *Il credulo deluso*, for the Teatro Nuovo in 1774.[11] Bellina notes that the verses in this version were frequently shortened, the relationship between characters was altered, and the genre indication was

---

7   For a detailed discussion of the mechanisms of exchange of opera between the two centers see: Lucio Tufano, "Nozze Napoletane. La Serva Onorata Di Giambattista Lorenzi e Niccolò Piccinni (1792)," *Mozart-Studien*, no. 21 (2012): 279–336.

8   Ibid.: 280–81.

9   Michael F. Robinson, *Naples and Neapolitan Opera* (Oxford: Clarendon Press, 1972), 88.

10 Gordana Lazarevich, "The Neapolitan Intermezzo and Its Influence on the Symphonic Idiom," *Musical Quarterly* 57, no. 2 (1971): 294–313, 295.

11 Anna Laura Bellina, "Goldoni, Paisiello e La Luna Nuova," in *Commedia e Musica al Tramonto dell'Ancien Régime: Cimarosa, Paisiello e i Maestri Europei*, ed. Antonio Caroccia (Avellino: Conservatorio di Musica Domenico Cimarosa, 2017), 189–213.

changed from dramma giocoso to "commedia."[12] This opera also included Neapolitan-speaking characters.[13]

The transmutation of *Le nozze di Figaro* into *La serva onorata* owes much to the Neapolitan *vis comica*—that had resulted in a distinct musical and literary comic style. This style pervaded eighteenth-century music genres, including intermezzi and opere buffe. The *villanella*—a Neapolitan song form—was a precursor of these genres. Theatrical comedies flourishing in Italy in the early sixteenth century typically legitimized instinctive behavior and elevated the supposedly vulgar. They set out to reflect the characteristic behavior, songs, and dialects of peasants, as perceived by the bourgeoisie. In this environment a more spontaneous, earthy alternative to the madrigal developed. The type of song that emerged came to be termed *canzone villanesca alla napoletana* or simply *villanella*.[14] The Neapolitan authors of *La serva onorata* followed this comedic style by distinguishing the language and preoccupations of the servant classes from those of the nobility more clearly than *Le nozzze di Figaro* does.

Neapolitan intermezzi flourished from approximately 1685 to 1750. Usually involving only two singing characters, they began as *scene buffe* or comic interludes between the acts of serious opera.[15] Intermezzi exploited operas' minor characters—ordinary people in everyday situations, speaking the language of the lower social strata rather than the high-flown language of high-status characters. Pronounced physical gestures were the norm. The comedic requirements of intermezzi resulted in performance markings additional to conventional musical notation. Troy terms the vocal style "comic realism," noting that singers would laugh, howl, sigh, cough, and imitate physiological phenomena such as heartbeats or the sounds of inanimate objects like whip cracks; "realistic" humor derived from specific directions for vocal delivery, which might include *ridendo* (laughing), *con ira* (angrily), *sospirando* (sighing), *piangendo* (weeping), *smaniando* (raving), and variation in voice timbre such as humming and falsetto. Vocal representations of sobbing, sighing, laughing, stuttering, and yawning were also

---

12 Ibid.

13 Paisiello set a one-act revision by an anonymous librettist of *Il mondo della Luna* in St Petersburg in 1783. This was reprised apparently in its original form in Naples in 1784. See Stefano Faglia, ed., *Il Mondo Della Luna: Opera in Un Atto* (Parma: Oca del Cairo, 2000).

14 Donna G. Cardamone, "Villanella," in *Grove Music Online*, Oxford University Press, 2001, https://doi.org/10.1093/gmo/9781561592630.article.29379.

15 Lazarevich, "The Neapolitan Intermezzo and its Influence on the Symphonic Idiom": 294–5.

indicated in the scores.[16] Many of these elements of the Neapolitan *vis comica* are present in *La serva onorata*. They are implied—if not directly specified—in the text and musical settings of the Neapolitan servant characters, where there is ample scope for physical and vocal gestures. According to Piccinni's biographer Pierre-Louis Ginguené, satisfying Neapolitan theatrical tastes was consistent with the composer's foremost compositional aim—to portray natural human behavior, including the expression of emotions.[17]

Actors who exercised agency in this transmutation of the Da Ponte and Mozart opera included the impresario, librettist, composer, and performers. Familiar with the tastes of Neapolitan comic opera audiences and the abilities and particular comedic skills of the available performers, the impresario engaged a librettist to transform the text accordingly and a composer to set it to music. The composer took into account the vocal skills and performance specializations of the singers in his setting, and exercised his agency, by making changes to the revised libretto in response to the performers, who in turn exercised their own agency to adapt the work to their aptitudes.

Impresario and Librettist

In eighteenth-century Naples it was common for an impresario to request a reputed librettist to produce an approximate version catering to Neapolitan tastes of an opera libretto imported from elsewhere. These two figures were primary agents in the transmutation undergone by the Mozart/Da Ponte opera. The impresario would advise as to the singers available for the production. Neither the libretto nor the score was considered inviolable, and it was aesthetically legitimate to adapt the work for the singers available. Carl Dahlhaus observes that a successful libretto would provide the composer with a scenario amenable to "the structure and sense of the musical forms of the time."[18] Lorenzi was one of the most esteemed librettists of Neapolitan comic opera. His background was in the *commedia dell'arte* tradition and he wrote some spoken-word comedies as

---

16 Charles E. Troy, *The Comic Intermezzo: A Study in the History of Eighteenth-Century Italian Opera* (Ann Arbor: UMI Research Press, 1979), 92.

17 Pierre-Louis Ginguené, *Notice Sur La Vie et Les Ouvrages de Nicolas Piccinni* (Paris: Veuve Panckoucke, 1800), 108.

18 Carl Dahlhaus, "The Dramaturgy of Italian Opera," in *Opera in Theory and Practice, Image and Myth*, vol. 6, *The History of Italian Opera*, part 2, *Systems*, ed. Lorenzo Bianconi and Giorgio Pestelli (Chicago: University of Chicago Press, 2003), 86.

well as libretti. Beginning in 1755, he produced over thirty opera buffa libretti, which were set mainly by Paisiello, Cimarosa, and Piccinni.[19]

By this late stage of his career Lorenzi was well versed in the expectations of local theater management and audiences. The sequence of musical elements in *La serva onorata* approximates the standard schema of Neapolitan comic opera of the late eighteenth century, as sardonically described in the anonymous preface to the second volume of Giambattista Lorenzi's *Opere teatrali*, vol. 2.[20] According to the preface, the Neapolitan *commedia per musica* must have two acts and include the following elements:

> [A]lways a boisterous operatic opening for many voices; a cavatina for the first appearance of the *prima buffa* or a short duet for the first encounter between her and the *primo buffo*; a trio, quartet, or quintet in the fourth or fifth scene of the work which often greatly embarrasses the poet as the climax of the scenario is not yet sufficiently developed, so it always lacks interest; the penultimate aria of the act by the *primo buffo*, then the last aria by the *prima buffa*. The first act finally concludes with a finale of seven or eight scenes which must end with the involvement of all the actors who say the same words, whether or not these are suitable to their characters, making with voices and instruments a noisy sinfonia with imitations, canons, fugues, and strettas, leading with much noise and clamor the end of the act. The curtain falls as if everything were finished and after a quarter of an hour it rises again to begin the second act. After a brief scene the minor character must sing the so-called *aria del sorbetto*; afterwards there usually comes a duet between the two *buffi*, then an aria by the tenor with its accompanied recitative; finally another ensemble piece between the main characters and then a finale similar to the first.

Librettist and Composer—Trans-Genre Remodeling

The Neapolitan authors of *La serva onorata* undertook a trans-genre remodeling of Da Ponte and Mozart's work—from opera buffa to Neapolitan *commedia per musica*. The opera is in two acts, with six characters and no chorus. Although Da Ponte's plot is modified, with completely new elements added, there remain

---

19 Anthony DelDonna, "Giovanni Battista Lorenzi (1721–1807) and Neapolitan Comic Opera in the Late Eighteenth Century," in *Genre in Eighteenth-Century Music*, ed. Anthony DelDonna (Ann Arbor: Steglein Publishing, 2008), 52–85.

20 Giambattista Lorenzi, *Opere Teatrali*, vol. 2 (Napoli: Stamperia Flautina, 1813), iv–v.

numerous points of concurrence. Many musical numbers in *La serva onorata* are based on the same texts as those in *Le nozze di Figaro*, intact or paraphrased. Da Ponte's verses remain recognizable, but often altered in length, metrical and strophic structure, and dramatic function.

In eighteenth-century Italian comic operas there were often discrepancies between the libretto, which was published in advance, and the score used for performance, which was not published at the time. The differences were usually not very substantial.[21] Logistical and time constraints determined the extent to which the composer could collaborate with the librettist. What is unusual about *La serva onorata* is the degree of disparity. The score omits 275 lines of the libretto text. Of these 134 belong to closed pieces. One aria is omitted, and two new ones are added.[22] The magnitude of the discrepancy suggests a fragmented creative process subject to multiple influences in response to which the composer exercised his agency.

Figure 1 shows the character names which have been modified, apparently to suit local preferences. A distinguishing feature of the Neapolitan revision is the way the revised title of the opera shifts the focus from the male servant (Figaro) to the female servant (Livietta).

Figure 1. Characters in *La serva onorata* (with the corresponding ones from *Le nozze di Figaro* shown where they are not obvious), singers, their voice parts and musico-dramatic roles (as they appear in the index of theatrical productions for the 1792–93 season)[23]

Character	Singer	Voice	Musico-dramatic role
Livietta (Susanna)	Anna Coltellini	Soprano	*Prima buffa*
La Contessa Metilde	Maria Brunetti	Soprano	*Prima donna giocosa*
Michelino (Cherubino)	Anna Sala	Soprano	*Seconda donna*

---

21 Franca Saini, "Introduction," in *Il Mondo Della Luna: Opera in Un Atto*, ed. Stefano Faglia (Parma: Oca del Cairo, 2000), 28–34, 29.

22 Tufano, "Nozze Napoletane": 279–336, 291.

23 Roberto Verti, ed., "Indice de' Teatrali Spettacoli Di Tutto l'Anno Dalla Primavera 1792 a Tutto Il Carnevale 1793, (Milano s. a.), 124," in *Un Almanacco Drammatico: L'Indice de' Teatrali Spettacoli: 1764–1823* (Pesaro: Fondazione Rossini, 1996).

Nardillo Barracca (Figaro)	Antonio Casaccia	Bass	*Primo buffo Napoletano*
Don Fazio (Don Basilio)	Luigi Martinelli	Bass	*Primo buffo Toscano*
Il Conte Ubaldo	Antonio Benelli	Tenor	*Primo mezzo carattere*

From *Le nozze di Figaro*, five characters and associated plot elements have been removed. The characters are Marcellina, Bartolo, Don Curzio, Barbarina, and Antonio. The related plot elements are Marcellina's claim on Figaro and the revelation that she and Bartolo are his parents; Antonio's reluctance to permit Susanna's marriage to Figaro; disguising the page as a girl to embarrass the count; and Barberina's loss of the pin and the associated aria. A new plot element is the count making Barracca (equivalent to Figaro) a sergeant of his regiment so that he may escort Michelino (the page) to his regiment. The count's real agenda is to get Barracca out of the way so he can pursue Livietta (equivalent to Susanna). Don Fazio—unlike Basilio the unctuous schemer—is an ingenuous, gullible person, though he eventually sees through the count.

Figures 2 and 3 show how the closed pieces of the opera, as represented in the score rather than the published libretto, complied closely with the Neapolitan *commedia per musica* schema.

Figure 2. Compliance with the requirements of the Neapolitan *commedia per musica* in Act I of *La serva onorata*

Neapolitan *commedia per musica*	*La serva onorata*: Act I
Boisterous operatic opening	1. Quartetto: Livietta, Conte, Barracca, D. Fazio, "Vedi un poco, mio sposino"
	2. Aria: D. Fazio, "Che dite? Che vi pare?"
Duet, first encounter of buffi	3. Duetto: Livietta, Barracca, "Si a caso maddamma"
	4. Cavatina: Contessa, "Porgi, Amor, qualche ristoro"
	5. Aria: Michelino, "Se un vago visetto"

	6. Aria: La Contessa, "Passami, ingrato, il core"
Trio, quartet or quintet in the 4th or 5th scene	7. Quartetto: Livietta, Il Conte, Barracca, D. Fazio, "Ah che veggio! Crude stelle!"
	8. Aria: Il Conte, "Quei mesti suoi sospiri"
Penultimate aria: *primo buffo*	9. Recitativo accompagnato and aria: Barracca, "Ombre onorate. Ecco, crudel lotamma"
Aria: *prima buffa*	10. Aria: Livietta, "Narcisetto mio carino"
Finale of seven or eight scenes	11. Finale: "Aprite presto, aprite"

Figure 3. Compliance with the requirements of the Neapolitan *commedia per musica* in Act II of *La serva onorata*

Neapolitan *commedia per musica*	*La serva onorata*: Act II
Aria del sorbetto	12. Canzoncina: Michelino, "Voi che sapete"
Duet: two buffi	
	13. Duetto: Livietta, Il Conte, "Crudel, perché finora"
	14. Aria: Livietta, "Ah ceffaccio d'assassino"
Aria with accompanied recitative: tenor	15: Aria: Il Conte, "Vi sento, sì, vi sento"
Ensemble piece: main characters	16. Quintetto: Livietta, Il Conte, La Contessa, Barracca, D. Fazio, "Uno schiaffo ad un par mio!"
	17. Duetto: Livietta, La Contessa, "Che soave zeffiretto"
	18. Aria: La Contessa, "Dove sono i bei momenti"
	19. Aria: D. Fazio, "In quegli anni"

	20. Aria: Barracca, "Aprite, aprite l'uocchie"
A finale of seven or eight scenes	21. Finale: "Ombre care, amica notte"

Figures 4 and 5 show the closed pieces that involve the remaining six characters in *Le nozze di Figaro* and those in *La serva onorata*. The order of events is largely respected although many scenes are merged or substituted.

Figure 4. Closed pieces in the first halves of *Le nozze di Figaro* and *La serva onorata*

Act	*Le nozze di Figaro*	Act	*La serva onorata*
I	1. Duetto: "Cinque, dieci"	I	1. Quartetto: "Vedi un poco, mio sposino"
	2. Duetto: "Se a caso madama"		2. D. Fazio, "Che dite? Che vi pare?"
	3. Figaro, "Se vuol ballare"		3. Duetto: "Si a caso maddamma"
	6. Cherubino, "Non so più cosa son"		4. La Contessa, "Porgi, Amor, qualche ristoro"
	9. Figaro, "Non più andrai"		5. Michelino, "Se un vago visetto"
II	10. La Contessa, "Porgi, Amor, qualche ristoro"		6. La Contessa, "Passami, ingrato, il core"
	11. Cherubino, "Voi che sapete"		7. Quartetto: "Ah che veggio!"
	12. Susanna, "Venite inginocchiatevi"		8. Il Conte, "Quei mesti suoi sospiri"
	13. Terzetto: Susanna, "Or via sortite"		9. Barracca, "Ecco, crudel lotamma"
	14. Duetto: "Aprite, presto aprite"		10. Livietta, "Narcisetto mio carino"
	15. Finale: "Ecci omai, garzon malnate"		11. Finale: "Aprite presto, aprite"

Figure 5. Closed pieces in the second halves of *Le nozze di Figaro* and *La serva onorata*

	Le nozze di Figaro		*La serva onorata*
Act		Act	
III	16. Duetto: "Crudel, perchè finora"	II	12. Michelino, "Voi che sapete"
	17. Conte, "Hai gia vinto la causa"		13. Duetto: "Crudel, perchè finora"
	19. Contessa, "Dove sono I bei momenti"		14. Livietta, "Ah ceffaccio d'assassino"
	20. Duetto: "Sull'aria"		15. Il Conte, "Vi sento, sì, vi sento"
	22. Finale: "Ecco la marcia"		16. Quintetto: "Uno schiaffo ad un par mio"
IV	25. Basilio, "In quegl'anni"		17. Duetto: "Che soave zefiretto"
	26. Figaro, "Aprite un po' quegl'occhi"		18. La Contessa, "Dove sono I bei momenti"
	27. Susanna, "Deh vieni, non tardar"		19. D. Fazio, "In quegli anni"
	28. Finale: "Pian, pian le andrò più presso"		20. Barracca, "Aprite, aprite l'uocchie"
			21. Finale: "Ombre care, amica notte"

Whereas two duets begin Da Ponte's and Mozart's opera, *La serva onorata* starts with the more conventional *introduzione*. Given the imperative to shorten the work, an opening ensemble featuring four of the six characters is an economical way to establish the relationships that will drive the plot. Taking one secondary element from the corresponding duet—Livietta's display of her new little hat—it covers a great deal of dramatic ground, including Livietta's concern about the count's designs on her and his explicit advances, Barracca's apprehension, and Don Fazio's ingenuous faith in his master's honorable intentions. The excerpt in figure 6 demonstrates these relationships and the straightforward language of the servants Livietta and Barracca. We immediately see Livietta's directness. It contrasts with the lighter, somewhat flirtatious style of Susanna in *Le nozze di Figaro*, and this shift in rhetorical tone reinforces the social separation between the servants and nobility. The *introduzione* also establishes at the outset the centrality of Livietta's character in the opera. Figure 7 shows the recitative that immediately precedes Don Fazio's aria "Che dite, che vi pare?" Again, the talk of the servants has a no-nonsense character.

Figure 6. Excerpt from the *introduzione*

IL CONTE, *a Livietta.*	COUNT, *to Livietta.*
Son due stelle quegli occhietti.	Those eyes are two stars.
LIVIETTA.	LIVIETTA.
Non si affanni, non si appletti.	Cool down, don't be so hasty.
IL CONTE.	COUNT.
E' saetta ogni tuo sguardo…	Your every glance is a lightning bolt…
LIVIETTA.	LIVIETTA.
Più decoro, più riguardo.	More decorum, more respect.
BARRACCA, *a Fazio.*	BARRACCA, *to Fazio.*
Se remmesca soccelleza.	His excellency takes liberties.
FAZIO.	FAZIO.
Sono grazie che ti fa.	These are favors he grants you.
BARRACCA.	BARRACCA.
(Ma vi' comme la scajenza	(But look how misfortune
vò co mmico pazzià!)	wants to play with me!)
IL CONTE, FAZIO, *a Livietta.*	COUNT, FAZIO, *to Livietta.*
Via, più docile e clemente;	Come, be more easygoing and
Via, non tanta austerità.	lenient; come, not so much
LIVIETTA.	sternness.
Un amore impertinente	LIVIETTA.
L'odio mio sempre sarà.	A love without respect
	will always be odious to me.

Figure 7. Excerpt of secco recitative before D. Fazio's aria: "Che dite, che vi pare?"

Il Conte.
    Livietta mia,
    Tra poco ti darò dell'amor mio
    Un forte saggio. Addio.
Livietta.
    (Rotta di collo.)
Il Conte.
    Caro Barracca, il tuo presente stato
    Mi fa pietà!
    Correggerò l'errore.
    Basta. Mio caro, addio; sarai signore.
    (L'abbraccia e bacia e va via.)
Barracca.
    (Che bontà schefenzosa!)
Fazio.
    Può da più chiaro fonte
    Nascer più puro, e virtuoso amore?
    Che dite adesso? È un Cesare?
    Si dà cuore più bello?
    Che generosità! Che gentilezza! ...
    Mi viene il pianto per la tenerezza.

Count.
    My dear Livietta,
    I will soon give you strong proof of my love. Farewell.
Livietta.
    (That could break your neck.)
Count.
    Dear Barracca, I feel pity for your present situation!
    I will correct the error.
    Enough. My dear, farewell; you'll be a gentleman.
    (He hugs and kisses him and leaves.)
Barracca.
    (What a lousy benevolence!)
Fazio.
    Could a purer and more virtuous love
    be born of such a limpid source?
    What do you say now? Is he a Caesar?
    Is there a more beautiful heart?
    What generosity! What kindness!
    ...
    The tenderness brings me to tears.

The countess's cavatina "Porgi, Amor" and the duetto "Se a caso madama" have virtually identical texts to the corresponding pieces in Da Ponte's libretto (apart from Barracca's Neapolitan dialect in the latter). However, as figure 8 shows, the text of the page's aria—"Se un vago visetto"—is quite different from "Non so più cosa son." The subject matter in both cases is adolescent confusion around infatuation and love. The piece in *La serva onorata* is shorter, presumably because of time constraints, and so does not convey emotional complexity to the same degree.

Figure 8. Comparison of Cherubino's "Non so più cosa son" with Michelino's "Se un vago visetto"

CHERUBINO.	MICHELINO.
Non so più cosa son, cosa faccio,	Se un vago visetto
or di foco, ora sono di ghiaccio,	incontro talor,
ogni donna cangiar di colore,	mi balza nel petto, mi palpita il cor.
ogni donna mi fa palpitar.	Un foco improviso
Solo ai nomi d'amor, di diletto,	mi corre nel seno,
mi si turba, mi s'altera il petto,	e Amor di quel viso
e a parlare mi sforza d'amore	poi servo mi tien.
un desio ch'io non posso spiegar.	Mi dite voi matto?
Parlo d'amor vegliando,	Rispondo di sì;
parlo d'amor sognando,	ma son così fatto,
a l'acque, a l'ombre, ai monti,	ma nacqui così.
ai fiori, a l'erbe, ai fonti,	
a l'eco, a l'aria, ai venti	
che il suon de' vani accenti	
portano via con sé.	
E se non v'è chi m'oda,	
parlo d'amor con me.	

I do not know anymore what I am, what I do,	If I encounter sometimes
One moment I'm on fire, the next moment I am cold as ice,	a lovely little face,
Every woman changes my color,	my heart jumps in my chest, my heart beats faster.
Every woman makes me tremble.	A sudden fire
At the very mention of love, of delight,	runs through my breast,
I am greatly troubled, my heart stirs within my chest,	and Love of this face
It compels me to speak of love	then holds me captive.
A desire I can not explain.	You say I'm crazy?
I speak of love while I'm awake,	I reply yes;
I speak of love while I'm dreaming,	but I am made this way,
Water, shade, mountains,	but I was born this way.
Flowers, grass, fountains,	
echo, air, and the winds,	
The sound of my hopeless words	
are taken away with them.	
And if I do not have anyone near to hear me	
I speak of love to myself!	

Of particular note is the equivalence of Figaro's "Non piu andrai" and Livietta's aria "Narcisetto mio carino." In fact, neither of Livietta's arias are derived from those of Susanna. Figure 9 shows the similarities in the text, rearrangement of the order of lines and differences in versification. In "Narcisetto mio carino" Livietta encourages Michelino to seek military glory with a cruel irony–a trait absent in Susanna's character. Her inheriting one of Figaro's arias and as a result acquiring a more down-to-earth character reinforces the centrality of Livietta's character in this opera.

Figure 9. Texts of "Non più andrai" and "Narcisetto mio carino"

Figaro.	Livietta.
Non più andrai, farfallone amoroso,	Narcisetto mio carino,
Notte e giorno d'intorno girando;	Amorino mio vezzoso,
Delle belle turbando il riposo	delle belle oggi il riposo
Narcisetto, Adoncino d'amor.	Tu non devi più turbar.
Non più avrai questi bei pennacchini,	Tra guerrieri, poffar Bacco,
Quel cappello leggero e galante,	Schioppo in spalla, e stretto sacco,
Quella chioma, quell'aria brillante,	Dell'onore pel sentiero
Quel vermiglio donnesco color.	Devi altero camminar.
Tra guerrieri, poffar Bacco!	Michelino alla vittoria,
Gran mustacchi, stretto sacco.	Alla gloria—militar.
Schioppo in spalla, sciabla al fianco,	Quel tuo ballo oggi tu devi
Collo dritto, muso franco,	Lallarà...larà...scordar:
Un gran casco, o un gran turbante,	E al concerto di moschetti,
Molto onor, poco contante!	Di tamburi, e clarinetti,
Ed invece del fandango,	Per il fango, e per le nevi
Una marcia per il fango.	Una marcia devi far.
Per montagne, per valloni,	Michelino, alla vittoria,
Con le nevi e i sollioni.	Alla gloria—militar.
Al concerto di tromboni,	Se una palla nella testa
Di bombarde, di cannoni,	Poi ti viene visitar,
Che le palle in tutti i tuoni	La tua sorta saria questa
All'orecchio fan fischiar.	Da poterti immortalar.
Cherubino alla vittoria:	Michelino alla vittoria,
Alla gloria militar.	Alla gloria—militar.

The page's canzone "Voi che sapete" has identical text in both operas, though the order of the verses is changed. However, it is moved to the beginning of the second act in *La serva onorata*—fulfilling the requirement for an *aria del sorbetto* in that position. And it has a different dramatic function. We see the page wandering around the garden, having disguised himself as a peasant girl after he has jumped from the balcony. He fears the count and is trying to regain the countess's attention. In *Le nozze di Figaro*, by contrast, the canzone is his ardent protestation of infatuation with the countess. It appears the Neapolitan authors pragmatically decided that there was no need to develop this minor character to such an extent.

There are several points of concurrence between the libretti during the second half of both operas. In the duet "Crudel, perchè finora" Lorenzi replaces the last two lines, in which the characters are singing different words, with three different lines. Livietta's statement—"Ah what an ordeal is mine! / I'm lying with such anxiety. / Love, you know it, you see it"—is more dramatic than Susanna's rather playful line: "Excuse me if I lie, / you who understand love." In keeping with the requirement to maintain a separation between the classes, the score does not imply an emotional connection between the count and the servant. Piccinni's setting is musically pleasing, with, for example, Livietta imitating the count's phrases, and both of them singing a long melisma in parallel thirds on the words "lo vede"/ "brillarmi"; but it offers a concurrent revelation of their respective emotions and concerns. There is little variation in mood and, in particular, no emotional contest between the count and Livietta. It is a static statement by two individuals who are remote from each other on the social scale, and whose interaction as equals would be undesirable on the Neapolitan stage.

Figure 10. A comparison of the final verses of "Crudel, perchè finora."

Le nozze di Figaro	*La serva onorata*
IL CONTE. 　Mi sento dal contento 　pieno di gioia il cor.	COUNT. 　Ah qual momento, oh Dio, 　Di gioia, e di contento! 　Sento brillarmi il cor.
SUSANNA. 　Scusatemi se mento, 　voi che intendete amor.	LIVIETTA. 　Ah qual cimento è il mio! 　Con quale affanno io mento, 　Lo sa, lo vede Amor.

Lorenzi chooses to put the countess's aria "Dove sono i bei momenti" after "Che soave zefiretto"—the so-called "letter duet." In Da Ponte's 1786 libretto the aria has three quatrains.[24] Lorenzi shortens this to two quatrains, adopting the first two lines of the second quatrain. One possible explanation is that in Da Ponte the text of the last quatrain leads towards the letter duet by expressing a hope of changing the count's ingratitude. This is not necessary in Lorenzi's libretto because the trick has already been set up, and there is time now to slow the pace for a quiet reflection:

24　Wolfgang Amadeus Mozart and Lorenzo Da Ponte, *Le nozze di Figaro* (libretto), Mozart-Libretti—Online-Edition, Internationale Stiftung Mozarteum, 2014, https://dme.mozarteum.at/DME/libredition/synopse.php?idwnma=5677&v1=1&v2=9&line=0&end=202, 57.

Figure 11. A comparison of the texts of "Dove sono i bei momenti."

Le nozze di Figaro	La serva onorata
LA CONTESSA.	CONTESSA.
Dove sono i bei momenti	Dove sono i bei momenti
Di dolcezza, e di piacer:	Di dolcezza, e di piacer:
Dove andaro i giuramenti	Dove sono i giuramenti
Di quel labbro menzogner?	Di quel labbro menzogner?
Perché se mai in pianti e in pene	Ah perché se in pianti e pene
per me tutto si cangiò,	Per me tutto si cangio,
la memoria di quel bene	Perché, oh Dio, di quel mio bene
dal mio sen non trapassò?	La memoria mi restò?
Ah se almen la mia costanza	
Nel languire amando ognor,	
Mi portasse una speranza	
Di cangiar l'ingrato cor!	

The texts of the "letter duets" and "In quegli anni" are practically identical in the two operas. Barracca's aria "Aprite, aprite l'uocchie" is a Neapolitan dialect version of Figaro's "Aprite un po' quegl'occhi." However, as figure 15 and examples 6, 7, 8, and 9 demonstrate, the Neapolitan authors have added verses and musical attributes that showcase Antonio Casaccia's comic acting skills.

The Singers and the Added Arias

Singers had as much influence on the final realization of an eighteenth-century comic opera as composers and librettists. The work was adapted to suit the singers, rather than their adjusting their performance style to the work.[25] The salaries for the season of Antonio Casaccia, Antonio Benelli, and Anna Coltellini were well above those of the other three cast members.[26] It could be inferred that these pay rates are proxies for the singers' fame and for audiences' expectations of the amount, quality, and kind of music they would perform. If so, these performers would expect to have a significant influence on the text and music of the opera. In addition, as *primo buffo Toscano*, Luigi Martinelli could expect more than the one aria allocated to Basilio, the corresponding character in Da Ponte and

---

25 Dahlhaus, "The Dramaturgy of Italian Opera," 47.
26 Tufano, "Nozze Napoletane": 279–336, 289.

Mozart's opera. It is also pertinent that *Figaro* was an exceptionally long work with many more characters. The character Don Fazio would be expected to adhere to the convention of one aria per act, rather than follow the precedent of Basilio.

Fazio's aria "Che dite? Che vi pare?" (What do you say? What do you think?) has no parallel in *Le nozze di Figaro*. He praises the count's goodness and generosity regarding the marriage of the servants. The picture of an idyllic relationship between nobility and servants—a trope used unironically in sentimental literature of the period—can be read as tongue-in-cheek. The aria allows Martinelli to showcase his ability to sing rapid flowing phrases with melodic leaps in the upper register. It pauses the action of the count's pursuit of Livietta, his foreshadowed but as yet undisclosed "proof" of his love, her determined resistance and Barracca's cynical decrying of Ubaldo's wiles. Figure 12 and example 1 show the declamatory ad libitum section (measures 79–85) in which Fazio gives an overblown description of Barracca. The section interrupts the musical flow temporarily with quasi recitativo accompagnato: "Lo fece la natura, poi disse: 'basta quà.'" (Nature made him, then said: "this is enough.") This is the climax, textually and musically, of the aria. It exemplifies a structural characteristic of Piccinni's comic operas—a rapid shift in dramatic tone from the farcical to the mock-serious.

Figure 12. Excerpt from Don Fazio's aria: "Che dite, che vi pare?"

Don Fazio.	Don Fazio.
Che grazia singolare!	What special grace!
Che taglio! Che figura!	Such style! Such a figure!
Lo fece la natura,	Nature made him,
poi disse: "basta qua."	then said: "this is enough."

EXAMPLE 1. Don Fazio's aria "Che dite, che vi pare?" measures 73–87.

Antonio Benelli is described in the printed libretto as "virtuoso della real cappella." He worked in the theaters devoted mainly to comic operas—the Teatro Nuovo in 1790 and 1791, and the Teatro dei Fiorentini from 1792 to 1798. In keeping with Benelli's musico-dramatic role of *primo mezzo carattere,* Count Ubaldo is a more complex character than the rather one-dimensional personage in Da Ponte and Mozart's opera. He shows evidence of a conscience, but manifests a moral decline into predatory passion, almost attempting to rape a servant girl, who is in fact the page in disguise. His act one aria "Quei mesti suoi sospiri" reveals remorse for the pain his behavior has caused the countess—something foreign to Da Ponte and Mozart's Count. There is no parallel to this aria in *Le nozze*.

Figure 13. The count's aria "Quei mesti suoi sospiri" with an excerpt of the preceding recitative.

La Contessa.	Countess.

Barbaro, e puoi ancora
Ostinato oltraggiarmi ? E di che mai
Improverar mi puoi? In me non trovo
Delitto alcun, se pur non è delitto
L'essere a te fedele:
L'amar te solo, idolo mio crudele.
	Brute, and then you still
	stubbornly insult me? And for
	  whatever
	can you reprimand me? I don't find
	in myself any crime, unless it's
	  a crime
	to be faithful to you;
	to love you alone, my cruel idol.

Il Conte.	Count.
M'intenerisce! Ah troppo sospettoso, Troppo ingiusto son io! Quei mesti suoi sospiri. Quei suoi dogliosi accenti , Si fanno miei martiri Si fanno miei tormenti, E sono quelle lagrime Fulmini nel mio cor. Più non resisto, o Dio ! Anima mia, perdono: Assai convinto io sono. Del tuo fedele amor; Nè più cagion, ben mio, Sarò del tuo dolor.	She moves me! Ah too suspicious, too unjust am I! What a terrible nature is mine! Those miserable sighs of hers, those sorrowful accents become my tortures, become my torments. And those tears are storms in my heart. I cannot resist any longer, o God! Forgive me, my life: I am quite convinced of your faithful love; I will no longer be a cause, my love, of your suffering.

The score excerpts show features of a *mezzo carattere* aria. Example 2 has sustained notes in the upper register and dramatic pauses. A heightening of emotional tension is apparent in the *allegro vivace* section (example 3). Long melismatic phrases are present in example 4. In example 5 the harmony proceeds through an augmented sixth to a D minor chord on the final syllable of *dolor*, the progression implying anguish, which would be expected of a *mezzo carattere*.

EXAMPLE 2. The count's aria "Quei mesti suoi sospiri," measures 9–28.

EXAMPLE 3. The count's aria "Quei mesti suoi sospiri," measures 43–8.

EXAMPLE 4. The Count's aria "Quei mesti suoi sospiri," measures 54–65.

EXAMPLE 5. The count's aria "Quei mesti suoi sospiri," measures 94–105.

A comparison of the count's arias in the second halves of *Le nozze di Figaro* and *La serva onorata* reveals similar verse structures and much identical text, but a different emotional trajectory (figure 14). Lorenzi's Count first describes the voices of a sweet love competing with the reprimands of honor—"rimproveri di onore." Finally the dominant emotions are his desire for vengeance and affection for Livietta—"My heart trembles, and awaits vengeance, and it will have it." He no longer hears the reprimands of honor—the voices of a sweet love have overcome his scruples. As in the count's act one aria the text here, with its range of emotions, is adapted to suit Antonio Benelli's *primo mezzo carattere* status.

Figure 14. A comparison of the texts of the count's aria in the second halves of the operas.

Le nozze di Figaro	*La serva onorata*
IL CONTE.	COUNT.
Vedrò, mentr' io sospiro,	Vi sento, sì vi sento
Felice un serve mio ?	Voci di un dolce amore:
E un ben, ch in van desio,	Rimproveri di onore,
Ei posseder dovrà ?	Anche vi sento in sen.
Vedrò per man d'amore,	Ma che! veder dovrei
Unita a un vile oggetto,	Unita a un vile oggetto,
Chi in mi destò un affetto,	Chi amor mi desta in petto
Che per me poi non ha!	Chi è l'unico mio ben?
Ah no! lasciarti in pace,	Ah no, non voglio in pace
Non vò questo contento,	Soffrire il suo contento,
Tu non nascesti, audace,	Non nacque no l'audace
Per dare a me tormento;	Per dare a me tormento.
E forse ancor per ridere,	Frème il mio core, e aspetta
Di mia infelicità.	Vendetta, e l'averà.
Già, la speranza sola	Rimproveri di onore,
Delle vendette mie	No, che non più vi sento:
Quest' anima consola;	Voci di un dolce amore,
E giubilar mi fa.	Voi trionfate già.

Casting the celebrated *primo buffo napoletano* Antonio Casaccia—"Casacciello"—in the principal male role of Nardillo Barracca offered opportunities for and imposed constraints on the Neapolitan authors. They could exploit his renowned comic acting skills but had to acknowledge the power conferred by his fame and accommodate changes he might request. The Casaccia family of singers were among the greatest exponents of Neapolitan opera buffa from the mid-eighteenth century to the late nineteenth. His year of birth is unknown, but Antonio Casaccia was probably in his fifties in 1792. He was active on the comic opera stage in Naples from 1758 to 1793, the year of his death. Several contemporary commentators, including the Earl of Mount Edgcumbe, Giacomo Gotifredo Ferrari, Michael Kelly and Charles Burney, wrote about the singer and his popularity. Edgcumbe, who saw him perform in 1785, noted that he was "a man of enormous corpulence."[27] Ferrari remembered him at about the same time as "sempre pronto per far ridere."[28] Kelly—who studied in the city in 1779–80 and subsequently created the roles of Don Basilio and Don Curzio in Mozart's *Le nozze di Figaro*—wrote that Casacciello was "the idol of Naples. Whenever he appeared on the stage, the house was in a tumult of applause."[29] Charles Burney, who saw him twice in Piccinni's *Gelosia per gelosia* in 1770, gave him particularly high praise. Burney criticized the singing of the cast in the performances, and observed that Casaccia's appeal was independent of his vocal ability:

> There was, however, a comic character performed by Signor Casaccia, a man of infinite humour; the whole house was in a roar the instant he appeared; and the pleasantry of this actor did not consist in buffoonery, nor was it local, which in Italy, and, indeed, elsewhere, is often the case; but was of that original and general sort as would excite laughter at all times and in all places.[30]
>
> The singing, as I before observed, is wretched; but there is so much *vis comica* in Casaccia, that his singing is never thought of . . .[31]

Casacciello's corpulence and stage presence, the evident favor he enjoyed with the Neapolitan audience and the fact that he always sang in the local dialect meant that the leading male role would be substantially transformed between Vienna and Naples. In the solo numbers the Neapolitan authors demonstrate

---

27　Richard Edgcumbe, Earl of Mount Edgcumbe, *Musical Reminiscences of the Earl of Mount Edgcumbe, Containing an Account of the Italian Opera in England from 1773 to 1834* (New York: Da Capo Press, 1973), 40.

28　Giacomo Gotifredo Ferrari, *Aneddoti Piacevoli e Interessanti Occorsi Nella Vita Di Giacomo Gotifredo Ferrari, Da Roveredo, Operetta Scritta Da Lui Medesimo* (Palermo: Remo Sandron, 1907), 146.

29　Michael Kelly, *Reminiscences*, vol. 1 (London: Henry Colburn, 1826), 47.

30　Charles Burney, *The Present State of Music in France and Italy: Or, The Journal of a Tour through Those Countries, Undertaken to Collect Materials for A General History of Music* (London: T. Becket and Co., 1771), 292.

31　Ibid., 314.

a willingness to breach the theatrical fourth wall to exploit his comic potential, at the expense of dramatic continuity and plausibility. It is clearly demonstrated in his aria in act one, scene twelve (figure 15). At a point where the plot is well advanced, its content is completely extraneous to the drama. Livietta proposes to her fiancée that, in imitation of the *primo uomo* in an opera seria, he should thwart the count's designs by planning to kill her rather than surrendering her to him. Making a reference to the castrato Farinelli, Barracca agrees to this proposal. After the initial accompanied recitative "Ombre onorate" the aria "Ecco, crudel lotamma" has four distinct sections. In the first (*Andante moderato*, C, measures 13–31) the allusion to a eunuch following the mention of Farinelli prompts Piccinni to close the predominantly syllabic setting of the first quatrain with an extended melisma in imitation of a castrato volatina figure (example 6).

Figure 15. Barracca's Act One aria: "Ecco, crudel lotamma"

Barracca.	Barracca.
Ecco, crudel lotamma,	Here, cruel nasty one,
versa il tuo sangue e zuco;	spill your blood and juice;
tu mi bramasti eunuco,	you want me to be a eunuch,
io ti farò tremar.	I will make you tremble.
Mmalora, so' agghiajato;	Damn, I'm frozen;
stuzzeca 'n'auto poco,	provoke me a bit another way,
sciosceme chiù lo fuoco,	stoke the fire more,
si no restammo ccà.	or else we'll stay as we are.
Lo Conte che pretenne	The count has a claim on you
Cospetto a me? Sei morta!	ahead of me? You're dead!
La botta è ghiuta storta,	The blow went sideways,
Sign'è ch'aje da campà.	it's a sign that you're destined to live.
Furie, dragune e bipere,	Furies, dragons and vipers,
Gatte tremende e zoccole,	huge cats and mice,
Stracciateme, ruditeme,	tear me apart, gnaw at me,
Strisciateme, zucateme,	scratch me, suck at me,
E nel mio sen destatemi	and in my breast awaken
Fiere bestialità.	wild beastliness.
Ma 'na cornetta flebile	But a feeble cornet
par che mi parla e dice:	seems to speak to me and say:
"Tu morirai felice,	"You will die happy,
quest'è la verità."	this is the truth."

EXAMPLE 6. Barracca's aria "Ecco crudel lotamma," measures 25–31.

Barracca then expresses concern that he's cooling off and suggests his passions need to be reignited. Line ten climaxes after a crescendo with the exclamation: "Sei morta!" (measure 43). This suggests a gesture of a stabbing towards his fiancée and is followed by a pause. He then explains that the strike has missed the target and that Livietta is going to live. In the next section (*Allegro*, C, measures 51–78) he summons up various fictitious monsters and verminous animals from the back streets of Naples and invites them to inflame his anger. This motivates the last four lines which are set in two sections: Andante (measures 79–91) and Allegro (measures 92–131). Barracca claims dramatically to hear a faint trumpet apparently predicting Livietta's fate: "You will die happy—and this is the truth!" This is a mock-serious aria with textual and musical allusions to opera seria. It provides enormous scope for Casaccia's comedic theatrical skills. It is noteworthy that there is no trace of its text in the printed libretto, which instead has an aria: "Quanno afferro 'na Carrera" in the previous scene, which Piccinni did not set to music. It could be inferred that Casacciello had significant input into his act one aria.

Figure 16. Text of the falsetto section of Barracca's aria "Aprite, aprite l'uocchie."

BARRACCA.
 "Uh mamma, che bregogna!
 Bell'ommo, fatte llà."
 Crederle n'abbesogna,
  so' tutta fauzetà.

BARRACCA.
 "Oh mamma, such shame!
 Nice man, go away."
 There is no need to believe them,
 They are all false.

EXAMPLE 7. Barracca's aria "Ecco crudel lotamma," measures 25–31.

The position of Barracca's act two aria—"Aprite, aprite l'uocchie"—confirms the singer's prestige: it is the last solo number of the score, immediately preceding the finale. Like Da Ponte's text it expresses cynicism about the virtue and sincerity of women. Piccinni again opts for a structure of differentiated sections. The first (Andante con moto, 3/4, 88 measures) comprises the first twenty-one lines. For the first eight lines (measures 1–33), Barracca, addressing credulous men of the audience in a good-natured benevolent tone, notes that they believe their young women to be noble and upright. In verses 9–10 he depict these honest young women rising up, protesting to their mothers about the shame their men have brought them, and telling them: "nice man, go away." Piccinni takes the opportunity to set these lines as falsetto with a lamenting tone (measures 34–46; see figure 16, example 7).

In the two measures before the next section (measures 87–88) there are several fermata marks: "Parentesi, parentesi"—"pause, pause." This suggests that Barracca turns to the audience and, moving downstage, addresses them directly with a confidential air, seeking their alliance. In this section (Andantino moderato, C, measures 89–124), he appears to be sympathetic to the women in the audience. The first twelve measures are in the parallel minor, suggesting a frank parody of sincere pathos (example 8). In the final section (Allegro C, measures 125–175) all the negative descriptions of women from the Andante con moto section are reprised in declamatory eighth-note phrases with repeated exhortations to the men to open their eyes and save themselves (example 9).

The settings of Barracca's arias give numerous opportunities for telling physical and vocal gestures and communication with the audience—such as pauses, sudden dynamic changes and variations in timbre. Their content and style are most likely explained by the personality (and enormous popularity) of the singer, who had the power to impose his preferences for textual and musical content—or at least to propose them to the librettist and composer with some success.

Anna Coltellini was a daughter of librettist Marco Coltellini and she frequently appeared in comic operas alongside her more famous sister Celeste. As indicated in figures 6, 7, 9, and 17, Livietta bears little resemblance to the Susanna of Da Ponte and Mozart. She is earthy, instinctual, direct, sometimes abrasive, and prone to emotional outbursts. Lorenzi had written an act two aria for her, entitled "Ah Livietta poveretta," which appears in the published libretto. The text there shows Livietta saddened by Barracca's unflattering description of her—actually only intended to discourage the count's interest. The emotion expressed is sentimental and rather out of keeping with her personality. The setting

EXAMPLE 8. Barracca's aria "Aprite, aprite l'uocchie," measures 87–98.

EXAMPLE 9. Barracca's aria "Aprite, aprite l'uocchie," measures 125–134.

of the text may have required a refined vocal technique that was beyond Anna Coltellini—examination of her two arias suggests that Piccinni composed them with an awareness of limitations in her vocal ability. The substituted act two aria "Ah ceffaccio d'assassino" delineates to perfection the character of Livietta, showing to the full her determination and guile while allowing the performer to showcase her comedic skills. These skills rely on vivacity and physical gestures in her performance rather than vocal technique.

Figure 17. Livietta's aria "Ah ceffaccio d'assassino."

LIVIETTA.

Ah ceffaccio d'assassino,
Ah linguaccia maledetta!
Una furia, una saetta
per te voglio diventar.
    Ma mancar mi sento il fiato,
Mi soffogano le pene.
Per pietà, chi mi sostiene,
Chi un ristoro o Dio mi dà!
Vi ringrazio bel Signore
Dell'affetto, del buon cuore
della vostra carità.
Crepa tu, che ben ti sta!
    (Come freme il poveretto!
Questi colpi di martello
Qualche amante matterello
Fà a noi savio diventar,
Fà a noi savio ritornar).

LIVIETTA.

Ah ugly mug of an assassin,
Ah accursed backbiter!
A fury, a thunderbolt
I want to be for you.
    But I am losing breath,
sorrows suffocate me.
For pity's sake who will support me,
Oh God who will revive me!
I thank you lovely Sir
for your fondness, your good heart,
for your kindness.
You die, for it serves you right!
    (How the poor little one
trembles!
These hammer blows
like a beloved rolling pin
make us become wise,
restore our sense.)

Consistent with the stereotypical character of the Neapolitan servant class, Livietta reacts with immediate fury to Barracca's description of her. Marked Allegro, the aria is in cut common time and starts abruptly without a ritornello. It has four sections, each with a different emotional profile. The first quatrain is furious invective, beginning: "Ah ugly mug of an assassin!" At measure 33 she pretends to faint and appeals to the count for help (example 10). Her counterfeit swoon parodies a literary and theatrical trope—the sentimental heroine's fragility.

When the count responds she miraculously recovers, turns to Barracca and resumes her tirade. After setting the complete text, Piccinni proceeds to repeat it, jumbling the order and accentuating various elements (example 11). Livietta alternates between flirting with the count to make her fiancé jealous and telling Barracca to die for it serves him right. Anna Coltellini had a sparkling repertoire of fury, false languor, flattery, and unpredictable movements.

EXAMPLE 10. Livietta's Act Two aria "Ah ceffaccio d'assassino," measures 20–35.

EXAMPLE 11. Livietta's aria "Ah ceffaccio d'assassino," measures 140–7.

The Composer

Returning to Naples after fifteen years in Paris, Piccinni felt the need to gradually re-establish himself in the city's theatrical environment and regain the public's favor. After composing a Lenten opera—his "azione sacra per musica" *Gionata* had been performed in March 1792—he presented *La serva onorata* for the appraisal of the comedy audience.[32] Although many of his serious operas had been well received in Italy, France and elsewhere, the comedy audience had been the main source of his fame in Naples. The reception of *La serva onorata* represented a test of his ability to re-connect with the city, and satisfying the audience's expectations was a creative imperative. The social class profile of comic opera theater patrons in Naples in the late eighteenth century is difficult to ascertain. However, rich data gleaned from the archives of the Banco di Napoli for the period 1776–1785 by Maione et al. suggests that audiences in general and

---

32 For a detailed discussion of Gionata and its sociopolitical significance, see: Anthony DelDonna, "At the Precipice of Revolution: Piccinni's Gionata (1792) as Drama and Diplomacy," in *Opera, Theatrical Culture and Society in Late Eighteenth-Century Naples* (London and New York: Routledge, 2016).

box subscribers were a mixture of nobility and bourgeoisie.[33] It appears that the aristocracy frequented the comic theaters out of conscious preference for the genres presented, whereas their subscriptions to the San Carlo theater—which presented opere serie exclusively—were largely intended to maintain social prestige.[34]

Piccinni was subject to certain constraints and influences, including the *commedia per musica* schema, and the singers' limitations, as well as their demands and requests. His setting responds to the requirements of the libretto, sometimes focussing on local effects rather than building the complex musico-dramatic coherence that characterized Mozart's opera. Piccinni opts for a more conventional "number opera" formula, the particular numbers generally responding to issues raised in the secco recitative. The marked deviation from Lorenzi's libretto indicates a fragmentary compositional process, in which Piccinni may have struggled to meet competing demands. Nevertheless, his creative choices were not entirely constrained, as many characteristics of his mature compositional style are evident.

The countess's arias in particular reveal the sympathetic, heartfelt, intimate qualities for which Piccinni is renowned. For example, sudden seamless transitions from major to parallel minor to express yearning or ardent appeal are found in her arias "Porgi amor" and "Dove sono I bei momenti?" In "Passami ingrato il cor" impassioned tension is created by interrupting the musical flow with an interpolated recitativo accompagnato section, as the countess beseeches the count to hear her pleas: "Crudel, to non mi ascolti? Tu vuoi la morte mia?" (measures 55–9). Variations in the form and styles of closed pieces with the sole aim of supporting the drama—this flexibility was characteristic of this composition—are evident. Typical also is his exploitation of the expressive capabilities of instruments to support the vocal line without distracting attention from it. In particular, he uses clarinets extensively to create various moods. An example is their response in parallel thirds and sixths to the count's phrases in the first part of the aria "Quei mesti suoi sospiri" (example 2), accentuating the remorseful sentiment in the text.

---

33 Giulia Di Dato et al., "Notizie Dallo Spirito Santo: La Vita Musicale a Napoli Nelle Carte Bancarie (1776–1785)," in *Domenico Cimarosa: Un "napoletano" in Europa*, vol. 2, ed. Paolo-giovanni Maione and Marta Columbro (Lucca: Libreria Musicale Italiana, 2004), 665–1197.

34 Ibid., 668.

Conclusion

With royal support as its apparent raison d'être, *La serva onorata* reveals much about the manifold determinants and mechanisms of adapting a comic opera to the late eighteenth-century Neapolitan milieu. We have seen how the social influences of audience expectation, local tastes, culture, and theater management, as well as the particular skills, limitations, and professional requirements of performers, shaped the transmutation of Da Ponte and Mozart's *Le nozze di Figaro* into a successful Neapolitan *commedia per musica*. In spite of the constraints, both librettist and composer found ways to elaborate a work that showcased their mature skills. The title of the opera—"The respected maidservant"—implies that the work complies with a particular comedic imperative of the *villanella*: ennoblement of the instinctual, natural and sometimes vulgar behavior of the Neapolitan servant classes as they were popularly perceived. It also suggests that the work owes much to the Neapolitan lineage of Serpina—the assertive maidservant in Pergolesi's 1733 intermezzo *La serva padrona*.

Bibliography

Bellina, Anna Laura. "Goldoni, Paisiello e La Luna Nuova." In *Commedia e Musica al Tramonto dell'Ancien Régime: Cimarosa, Paisiello e i Maestri Europei*, edited by Antonio Caroccia, 189–213. Avellino: Conservatorio di Musica Domenico Cimarosa, 2017.

Burney, Charles. *The Present State of Music in France and Italy: Or, The Journal of a Tour through Those Countries, Undertaken to Collect Materials for A General History of Music*. London: T. Becket and Co., 1771.

Cardamone, Donna G. "Villanella." In *Grove Music Online*. Oxford University Press, 2001. https://doi.org/10.1093/gmo/9781561592630.article.29379.

Dahlhaus, Carl. "The Dramaturgy of Italian Opera." In *Opera in Theory and Practice, Image and Myth*. Vol. 6, *The History of Italian Opera*, Part 2: *Systems*, 2, edited by Lorenzo Bianconi and Giorgio Pestelli, 1–45. Chicago: University of Chicago Press, 2003.

DelDonna, Anthony. "At the Precipice of Revolution: Piccinni's Gionata (1792) as Drama and Diplomacy." In *Opera, Theatrical Culture and Society in Late Eighteenth-Century Naples*, 193–226. London and New York: Routledge, 2016.

———. "Giovanni Battista Lorenzi (1721–1807) and Neapolitan Comic Opera in the Late Eighteenth Century." In *Genre in Eighteenth-Century Music*, edited by Anthony DelDonna, 52–85. Ann Arbor: Steglein Publishing, 2008.

———. *Instrumental Music in Late Eighteenth-Century Naples: Politics, Patronage and Artistic Culture*. Cambridge: Cambridge University Press, 2020.

Di Dato, Giulia, Teresa Mautone, Maria Melchione, Carmelina Petrarca, and Paologiovanni Maione (coordinatore). "Notizie Dallo Spirito Santo: La Vita Musicale a Napoli Nelle Carte Bancarie (1776–1785)." In *Domenico Cimarosa: Un "napoletano" in Europa*, edited by Maione Paologiovanni and Marta Columbro, Marta, 2: 665–1197. Lucca: Libreria Musicale Italiana, 2004.

Edgcumbe, Richard, Earl of Mount Edgcumbe. *Musical Reminiscences of the Earl of Mount Edgcumbe, Containing an Account of the Italian Opera in England from 1773 to 1834*. New York: Da Capo Press, 1973.

Faglia, Stefano, ed. *Il Mondo Della Luna: Opera in Un Atto*. Parma: Oca del Cairo, 2000.

Ferrari, Giacomo Gotifredo. *Aneddoti Piacevoli e Interessanti Occorsi Nella Vita di Giacomo Gotifredo Ferrari, Da Roveredo, Operetta Scritta da lui Medesimo*. Palermo: Remo Sandron, 1907.

Ginguené, Pierre-Louis. *Notice Sur La Vie et Les Ouvrages de Nicolas Piccinni*. Paris: Veuve Panckoucke, 1800.

Kelly, Michael. *Reminiscences*. Vol. 1. London: Henry Colburn, 1826.

Lazarevich, Gordana. "The Neapolitan Intermezzo and Its Influence on the Symphonic Idiom." *Musical Quarterly* 57, no. 2 (1971): 294–313.

Lorenzi, Giambattista. *La serva onorata: dramma giocoso per musica da rappresentarsi nel Teatro de' Fiorentini per seconda opera del corrente anno 1792*. Napoli: Per Vincenzo Flauto, 1792.

Mozart, Wolfgang Amadeus, and Da Ponte, Lorenzo. *Le nozze di Figaro* [libretto]. Mozart-Libretti—Online Edition. Internationale Stiftung Mozarteum, 2014. https://dme.mozarteum.at/DME/libredition/synopse.php?idwnma=5677&v1=1&v2=9&line=0&end=202.

Notizie del mondo. Naples: September 8, 1792.

Piccinni, Niccolò. *La Serva Onorata*. Edited by Lucio Tufano and Lawrence Mays. Recent Researches in Music of the Classical Era. Middleton, Wisconsin: A-R Editions, Inc., n.d.

Robinson, Michael F. *Naples and Neapolitan Opera*. Oxford: Clarendon Press, 1972.

Troy, Charles E. *The Comic Intermezzo: A Study in the History of Eighteenth-Century Italian Opera*. Ann Arbor: UMI Research Press, 1979.

Tufano, Lucio. "Nozze Napoletane. La Serva Onorata Di Giambattista Lorenzi e Niccolò Piccinni (1792)." *Mozart-Studien*, no. 21 (2012): 279–336.

Verti, Roberto, ed. "Indice de' Teatrali Spettacoli Di Tutto l'Anno Dalla Primavera 1792 a Tutto Il Carnevale 1793, (Milano s. a.), 124." In *Un Almanacco Drammatico: L'Indice de' Teatrali Spettacoli: 1764–1823*. Pesaro: Fondazione Rossini, 1996.

Josephinism and Leopold Koželuh's Masonic Cantata *Joseph der Menschheit Segen*

Allan Badley

Like a number of his musical colleagues in Vienna in the 1780s, Leopold Koželuh was a Freemason. The date on which he attained the degree of Entered Apprentice is not recorded in Ludwig Abafi's authoritative *Geschichte der Freimauerei in Oesterreich-Ungarn*, nor is there any indication of whether he progressed to the second or third degree; but Koželuh's name appears in a list of new members of the Zu den drei Adlern lodge following its amalgamation with Zum Palmbaum in 1783.[1] Abafi includes Koželuh among the members of Zum Palmbaum, describing him as "Kapellmeister [and] music teacher to Archduchess Elizabeth, the wife of Franz II, who in 1792, was appointed Hofkapellmeister and Hofcompositeur."[2] He does not give any details of Koželuh's occupation or professional status when he was a member of Zum Palmbaum, a lodge whose members included the composer and civil servant Karl von Ordonez, Senior Master since 1777, and Franz Zöhrer, Kapellmeister to Count Palm at Regensburg.[3] It seems likely that Koželuh was active in Masonic circles from the early 1780s and he may have had Masonic connections in Prague before he moved to Vienna in 1778.

Freemasonry had a rather checkered history in Austria from the foundation of the first lodge in Vienna in 1726. There was strong opposition from the papacy to the growth of freemasonry throughout Europe, and the Holy Roman

---

1 Ludwig Abafi, *Geschichte der Freimauerei in Oesterreich-Ungarn von Ludwig Abafi / Mitglied der Petőfi-Gesellschaft in Budapest, Vierter Band* (Budapest: Ludwig Aigner, 1893), 269.
2 "Leop. Koželuch, Kapellmeister, Musiklehrer der Erzherzogin Elisabeth, Gemahlin Franz II., der im 1792 zum Hofkapellmeister und Hofcompositeur ernannte," in Abafi, *Geschichte der Freimauerei*, 265.
3 David Young, "Karl von Ordonez (1734–1786): A Biographical Study," *Royal Musical Association Research Chronicle 1983–1985*, no. 19 (1983–1985): 40.

emperor was expected to take an active part in its suppression. Under pressure from the clergy, Charles VI promulgated an edict in 1736 prohibiting freemasonry in the Low Countries, but he did not extend the ban to Austria because a number of influential members of the imperial court were active Masons.[4] The position of freemasonry in Vienna owed its initial prominence to Francis Stephen of Lorraine who joined "the craft" in May 1731, five years before his marriage to Archduchess Maria Theresia of Austria. He had sufficient influence to persuade his father-in-law, Charles VI, to ignore Pope Clement XII's 1738 bull *In Eminenti* condemning freemasonry;[5] and with Maria Theresia's accession and his subsequent election as Holy Roman emperor, some lodges even came to enjoy a kind of semiofficial status. Because of this they became a target for opponents of the emperor, who saw discrediting freemasonry as a means of undermining his authority. Sufficient damage was done to the society's reputation that in 1764 freemasonry was forbidden throughout Austria by imperial decree.[6] Within a year, Francis I was dead, and Joseph II the newly elected Holy Roman emperor and co-regent of the far-flung Habsburg domains. While Maria Theresia's distrust of freemasonry persisted during the fifteen-year co-regency, its reputation began to improve as a result of Joseph II's somewhat cynical support, and it underwent a radical transformation during the early years of his sole reign.[7]

Joseph's attitude to freemasonry was more tolerant than his mother's. Though not a Mason himself, and considering their mysteries and ceremonies pure charlatanry (*Gaukelei*), he nonetheless supported its nobler endeavors as compatible with his own reformist agenda, and conferred upon the organization the protection of the state. Joseph's Toleration Patent, issued on 13 October 1781, extended religious freedom to non-Catholic Christians living in the crown lands, legally allowing members of these minority faiths to hold "private religious exercises" in "clandestine churches."[8] While freemasonry was not explicitly mentioned in the Patent, it was swept up in its implementation, and its newfound status stimulated a rapid expansion. By 1785 there were dozens of

---

4   Lloyd Earl Mitchell, "The Influence of Freemasonry on Some of the Music of Wolfgang Amadeus Mozart" (M.Ed. thesis, Central Washington University, 1969), 5.

5   H. C. R. Landon, *1791 Mozart's Last Year* (London: Thames & Hudson, 1988), 55.

6   Mitchell, "The Influence of Freemasonry," 6.

7   Derek Beales, *Joseph II*, vol. 1, *In the Shadow of Maria Theresa, 1741–1780* (Cambridge: Cambridge University Press, 1987), 486.

8   Carlile Aylmer Macartney, ed., *The Habsburg and Hohenzollern Dynasties in the Seventeenth and Eighteenth Centuries* (New York: Harper & Row, 1970), 269–74.

lodges throughout the Habsburg territories and several thousand Freemasons. They were concentrated in the cities, in Vienna first and foremost, but also elsewhere, notably Lombardy, Belgium, and Hungary.[9] The Toleration Patent and other reforms helped to establish an intellectual climate in which freemasonry flourished, and with it a market for books, music, and other creative works connected to it.

In his magisterial two-volume study of Joseph II, Derek Beales argues against the prevailing view that freemasonry exerted a profound influence on Joseph's program of reform, and that most of the key figures in his administration were Masons. While a number of influential ministers were committed Masons, others were not, including the very powerful Prince Kaunitz. Moreover, deeply committed Freemasons such as Count Leopold von Kollowrat were among those who obstructed many of his proposed reforms. Around 1783 Joseph appears to have begun encouraging his ministers to join lodges, which Beales argues was a tactic intended to assert control over them,[10] but by the end of 1785 he was sufficiently concerned about their growing power and influence to take decisive action. On December 11 he drafted an idiosyncratically expressed patent on freemasonry:

> The so-called societies of Freemasons, about whose secrets I know nothing, as I have never been in the least curious to experience their charlatanries, are growing and spreading even to the small towns. These gatherings, if left entirely alone and uncontrolled, can lead to excesses harmful to religion, order and morality, and, especially, if the top people are bound closely together by fanaticism and behave unfairly towards underlings who are not in the same social relationship with them, [the lodges may] degenerate completely and engage in swindles.
>
> Formerly and in other countries Freemasons were forbidden and punished, and their lodge meetings were broken up because it was not known what their secrets were. Although they are also unknown to me, it is for me enough to know that these Masonic meetings yield some real benefit to the community, to the poor and for education, so that I shall do for them more than any other country has yet done namely ... to order that, so long as they do good, they shall be taken under the care and protection of the state, and their meetings are to be formally permitted.[11]

---

9   Derek Beales, *Joseph II*, vol. 2, *Against the World, 1780–1790* (Cambridge: Cambridge University Press, 2009), 527.

10   Ibid., 535.

11   Ibid., 539–40.

The most important immediate consequence of the patent was a major reorganization of the lodges. Joseph ordered that Viennese lodges be reduced to just three, forcing some to amalgamate and others to close. He also required lodges to furnish precise lists of their members, whether they attended meetings or not, and these were incorporated into the secret files of the court archives.[12] Unsurprisingly, membership of the lodges began to decline sharply and many Masons simply drifted away. Koželuh's transfer of his lodge membership to Zu den drei Adlern suggests a continuing interest in freemasonry, although there is little corroborating evidence.

Given the rapid expansion of freemasonry in Vienna following the Toleration Patent of 1781, it seems likely that Koželuh joined the Masons around this time. His reasons for doing so are unknown. They may have been idealistic reasons, such as the fellowship and intellectual stimulation of like-minded individuals. There were certainly many such Masons, but many more joined the society because it was fashionable. Beales notes that few records survive of activities in most lodges, but those that do indicate that their essential function and attraction was sociability.[13] Neither can self-interest be discounted, as Caroline Pichler observes in her memoirs:

> It was not useless to belong to such brotherhoods, which had members in all government departments and generally found a way of bringing heads, presidents and governors into their bosom. One brother helped another . . . those who did not belong to it encountered obstruction [in their careers], and this lured many into it.[14]

Pichler was well placed to make this observation since her father, Hofrat Franz Sales von Greiner, was a member of the influential Zur wahren Eintracht lodge,[15] and she must have had many opportunities to meet his fellow Masons at the Greiners' salon, a notable meeting place for artists, musicians, and intellectuals. Perhaps Koželuh's reason for becoming a Mason embraced intellectual, social, and pragmatic motives: such a combination was probably typical of his brothers, even the most enlightened. As an independent artist and later

---

12   Landon, *1791*, 58.
13   Beales, *Against the World*, 532.
14   Caroline Pichler, *Denkwürdigkeiten aus meinem Leben*, 2 vols., ed. E. K. Blümml, (Munich: Georg Müller, 1914), 1:93.
15   Paul Nettl, *Mozart and Masonry* (New York: Dorset Press 1987), 135.

the founder of a publishing house,[16] there is no question that Koželuh would have made use of his Masonic connections. Neither would this have been seen as inappropriate, because one of the fundamental obligations of a Mason was to help his brothers. But this does not rule out more idealistic motives; admittedly tenuous evidence of them lies in Koželuh's composition of the cantata *Joseph der Menschheit Segen*, the character of the lodges to which he belonged, and his continuing involvement after the enactment of Joseph's patent on freemasonry.

On 1 September 1783 the Zur gekrönten Hoffnung lodge, in partnership with Zu den drei Adlern and Zur Beständigkeit, performed Koželuh's new cantata *Joseph der Menschheit Segen*.[17] Koželuh's own lodge, Zum Palmbaum, together with Zu den drei Adlern and Zur Beständigkeit, were closely associated with Zur wahren Eintracht, the most intellectually distinguished of the Viennese Masonic lodges. Under the leadership of the distinguished metallurgist and scientist Ignaz von Born, it viewed itself as an academy of enlightened thought, establishing a library and a regular lecture series. Born's deputy, Baron Joseph von Sonnenfels, was Professor of Political Economy at the University of Vienna and a prominent legal reformer.

The lodge issued from 1784 to 1786 the *Journal für Freymaurer*, in which Sonnenfels published the text of his lecture "The Influence of Masonry on Civil Society." There Sonnenfels laid out what he believed were the benefits of the society, summarized here by Beales:

> He condemned despotism and the Jesuits, but also the less worthy among the masons, alchemists for example, while praising religious toleration and claiming that the lodges, if properly conducted, would increase the number of virtuous citizens and further the general wellbeing of humanity through the beneficent state. Masons should obey the ruler and his laws, respect religion and love the fatherland.[18]

But Beales argues that Zur wahren Eintracht was exceptional among the Viennese lodges and scorns the notion that Sonnenfels's philosophy dominated freemasonry in the 1780s. Indeed, he asserts that "those who were subjected to his lectures and writings—and many masons had not been—commonly

---

16 Koželuch founded the *Musikalisches Magazin*, which was later managed by his brother Antonín Tomas, in 1784.
17 Abafi, *Geschichte der Freimaurerei*, 208.
18 Beales, *Against the World*, 529–530.

found them turgid and boring."[19] The sentiments expressed by Sonnenfels echo strongly those found in Leopold Föderl's text for *Joseph der Menschheit Segen*. This places Föderl firmly in the idealistic Masonic camp, and also suggests that Koželuh, his collaborator, may have shared similar views.

When the work was composed, Leopold Föderl (1748–1817), a member of Zur Beständigkeit, was Professor of Poetry at the Akademisches Gymnasium in Vienna. Föderl had been ordained as a priest in 1772, and also appears to have been deeply involved in Masonic activities. In 1782 he was one of the wardens (*Aufseher*) of the lodge,[20] and he wrote and delivered odes to mark important events such as the installation of its Grand Master in 1784.[21] Föderl resigned his position at the Gymnasium in 1785,[22] and took up the post of parish priest in Weitra where he remained until 1803.[23]

Abafi describes the performance of *Joseph der Menschheit Segen* as part of a feast of thanksgiving for the protection Joseph II had bestowed on

---

19 Ibid.

20 Ludwig Lewis, *Geschichte der Freimaurerei in Österreich im allgemeinen und der Wiener Loge zu St. Joseph Inbesondere* (Vienna: Druck und Verlag der Typogr. -literar. – artistichen Anstalt L. C. Zamarski & C. Dittmarsch, 1861), 158.

21 "Ode an den hochwürdigen Großmeister der Distrikts – Loge zum neuen Bunde, Freiherrn von Gebler" (Tob. Fil.) [...] Bei der feierlichen Installirung der sehr ehrw. Johannis–Loge Zur Beständigkeit im Orient zu W[ien]. von Br[uder]. F[öderl]. Lewis, *Geschichte der Freimauerei*, 197.

22 Universität Wien, Universitätsarchiv: AT-UAW / CA 1.4.392 Stein, Anton; Federl, [Leop2 old], 1785.11.15 (Akt); Schachtelnummer 183, *olim* Fasc. 1, Lit S Nr 50: "Die Niederösa terreichische Regierung teilt dem Konsistorium mit, dass die durch den Austritt von Prof. Leopold Federl [Föderl] freigewordene Professur der Poetik am akademischen Gymnasium dem Anton Stein verliehen wurde."

23 *Das Waldviertel / Blätter für heimat= und Volkskunde des Niederösterreichischen Waldviertels* 3, no. 8 (December 1, 1930): 3, no. 8 (December 1, 1930): 135–137. The reference to Föderl is made on page 135 of Luise Hadl's article "Das Castellihaus und der Dichter." Föderl was a friend of the Castelli family and the first teacher of the poet Ignaz Franz Castelli (1781–1862), whose memoirs (Ignaz Franz Castelli, *Memoiren meines Lebens*, [Vienna and Prague: Kober & Markgraft, 4 vols, 1861–62]) provide much of the most important information in the article. "In his memoirs," Hadl writes, "the poet Castelli gratefully commemorates this fatherly friend, his knowledge and his noble nature. He had practiced many good things in the parish districts, had built up the parsonage quite a bit, had also contributed to sociability by founding a shooting society and a Musik Kapelle, was an excellent violin player and a kind advisor to his parishioners" (In seinen Lebenserinnerungen gedenkt der Dichter Castelli dankbar dieses väterlichen Freundes, seiner Kenntnisse und seines vornehmen Wesens. Er habe im Pfarrbezirke viel Gutes geübt, habe den Pfarrhof ganz neu aufgebaut, auch zur Geselligkeit durch Gründung einer Schützengesellschaft und einer Musikkapelle beigetragen, war vortrefflicher Violinspieler und ein gütiger Berater seiner Pfarrkinder.).

freemasonry.[24] For this occasion, Föderl produced a text that was celebratory in tone but also instructive as to how Joseph's actions had benefitted freemasonry and the wider world. In his first appearance in Föderl's text (no. 3, Melodrama), Joseph is described using the conventional royal image of the sun in splendor––"After many a gentle dawn / Joseph's sun shone forth at last in splendor" (Und sieh! Nach manchen sanftern Morgenröten / tratt endlich Josephs Sonne schön hervor)—in this case also perhaps appropriate because of its association with enlightenment.[25] "In the ritual and solely by its practice," Jacques Henry writes, "the freemason is accorded the possibility of leaving the 'secular world' in order to 'raise his heart in brotherhood and turn his gaze toward the light.'"[26] As the text for this particular movement unfolds, Föderl describes Joseph as "mankind's guardian spirit," crediting him with the return of a spirit of tolerance and thus a society in which the order could flourish and serve the welfare of both Masons and mankind.

It is unlikely that Joseph would have been impressed with the sycophancy, but he might have been pleased that a by-product of the Toleration Patent was an increase in practical charitable initiatives. These matters must have concerned Joseph in 1783 as he sought to implement complex and controversial reforms of monasteries throughout the kingdom.

While Joseph's desire for reform had a philosophical underpinning, he was pragmatic about its implementation. His view of the monasteries was that they must serve a practical end. In a letter to Franz Joseph, Ritter von Heinke written in 1780 he asserts:

> No sympathy should be shown to idleness; therefore all foundations, prelatures, canons, Carthusians, [Camaldese,] and other regulars who cannot or will not devote themselves to the benefit of their fellows are to be held to this as their first duty regardless [of their rules]; and, if their statutes do not permit it, their Orders are to be dissolved on that ground

---

24 "Zwei Wochen darnach, am 1. Sept., feierte die [Loge] das Johannisfest in Gemeinschaft mit der [Order]. Zur gekrönten Hoffnung und Zu den 3 Adlern und dasselbe gestaltete sich durch die dabei zum Vortrag gebrachte Cantate Föderl's zu einen Dankfest für den Schutz, welche Joseph II. der Freimauerei angedeihen liess" (Abafi, *Geschichte der Freimauerei*, 324).

25 James Parker, "Sun," heraldsnet, accessed 26 September 2019, https://www.heraldsnet.org/saitou/parker/Jpglosss.htm#Sun.

26 Jacques Henry, *Mozart the Freemason: the Masonic Influence on his Music Genius* (Rochester, VT: Inner Traditions, 2006), 22.

alone, and they can be turned into more useful and God-pleasing citizens of the state.[27]

By 29 November 1781 Joseph had reached a decision to dissolve all contemplative orders in his dominions, on the grounds that they were "entirely useless to society . . . they neither run schools nor look after the poor."[28] Action swiftly followed, and met with considerable resentment but no real opposition. Assets taken from the monasteries were used to fund the creation of new parishes, in order to provide more spiritual and practical support for parishioners. The diocesan boundaries had not changed in nearly eight hundred years in spite of big changes in political boundaries and population distribution, and clearly a rationalization of parishes was long overdue. Joseph's ecclesiastical commission, established in July 1782, was charged with implementing these policies and dealing with abuses relating to indulgences, forms of worship, processions, miracle-working pictures, brotherhoods, and other religious practices that met with his disapproval.

The sixth movement of *Joseph der Menschheit Segen* alludes to the indifference of the monks to the plight of the poor, and suggests the infatuation of credulous laymen had enriched monastic orders:

> Hail, mankind!
> The monks' deity Dagon has fallen,
> crushed by the Ark of the Covenant;
> the world learns from light to depart from the darkness.
> Reason and religion return,
> resplendent in their old glory.
> Even in the breast of the profane
> awakens delight in wiser benevolence.
>
> See how the layman marvels at the shame of infatuation.
> That for centuries he raced to fatten up
> that rich band of beggars, when God instructed!
>
> That he, smitten by stale wounds
> and tormented by a thousand pangs of conscience
> slept so long, numbed by holy mist—

---

27 Beales, *Against the World*, 279.
28 Ibid., 280.

Once—monks did this—he went unpityingly
to the truly poor, with gaze averted,
surged past the screams of the wailers
swiftly up to the clouds.

Indulged by the sweet flattery of the monks,
dazzled by their pious hypocrisy,
he did not see the tears of true misery.

But yes—he awakens, be comforted, you poor!
The long sorrow is at an end;
Idols are challenged
and collapse on their own disgraced faces.
This too is Joseph's work: here too there is light.

(Heil Menschheit dir! / Der Mönche Dagon fällt, / zertrümmert vor der Bundeslade nieder; / vom Lichte Finsternis zu scheiden lernt die Welt, / Vernunft, Religion kehrt wieder, / und prangt im alten Glanz. / Auch in profaner Brust / erwacht des klügern Wohltuns süße Lust. / Sieh! Wie der Laie staunt ob der Betörung Schande. / Daß er Jahrhunderte die reiche Bettlerbande, / als hieß es Gott, zu mästen lief! / Daß er von schalen Wundern hingerissen / bei tausend marternden Gewissensbissen, / von heil'gem Dunst betäubt so lange schlief' – / Einst – Mönche tatens – ging er ohn' Erbarmen, / mit weggewandten Blick den wahren Armen, / drang gleich des Jammernden Geschrei / bis an die Wolken hin, mit schnellem Schritt vorbei. / Verwöhnt durch der Mönche süßes Schmeicheln, / geblendet durch ihr frömmelnd Heucheln / sah er des wahren Elends Träne nicht. / Doch – er wacht auf, trost euch, ihr Armen! / Ausgelitten ist nun der lange Schmerz; / Idole sind bestritten, / sie stürzen hin auf ihr beschämt Gesicht. / Auch dies ist Josephs Werk: auch hier wird Licht!)

The association of monks with the Philistine deity Dagon, crushed by the Ark of Covenant according to 1 Samuel 5:2–5, may be surprising given Föderl's background as a priest.[29] However, it is consistent with the principle of

---

29 "When the Philistines captured the ark of God, they carried it from Ebenezer to Ashdod; then the Philistines took the ark of God and brought it into the house of Dagon and set it up beside Dagon. And when the people of Ashdod rose early the next day, behold, Dagon had fallen face downward on the ground before the ark of the LORD. So they took Dagon and put him back in his place. But when the rose early on the next morning, behold, Dagon had fallen face downward on the ground before the ark of the LORD, and the head of Dagon and both his hands were lying cut off upon the threshold; only the trunk of Dagon was left to him.

moving from darkness to light, from ignorance and superstition to enlightenment, espoused by the Masons and by Joseph himself. The aria that follows again expresses gratitude to Joseph for creating a world in which:

> [E]qual brothers of different faiths,
> Walk peacefully hand in hand
> Embraced by the bonds of tolerance.

(Von ihm quoll Segen auf uns nieder, / durch ihn gehn friedlich Hand in Hand, / verschiednen Glaubens gleiche Brüder, / umschlungen von der Duldung Band.)

The sentiments expressed in the texts quoted above are amplified in the eighth and penultimate movement.

> How gloriously the flag of peace
> Flutters on Vienna's noble walls!
> You, Joseph, raised it yourself for humanity,
> To last for ages to come.
>
> Weaned off frippery, awakened from a long sleep,
> The profane man comes running, vowing in tears of joy
> To be an honest accomplice in the struggle against distress.
>
> You too, moved brothers, do not tarry;
> Joseph's wishes are a Mason's command.
>
> O, do not return from these happy halls—
> do the bidding of the Almighty and of Joseph—
> till you have multiplied the sum of the happy
> and heard the rescued ones bless the Order.

(Wie herrlich schön auf Wiens erhabnen Mauern / die Friedens Fahne weht! / Aeonen durchzudauern / hast du sie Joseph selbst der Menschheit aufgesteckt. / Vom Tand entwöhnt, vom langen Schlaf geweckt, / Eilt der Profane her und schwört in Freuden Zähren / ein redlicher Gehilf dem Elend mitzuwehren. / Auch ihr, gerührte Brüder, säumet nicht, / was Joseph wünschet sei dem Maurer Pflicht. / O kehrt, dem Ewigen

---

This is why the priests of Dagon and all who enter the house of Dagon do not tread on the threshold of Dagon in Ashdod to this day." 1 Samuel 5:2–5 (RSV).

und Joseph zu gefallen, / erst dann zurück aus diesen frohen Hallen, / wenn ihr die Zahl der Glücklichen vermehrt / und die Geretteten den Orden segnen hört.)

Joseph's actions are portrayed as perfectly aligned with the ideals of freemasonry, and his "wishes are a Mason's command," his authority evidently second only to that of the Almighty.

This may well have been considered verging on sacrilege by some people, but the enthusiasm for freemasonry in the city where the Holy Roman emperor himself resided suggests that Catholics had no difficulty in reconciling their religious obligations and beliefs with those of freemasonry. Two successive abbots of the Benedictine monastery at Melk were said to have been "buried in their [Masonic] apron according to the custom of the house."[30]

As we have seen, Föderl's text alludes to Joseph's reform initiatives that were enthusiastically endorsed by Freemasons. Although the text is explicitly Masonic in sentiment and draws on Masonic imagery, Koželuh's publication of an arrangement of *Joseph der Menschheit Segen* for fortepiano and voices in 1784 by the Viennese publisher Torricella[31] suggests that it contains nothing his Masonic

FIGURE 1. Title page of *Joseph der Menschheit Segen*, Op. 11, arranged for fortepiano and voices (Vienna: Torricella, 1784).

---

30   Beales, *Against the World*, 276.
31   Leopold Kozeluch, *Joseph der Menschheit Segen, Eine Cantata mit Arien und Chören von L. F. Pr. d D. Gewidmet Dem Edlen Herrn Von P*, in *Musik gesetzet und für das Clavier eingerichtet* (Vienna: Torricella, ca. 1784).

brothers would have objected to being made public. The work is not described as a Masonic cantata, but the Masonic devices on the engraved title page would have identified it as such to non-masons even if their precise significance was not understood.

The commercial publication of Masonic musical works was not uncommon in the eighteenth century, and many of the collections used common Masonic devices such as the compasses and T-square on their title pages. These collections include songs that are clearly Masonic in their texts and the way they are set, and also other songs, often drawn from popular sources.[32] Masonic collections were published in England, France, the Netherlands and elsewhere, and the market for them was not confined to Masons. Masonic songs also appeared in more general collections such as Thomas Hale's 1763 *Social Harmony*,[33] whose lengthy list of subscribers represents a cross-section of society from schoolmasters, lawyers and clergymen to professional musicians and soldiers. A number of unmarried women also subscribed to *Social Harmony*, which demonstrates the extent to which freemasonry was visible and accepted in society.

Like all vocal works, *Joseph der Menschheit Segen* marries text and music. Koželuh's challenge was to set the text in a way that is musically interesting and appropriate to its content and symbolism. The uninitiated may recognize symbols but not fully understand them. There is ample evidence that certain Masonic devices and images were widely recognized in the 1780s, but their significance was likely understood only by initiates, even within the organization. A Master Mason would have a different understanding of the symbolic importance of a given device than a member who had been admitted only to the first or second degree. Thus, there are two potential levels of understanding: one obvious, the other complex and invisible (or inaudible) to the uninitiated. The way Koželuh treats certain aspects of Masonic symbolism in *Joseph der Menschheit Segen* shows that that he approached the task of setting the text with knowledge and sensitivity.

Numbers play an important symbolic role in freemasonry, and the numbers three and nine are particularly significant. The individual movements of the cantata are not numbered, but there are nine discrete sections if the first aria-chorus

---

32 For an overview of a number of such collections see, Nettl, *Mozart and Masonry*, 29–41.

33 Thomas Hale, *Social Harmony / Consisting of a Collection of / Songs and Catches / In two, three, four and five PARTS / From the Works of the most eminent Masters / To which are added / Several Choice Songs on / MASONRY / By Thomas Hale of Darnhall Cheshire / 1763*. (Liverpool: Hale & Son, 1763).

complex [no. 4] is counted as two interlinked movements. The number three is given far more prominence in the work, as might be expected given its ubiquity in Masonic compositions.

Koželuh's numerical allusions are sometimes made in an obvious way that can be grasped immediately by the uninitiated. At other times, however, the symbolism is illuminated more subtly, so that it might only be perceived or understood by masons.

The adagio *Introduzione*, in triple meter, begins with three imposing chords. While there is an obvious reference to the number three, the initiate will also recognize a reference to the three knocks that mark the beginning of every Masonic meeting. These chords are followed by a dotted eighth-sixteenth pair. This pattern is important in Masonic ritual music since it not only represents a ternary pattern—the dotted note is three times the duration represented by the dot (and is meaningless without its completion; that is, the shorter note that follows and completes the dotted figure)—but dotted patterns are associated with limping, which has great symbolic meaning: "Oedipus limped and the layman, precisely to recall this myth, limps when entering the lodge to be initiated."[34] While the dotted figure plays a minimal role in the unfolding of the introduction, it appears prominently in the central section of the second melodrama and is the dominant rhythmic pattern in the second aria, "Trockne sanft die heissen Zähren." The opening four-measure phrase is repeated in modified form, beginning on the submediant—an early allusion to the thirds relationship that is central in the work (see example 1).

The allegro that follows also contains multiple allusions to the number three, from the prominent writing in thirds which is an integral stylistic element of the primary theme, to a closing theme which contains three iterations of a pattern consisting of a dotted quarter-eighth pair followed by three eighth notes: the section ends with three tutti quarter-note chords. The recurrence of such

---

34   Henry, *Mozart the Freemason*, 32. The reference to Oedipus concerns the riddle of the Sphinx: "Which creature has one voice and yet becomes four-footed and two-footed and three-footed?" Oedipus correctly answers, "a man." A person crawls as infant, walks on two legs in the prime of life, and with a stick in old age. In Masonic ritual it is applied to the east, west and south of the lodge. A mason first receives light in the east from the Worshipful Master, or from the birth of the journey. Moving clockwise around the lodge, the brother approaches the south in the middle of the journey, analogous to the "noontime of life when half of our years lie before us and half behind us," and finally he arrives in the west at the end of the metaphorical day to his resting place. See "A Life in a Day," Masonrytoday.com, accessed 14 February, 2022, https://www.masonrytoday.com/index.php?new_month=11&new_day=25&new_year=2018.

Example 1. *Joseph der Menschheit Segen*, Introduzione, Adagio, s1–8.

patterns is clearly intended to be understood in terms of numerological symbolism. One curious aspect of this section, is that the unison passage beginning at measure 86, if the print is correct, remains at *piano* (see example 2). This theme reappears at the end of the movement, the unison passage now marked *forte* and the final three chords, which have been revoiced, the more emphatic for being punctuated by quarter-note rests.

Example 2. *Joseph der Menschheit Segen*, Allegro, measures 82–91.

It is unclear whether the movements assigned to the chorus—nos. 2, 5, and 9—were intended to be sung by an ensemble of soloists or by more substantial forces,[35] but the three-part texture, in this case consisting of two sopranos and bass, is one found in many contemporary Masonic vocal works and is clearly intended to be understood in terms of numerical symbolism. This is emphasized further in the opening chorus (no. 2) by its tonality, E-flat major, and in the

---

35 These movements are headed "Coro" in Koželuh's score.

second chorus (no. 5) by the use of triple meter. The reference to numerical symbolism in the final movement (no. 9) is explicit in the text rather than the music. The refrain "This do we swear by three times three, to honor the Masons' weal" (Dies schwören wir durch dreimal drei, beim Wohl der Maurerei), is sung four times which suggests that for Koželuh, musical concerns such as phrase construction took precedence in this instance over numerical symbolism although it is still arguably present in the scoring for three-part choir. However, this closing solo-chorus movement also alludes to the Masonic element of space. According to Henry, symbols of time and space are constituent parts of Masonic rituals, representing the world in its present state and its unfolding:[36]

> Space is "drawn" by the two rows into which the brothers are divided on either side of the Grand Master's chair, which is located at the Orient. Two brothers, the Wardens, stand for those two rows through a particular function. They represent all their brothers and speak in their name. Their responses, which alternate with the questions posed by the Grand Master, seem to formulate orally the limits of the space, especially at the opening and closing of the proceedings.[37]

This practice of alternating question and response invites a very obvious musical treatment and Nettl notes that antiphonal singing in German art song was first employed by Freemasons. The *Neue Freimäurer Lieder*, dedicated to the Zorobabel lodge in Copenhagen and dated St. John's Day, 5749 [1749], includes a number of songs which carry the direction "Now sings one, now sing all."[38]

The second symbol of space that Henry notes is the alternating black-and-white squares of the mosaic flooring at the center of the lodge. In musical terms, this can also be represented by a pattern of statement and response. In the finale of *Joseph der Menschheit Segen* we see just such an arrangement, with the soprano soloist's four couplets alternating with the refrain sung by the chorus. The final refrain, with its short expansion, leads to a brief instrumental coda which closes with a thrice-repeated figure (see example 3). This closing gesture also amplifies the idea of three times three in the text sung by the chorus, and this is anticipated by its use at the end of the previous monologue. As in the other choral

---

36 Henry, *Mozart the Freemason*, 34.
37 Ibid., 34–35.
38 Nettl, *Mozart and Masonry*, 36

EXAMPLE 3. *Joseph der Menschheit Segen*, closing tutti, measures 77-84.

movements, the vocal writing is homophonic throughout, suggesting brotherhood and unity of purpose.

The tonal scheme of *Joseph der Menschheit Segen* differs from large-scale works of the period, which typically have their outer movements cast in the same key. In *Joseph*, this does not happen: the overture is in G major and the final chorus is in B-flat major. This third relationship should not come as a surprise given the symbolic emphasis placed elsewhere on the number three. Indeed, the tonal relationship between individual movements takes this principle further as the schematic below demonstrates:

EXAMPLE 4. *Joseph der Menschheit Segen*, Solo-Chorus, "Dem Maurer Bunde treu zu handeln."

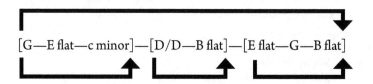

In the tonal sequence G—E flat—C minor—D—B flat—E flat—G—B flat, the second and third movements are both a third lower than their predecessor, while movements eight and nine are a third higher than movement seven. The central section of the movement, comprising the solo-chorus complex nos. 4 and 5 in D major and the sixth movement in B flat, is once again built on the relationship of a third.

While the tonal architecture of the work is highly unusual in itself, and its emphasis on thirds relationships may be understood as an extension of the numerical symbolism discussed above, another aspect to it warrants consideration. Koželuh appears to have chosen his keys according to their affective characteristics. Thus, we see a sequence of tonalities that carefully matches the structure and meaning of the text. Analyzed in terms of the characteristics typically ascribed by eighteenth- and early nineteenth-century musical theorists to musical keys, the work progresses from an invocation of true friendship and faithful love (G major) to aspiration for a better world (B-flat major).[39] The choice of G major for the opening movement has a layer of Masonic significance in that G is a cipher for God, the "Grand Architect."[40] Koželuh's careful placement of the two E flat movements—the key of love, of devotion, of intimate conversation with God—is significant.[41] The opening chorus expresses joy at the growing number of "brothers who worship wisdom" and hope that "the number of the happy may likewise be multiplied."[42] The second appearance of E-flat major is reserved for the aria [no. 7], which predicts that

> It shall be the delight of even the profane
> to tell the truly poor
> what Masons have done in silence.

---

[39] These descriptions are taken from Christian Daniel Friedrich Schubart's *Ideen zu einer Aesthetik der Tonkunst* (Vienna: J. V. Degen, 1806). For a detailed exploration of this topic, see Rita Steblin, *A History of Key Characteristics in the Eighteenth and Early Nineteenth Centuries*. (Ann Arbor: UMI Research Press, 1983).

[40] "The Meaning Behind the Masonic Letter 'G,'" *Northern Masonic Jurisdiction Scottish Rite* (blog) December 23, 2020, https://scottishritenmj.org/blog/masonic-letter-g.

[41] Steblin, *Key Characteristics.*

[42] Segen kam auf uns hernieder,
jeder Tag vermehrt die Brüder,
die der Weisheit huldigen.
Mit der Zahl der Weisen mehre
sich zu unsers Bundes Ehre
auch die Zahl der Glücklichen.

(Wahrer Armut schnell zu raten, / was in Stillem Maurer taten, / wird auch des Profanen Lust.)

D major, the brightest key employed in the work and one associated with victory and rejoicing,[43] is reserved for the first solo-chorus complex, a paean of praise to Joseph himself.

One of the unusual features of *Joseph der Menschheit Segen* is its use of melodrama, an innovative style that had been used with great success by Georg Benda in his melodramas *Ariadne auf Naxos* (Gotha, 1775), *Medea* (Leipzig, 1778), and *Pygmalion* (Vienna, 1779). Like a number of other composers of theater music, Mozart was fascinated by these works and incorporated melodrama in his incidental music to Baron Tobias von Gebler's play *Thamos, König von Aegypten* and in his partially complete Singspiel *Zaïde* (1779–1780), which may have been intended for Joseph II's new German-language Nationaltheater. He brought the score of *Zaïde* with him to Vienna in 1781 but abandoned it in a favor of working on *Die Entführung aus dem Serail*. *Joseph der Menschheit Segen* is thus one of the very earliest works composed in Vienna to incorporate melodrama. The inspiration for this came perhaps from Föderl, who was presumably acquainted with his fellow Mason, Baron von Gebler. But it seems unlikely that Koželuh would have been unaware of Benda's melodramas. He may have met Benda, who even composed works for Masonic rituals, through Masonic circles.

Two distinct styles of melodrama were cultivated in the eighteenth century, one in which the spoken text was punctuated by passages of expressive instrumental music in the manner of accompanied recitative, and the other, in which the spoken voice was superimposed on the accompanying music.[44] Koželuh employs the first of these styles, using the orchestra to anticipate the tone of the text to follow or amplify it in more extended sections. The bursts of instrumental music vary considerably in length and style within each of the melodrama movements, and this unpredictability is underlined by their tonal instability. In the first melodrama movement we also see Koželuh's preoccupation with numerical patterning. The movement opens with a turbulent ten-bar passage in C minor which anticipates the first line of spoken text: "Once barbarism and superstition flowed forth, / hurling

---

43 Schubart, *Ideen*.
44 For an excellent overview, see Peter Branscombe, "Melodrama," *Grove Music Online*, Oxford University Press, 2001, http://www.grovemusic.com.

themselves at long-sealed torrents ...." (Einst goß sich Barbarei und Aberglaube gleich lang verdämmten Fluten wild heran ...).

The passage breaks off on a V6/5 chord which sets up a truncated restatement of the opening material in the dominant (G minor) after the first lines of spoken text. This new statement of the theme breaks off in the same way to signal the reintroduction of the narration and is in turn followed by the final statement of the theme, this time condensed to six measures and in D minor. From this point in the movement, Koželuh employs several new and distinct musical ideas which can be seen to complement the text of the narrative. None of them shares any motivic material with the opening theme, but the last idea introduced proves to be the theme of the movement that follows, the song of praise to Joseph. Koželuh prepares the ground by introducing an earlier figure in D major which is restated in E minor and concludes with a cadence in B minor after which the "Joseph" theme is introduced. Thus, we see the juxtaposition of B minor and D major (the thirds relationship which also ushers in the first D major theme) and within the movement, an emphasis on three tonal areas: C minor, D minor/D major, and E minor. This progression of three tonal steps, often more simply expressed in a rising three-note pattern or sequence, is encountered elsewhere in Masonic works. According to Henry:

> Moving up steps to approach the altar or the temple has always been a universal symbol.... In the Lodge, in order to reach the Orient where the Grand Master is seated, you have to mount three steps. Moreover, these steps, designed as part of the ritual tableau at the center of the Masonic hall, are always visible to the freemason.... The listener easily perceives this especially descriptive form of imagery. The musical form appears to the ear just as the steps appear to the eye: the mark of a shift in levels.[45]

The tonal trajectory of this movement from C minor to D major also represents the central impulse in freemasonry: the movement from darkness into the light, reinforcing the tone and content of its text, which begins in deep despair and concludes with the arrival of Joseph.

While Föderl and Koželuh may have chosen to employ melodrama in three of the nine movements of *Joseph der Menschheit Segen* for clear dramatic reasons, it is also possible that they intended the narrator to be understood as analogous

---

45   Henry, *Mozart the Freemason*, 33.

to the Grand Master. Since we have no indication of who performed the work, we cannot know for certain whether the narrator's role was taken by an actor or even by Föderl himself. Perhaps as an official of the lodge, his reading of the text would have increased its gravitas for his fellow Masons, who viewed Joseph's rule as ushering in a new and glorious world.

Although *Joseph der Menschheit Segen* was published by Koželuh in 1784, there is no evidence of any later performance of the work in its original form. It was not the only work composed by a Mason in praise of Joseph II, but it was unusual for its scale and scope. The best-known example is Mozart's *Zerfliesset heut' geliebte Brüder*, K. 483, a setting of a text by Augustin Veith von Schittlersberg for tenor and three-part male chorus, composed in 1785 to mark the opening of the Neugekrönte Hoffnung lodge. Like Föderl, Schittlersberg was a Senior Warden at the Zur wahren Eintracht lodge, and his text, although far narrower in scope than Föderl's, nonetheless expresses similar sentiments in respect of Joseph's benevolent support of freemasonry. This is particularly apparent in the second section of the text, which Mozart assigns to the chorus:

> Let hearts and tongues
> unite to sing this hymn in praise to Joseph,
> the father who drew us closer together.
> Beneficence is the most beautiful of duties;
> he has watched us ardently perform it
> and crowns us with loving hand.

> (Vereineter Herzen und Zungen / sei Joseph dies Loblied gesungen, / dem Vater, der enger uns band. / Wohltun ist die Schönste der Pflichten; / er sah sie uns feurig verrichten / und krönt uns mit liebevoller Hand.)

Mozart was soon to compose more ambitious Masonic works, and Henry has argued that there is strong evidence of Masonic influence in many of his other works from the last few years of his life.[46] Not enough systematic work has been carried out on Koželuh's works to reach a similar conclusion about his oeuvre, but there is no question that Masonic elements can be detected in the cantata he composed in 1791 for the coronation of Leopold II in Prague.[47] The libretto was written by a fellow mason, August Gottlieb Meissner (1753–1807), Professor

---

46   Ibid., 54–104
47   *Kantate zur Krönung Leopolds II*, "Heil dem Monarchen," P.XIX:6.

of Aesthetics and Classical Literature at the University of Prague.[48] Although the work is far larger in scale than *Joseph der Menschheit Segen*, it reflects a similar creative ethos, and similarly looks forward with Josephine optimism to the dawning of a new age of peace and prosperity.

Bibliography

Abafi, Ludwig. *Geschichte der Freimauerei in Oesterreich-Ungarn von Ludwig Abafi / Mitglied der Petőfi-Gesellschaft in Budapest, Vierter Band*. Budapest: Ludwig Aigner, 1893.

Anon. "A Life in a Day." Accessed 14 February 2022. https://www.masonrytoday.com/index.php?new_month=11&new_day=25&new_year=2018.

———. "The Meaning Behind the Masonic Letter 'G.'" *Northern Masonic Jurisdiction Scottish Rite* (blog), December 23, 2020. https://scottishritenmj.org/blog/masonic-letter-g.

Beales, Derek. *Joseph II*. Vol. 1, *In the Shadow of Maria Theresia, 1741–1780*. Cambridge: Cambridge University Press, 1987.

———. *Joseph II*. Vol. 2, *Against the World, 1780–1790*. Cambridge: Cambridge University Press, 2009.

Castelli, Ignaz Franz. *Memoiren meines Lebens*. Vienna and Prague: Kober & Markgraft, 4 vols, 1861–62.

Branscombe, Peter. "Melodrama." *Grove Music Online*. Oxford University Press, 2001. https://doi-org.ezproxy.auckland.ac.nz/10.1093/gmo/9781561592630.article.18355.

---

48 See Walter Weber, "Meißner, August Gottlieb," Deutsche Biographie, accessed 15 February 2022, https://www.deutsche-biographie.de/sfz60084.html#ndbcontent.

Hadl, Luise. "Das Castellihaus und der Dichter." In *Das Waldviertel / Blätter für heimat= und Volkskunde des Niederösterreichischen Waldviertels*. 3, no. 8 (December 1, 1930): 135-137.

Hale, Thomas. *Social Harmony / Consisting of a Collection of / Songs and Catches / In two, three, four and five PARTS / From the Works of the most eminent Masters / To which are added / Several Choice Songs on / MASONRY / By Thomas Hale of Darnhall Cheshire / 1763.* Liverpool: Hale & Son, 1763.

Henry, Jacques. *Mozart the Freemason: The Masonic Influence on his Music Genius*. Rochester, VT: Inner Traditions, 2006.

Landon, H. C. Robbins. *1791 Mozart's Last Year*. London: Thames & Hudson, 1988.

Lewis, Ludwig. *Geschichte der Freimauerei in Österreich im allgemeinen und der Wiener Loge zu St. Joseph insbesondere*. Vienna: Druck und Verlag der Typogr. -literar. – artistichen Anstalt L. C. Zamarski & C. Dittmarsch, 1861.

Macartney, C. A., ed. *The Habsburg and Hohenzollern Dynasties in the Seventeenth and Eighteenth Centuries*. New York, Evanston, and London: Harper & Row, 1970.

Mitchell, Lloyd Earl. "The Influence of Freemasonry on Some of the Music of Wolfgang Amadeus Mozart." M.Ed. thesis, Central Washington University, 1969.

Nettl, Paul. *Mozart and Masonry*. New York: Dorset Press 1987.

Parker, James. "Sun." heraldsnet. Accessed 26 September 2019. https://www.heraldsnet.org/saitou/parker/Jpglosss.htm#Sun.

Pichler, Caroline. *Denkwürdigkeiten aus meinem Leben*. 2 vols. Edited by E. K. Blümml. Munich: Georg Müller 1914.

Schubart, Christian Daniel Friedrich. *Ideen zu einer Aesthetik der Tonkunskt*. Vienna: J. V. Degen, 1806.

Steblin, Rita. *A History of Key Characteristics in the Eighteenth and Early Nineteenth Centuries*. Ann Arbor: UMI Research Press, 1983.

Weber, Walter. "Meißner, August Gottlieb." Deutsche Biographie. Accessed 15 February 2022. https://www.deutsche-biographie.de/sfz60084.html#ndbcontent.

Young, David. "Karl von Ordonez (1734–1786): A Biographical Study." *Royal Musical Association Research Chronicle 1983–1985*, no.19 (1983–1985): 31–56.

Agency, Politics, and Opera Arrangements in Fanny Arnstein's Salons

Nancy November

> The tide runs in Vienna towards gross sensuality in the people;—mute obedience in the public officers;—gloom or dissoluteness among the high nobility, and towards the most complete despotism in the Government, which grasps with the iron claw of its emblem—the double eagle—the whole empire, and keeps it in its baneful embraces.[1]

Public morale was at a low ebb in early nineteenth-century Vienna. Although the Congress of Vienna (1815) involved a diplomatic redrawing of the map of Europe, Emperor Francis I (r. 1804–1835) was a dictator, primarily interested in personal power. With Clemens von Metternich, his foreign minister (1809–1848), he was taken up with reversion to monarchical rule and studied avoidance of another revolution. Suspected insurrections were closely monitored and suppressed under the 'system' operated by Metternich. Meetings of groups were under surveillance, and private letters and published plays went first to the censor. Inhibiting education but permitting light and amusing activities, like theatre going, walking, café visits and music-making, the program was designed to keep the public in a state of peaceful ignorance.[2] For their part, the Viennese strove to live innocuous lives, or lives that *looked* innocuous. Music-making in the Viennese home was widely perceived to be nonpolitical at the time and was therefore ubiquitous.

---

1   Charles Sealsfield [Karl Postl], *Austria as it is, or, Sketches of Continental Courts. By an Eyewitness/Österreich, wie es ist oder Skizzen von Fürstenhöfen des Kontinents; von einem Augenzeugen* (London: Hurst, Chance and Co., 1828), 215.

2   Donald G. Daviau, "Biedermeier. The Happy Face of the Vormärz Era," in *The Other Vienna: The Culture of Biedermeier Austria*, ed. Clifford A. Bernd, Robert Pichl, and Margarete Wagner (Vienna: Lehner, 2002), 17–18.

Fanny von Arnstein was one of several Viennese women who pushed back against the government by means of culture. She and her daughter Henriette von Pereira-Arnstein, Caroline Pichler (1769–1843), and Maria Theresa von Paradis (1759–1824), were leaders in a diplomatic rearrangement of the sociocultural map in early nineteenth-century Vienna. They achieved this by helping to develop a new music culture—or rearranging an old one—to reflect middle-class ideals and empower ordinary people, including many women. Their musical salons were an important arena of empowerment, where women could take on roles, make decisions and generally demonstrate leadership not offered them in public. I discuss how this was possible, with a case study of Arnstein's salons.

Viennese Musical Salons

We first need to understand the Viennese salons of the time. Rebecca Cypess has argued that the term "salon" can misleadingly evoke high society and exclusivity; whereas in the early nineteenth century it takes in events ranging from large informal gatherings to occasions within the intimate circle of family and friends.[3] Arnstein's salons were at the more lavish end of the spectrum, and they did attract prominent guests, including distinguished middle-class intellectuals such as Wilhelm von Humboldt, August Wilhelm Schlegel, and Friedrich Schlegel. During the Congress of Vienna she was also visited by famous aristocrats like the Duke of Wellington, the Prince of Talleyrand, and Prince Karl August of Hardenberg. Although she was of noble heritage, Arnstein frequently encountered prejudice against Jewish prominence in the upwardly mobile classes in Vienna. Her own salons were relatively open and inclusive in a time of widening class division.[4] In Vienna there was generally less mixing of the classes than in the Parisian salons of the late eighteenth and early nineteenth centuries, especially after the Congress.

The early nineteenth-century Viennese salon is best understood as a set of practices or processes, rather than as events involving a particular group of people in a specific environment.[5] We can understand the distinctively

---

[3] Rebecca Cypess, "Ancient Poetry, Modern Music, and the *Wechselgesang der Mirjam und Debora*: The Meanings of Song in the Itzig Circle," *Bach* 47, no. 1 (2016): 21–65.

[4] See my comments on this subject in *Cultivating String Quartets in Beethoven's Vienna* (Woodbridge: Boydell, 2017), 109–110.

[5] See especially Rebecca Cypess, *Women and Musical Salons in the Enlightenment* (Chicago: University of Chicago Press), 7.

practice-oriented character of Viennese salons by considering the kinds of activity they pursued. These salons frequently mixed the arts—music, poetry, theatre—and involved audience participation. Such mixed entertainments included *Geschichten spielen* (pantomiming of scenes from famous plays); *tableaux vivants* or *lebende Bilder* (posing to resemble scenes in famous historical paintings); and *Attitüden* (acting out emotions as depicted in paintings).[6] Interest in theatre extended to the explicit imitation of public performances and performers. The theatrical character of salons, which often interleaved musical numbers with theatrical recitations, was quintessentially Viennese, as was a strong emphasis on music.

Nineteenth-century *Salonmusik*, like the nineteenth-century salon itself, can be understood as an integrated practice with specific objects or products. In the salons, composers and performers, professionals and amateurs, intellectuals and artists, listeners and critics met on terms at least superficially more informal than the concert hall. As Sonnleithner observed of Viennese salons: "the most eager friends of the true art of music gladly joined this circle, and participated as willingly as they listened."[7] Scores and works were adapted by the performers to meet the social and cultural needs of the moment. Instrumentation was freely changed, and "arrangements" of various sorts were produced—in new performing scores or in improvised, un-notated versions—to serve the aims of musical sociability, entertainment, and *Bildung*. Within the salon, musical scores enabled sociable interaction, allowing the rise of musical practices that might otherwise never have happened, by people who otherwise lacked such opportunities—especially female performers.

Sonnleithner's memoirs, reporting on musical salons of the early nineteenth century, suggest that the standards among Viennese musical "dilettantes" was relatively high:

> Even if the results of our dilettantes cannot easily compete with the more careful performance of outstanding professional artists, when they are effectively prepared such results contribute to the spread of knowledge

---

6 Wiebke Thormählen, "Playing with Art: Musical Arrangements as Educational Tools in Van Swieten's Vienna," *Journal of Musicology* 27, no. 3 (2010): especially 370.

7 Leopold von Sonnleithner, "Musikalische Skizzen aus 'Alt-Wien,'" *Recensionen und Mittheilungen über Theater, Music und bildende Kunst* 7, no. 47 (24 November, 1861): 739.

of solid musical works of art and thereby to an enhancement of taste as a whole.[8]

We also see here that Viennese salons acquired an educative function, improving performance standards by requiring preparation, and enhancing public taste by developing musical literacy.

The musical repertoire of these salons was largely tailored to domestic performance. Opera arrangements in various forms made up a sizeable portion of the repertoire. At the Viennese salons of Joseph Hochenadl, around 1820, for instance, the following excerpts from operas, songs, and sacred vocal works were heard between the instrumental music (accompanied by Hochenadl's daughter Katharina at the piano, and his son Thomas, a cellist, "for reinforcement"):

Wolfgang Amadeus Mozart, first finale from *Don Giovanni* (1787); arias for soprano from *Die Zauberflöte* (1791).
Ludwig van Beethoven, "Adelaide."
Joseph Haydn, duet from *The Seasons*.
Louis Spohr, tenor aria from *Faust* (Singspiel, 1813—when Spohr had taken up a post at the Theater an der Wien).
Joseph Weigl, pieces from *L'Uniforme* (heroic-comic opera, 1800).
Ferdinando Paër, duets from *Camilla* (1798–99) and *Agnese* (opera semi-seria, 1809); trio and finale from *Sargino* (heroic-comic opera, 1803).
Gasparap Spontini duet from *Die Vestalin* (*La Vestal*, 1807).
Franz Schubert, "Das Erlkönig" (1815), "Gretchen am Spinnrade" (1814).
Friedrich Ernst Fesca, "Die Geburt" (ca. 1819).
Étienne Mehul trio from *Beiden Füchsen* (*Une folie*) (comedie en vers mêlée; 1802).
Friedrich Götz, composer of opera duets and trios, and theatre director in Berlin.
Gioachino Rossini, duet, trio, and finale from *L'Italiana in Algeri* (1813); aria from *Sigismondo* (1814) aria and duet from *Semiramide* (1823) trio from *Zelmira* (1822).
Simon Mayr, duet from *Ginevra di Scozia* (1801).
Ernesto Nicolini, aria, duet, and finale from *Carlo magno* (1813); aria from *Quinto Fabio* (1811).
Valentino Fioravanti, quintet from *I virtuosi ambulanti* (1807); scale trio from *Le cantarici villane* (1801).
Giovanni Paisiello, aria from *La Molinara* (1788).
Saverio Mercadante, duet from *Elisa e Claudio* (1821).

---

8   Ibid.: 177; translation by Alexandra A. Vago in her Musical Life of Amateur Musicians in Vienna, ca. 1814–1825: A Translated Edition of Leopold von Sonnleithner's "Musiklaische Skizzen aus 'Alt-Wien,'" (MA thesis, Kent State University, 2001), 3.

Puccita [or Vincenzo Pucitta?], duet for two sopranos.
Pierre Rode, variations [possibly the Variations on "Nel cor più non mi sento" from Paisiello's *La Molinara* (1821)].
Johann Nepomuk Hummel, "La Sentinelle" (arr.; original for three voices, guitar, piano, violin, two cellos [ad lib]).
Ignaz Moscheles "Der Abschied des Troubadours" (arr.; original for violin, guitar and piano, by Moscheles, Mayseder, and Guiliani).
Most popular choruses: Nikolaus von Krufft, "Die Wanderer im Walde"; Luigi Cherubini, Introduction from *Elisa* (1794); Carl Maria von Weber "Lützows Jagd"; Johann Peter Pixis, "Räubenchor" from *Almazinde* (1820); and Andreas Romberg's "Die Macht des Gesanges".

The distinctive aspects of the Viennese salon—theatricality, music, and especially opera performed in arrangements by talented amateurs—dominated in the early nineteenth century, as musical salons became a vehicle for middle-class aspiration. The rich salon culture was supported by both the middle class and the aristocracy. It contributed much to the vitality of Viennese musical life, especially around the time of the Congress of Vienna. Chamber music flourished among the upwardly-mobile classes, partly because the Viennese nobility and rulers were themselves often interested or involved in music—Francis I, for example, was an amateur violinist; and his second wife Maria Theresia was a competent pianist. They were emulated by aspiring families in new salons that now opened up, but remained distinct from those of the nobility.

The new salons of the bourgeoisie in early nineteenth-century Vienna involved some emulation of the rulers, but they also developed a subversive character, especially around the time of the Congress. A desire for enjoying all things domestic was cultivated by the government under Metternich's system, since it kept people (especially men) at home and engaged in apparently innocuous pursuits, rather than meeting with others, and possibly conspiring to revolt.[9] But while salons ostensibly cultivated civil harmony and sought to avoid political agitation, the reality could be otherwise. Arnstein's salon, for example, took on a covert function of fostering political activism, and ultimately became known as a center of conspiracy against Napoleon, attracting great attention after Napoleon's defeat and particularly during the Congress of Vienna. The salon ended in 1818, when Arnstein died.

---

9   See also Daviau, "Biedermeier. The Happy Face of the Vormärz Era," 23.

There were several ways, more or less overt, that a musical salon could become political. First, the theatrical pursuits of the salon, including the performance of opera, allowed the participants to try on roles that might otherwise be forbidden to them, as in manservant Leporello's subversive critique of his master in *Don Giovanni*. Trying on these roles was a way of defining oneself in contradistinction to the aristocracy/ruling class, and thus exerting a kind of power. Rescue plots were in vogue around 1800, in the wake of the French Revolution, in operatic hits like Spontini's *La Vestal* or Weigl's *L'Uniforme*, involving, heroism, political freedom, and personal choice as in marriage for love. These politically suggestive plots were not necessarily censored if the political element was incorporated indirectly. And even when it seemed to offer sheer entertainment or straightforward escapism, private-sphere music-making also helped to define musicians' sense of freedom—a freedom of choice regarding what they heard, where they heard it, and how. Here we can already speak of a cultivation of agency, understood as simple autonomy.

To be sure, the extent to which a salon, musical or not, was taken up with politics varied with the host and his or her connections. But Brian Vick points out the error of viewing salons as a "feminine" or "limited" environments, where contentious topics were to be avoided. In fact, the salons, and the music-making they hosted, often served serious political and religious purposes and involved a great deal of debate among a fascinating cross-section of society.[10]

Agency in Arnstein's Musical Salons

Fanny Arnstein, daughter of the banker of Friedrich II of Prussia, grew up in Berlin in a wealthy and sociable family. Marrying Viennese banker Nathan Adam Arnstein in 1776, she moved to Vienna where she founded her first salon, the first Jewish salon in the city, four years later. She virtually dominated Vienna's salon life between 1780 and 1818. Subsequently her daughter Henriette von Pereira-Arnstein would become an important salon hostess herself. The Jewish bankers of Vienna, to whom these women were related, were generally excluded from the social circles of Austrian aristocrats,[11] so these families fostered their own salons, which came to be centers of learning and art.

---

10 Brian Vick, "Salon Networks," in *The Congress of Vienna: Power and Politics after Napoleon* (Cambridge, MA: Harvard University Press, 2014), 112–52.
11 See also Alice M. Hanson, *Musical Life in Biedermeier Vienna* (Cambridge: Cambridge University Press, 1985), 114.

Around 1800 Arnstein's salon became the center of a cooperating salon network of intellectual and musical women in Vienna, with close ties to Berlin where Arnstein's sisters, Sara Levy and Rebecca Ephraim, lived.[12] Her sisters directed lively musical and literary salons, and Levy visited Arnstein's salon in Vienna. In 1800 Arnstein's other sister Caecilie Wulff (1760–1836) married Bernhard von Eskeles, an associate of Arnstein's husband Nathan von Arnstein, and came to Vienna; in 1805 Rebecca also moved to Vienna. Other women in Arnstein's circle kept literary salons themselves: Bernhard von Eskeles's sister Eleonore Fliess; Arnstein's nieces Regina Frohberg and Marianne Saaling; Mariane von Eybenberg and Dorothea Schlegel, wife of Friedrich Schlegel. Sara, Fanny, and Caecilie were all musical themselves.

An account by Johann Pezzl, a playwright and Enlightenment writer who lived in Vienna from 1784, gives an impression of Fanny's early salons and how she helped to define the new tone of the Viennese salon. Pezzl carefully avoids mentioning anyone by name (on grounds of protecting their modesty). But he writes about certain influential women in connection with "a core of businessmen who work hand in hand with the stars of first magnitude in the state"—the businessmen Arnstein's husband, Nathan:

> As these persons' gatherings are not quite so rigorously barricaded against honest, but earthly beings as those of the nobility, the enlightened way of thinking is spread through them to many others, and through these again to many classes of the public. Here it is helpful that some ladies from these houses combine the masculine way of thinking with feminine charm, and are thereby doubly agreeable. . . . These are Musarion's pupils: their company is as instructive and tasteful as it is charming; in their houses one does not yawn while away the evenings with miserable card-shuffling. Little concerts, confidential chats among friends, literary novelties, discussions about books, travel, works of art, the theatre; the events of the day, and interesting news related, judged and illuminated with a little spice, make up the entertainment, and shorten the long winter evenings for the intimate circle. There one makes the acquaintance of most of the resident scholars as well as the foreign ones who occasionally travel through Vienna.[13]

---

12 See also Rebecca Cypess and Nancy Sinkoff, eds., *Sara Levy's World: Gender, Judaism, and the Bach Tradition in Enlightenment Berlin* (Rochester: University of Rochester Press, 2018).

13 Johann Pezzl, *Skizze von Wien* (Vienna and Leipzig: Krauss, 1786), 89–91 (my translation).

Nathan was upwardly mobile. He was ennobled by Emperor Francis and became the first unconverted Jewish baron in Austria in 1798. But, as Pezzl makes it clear, certain women in Viennese society, operating primarily as charming hostesses, became in Michael Wise's words "a sort of muse for intellectual exchange and progressive activity—that helped pave the way for a more liberal era in which no longer the aristocracy alone, but an enlightened bourgeoisie, determined the cultural agenda."[14]

Arnstein's approach was affiliative, by creating emotional bonds and collaborative conditions, and democratic, by building consensus by encouraging participation. She brought together a great variety of thinkers in her salons. This was a new degree of societal mixing, affording a new freedom of exchange, as Wise describes:

> Here one could listen to free speech and good music, converse about writers—including those with rebellious or progressive leanings—without being prevented by an abbé, meet interesting foreigners, artists and scholars, such as were never admitted among the high nobility.[15]

Arnstein's salons created a kind of chemical experiment in the sense implied in the Fragments of Friedrich Schlegel (1772–1829). These provocative aphorisms appeared in his literary magazine *Athenaeum*, published 1798–1800, and might well have been discussed in the salons of Arnstein, some of which were attended by Schlegel himself. For Schlegel "chemistry" is a metaphor for thinking, philosophizing, and especially wit ("reason is mechanical, wit chemical, and genius organic spirit"), which he saw as leading to some kind of change of state, or transformative process.[16] Arnstein operated not by the force of her own personality or opinions, but bringing the right mix of people together, and by modelling the process of interacting—with conversation (in various languages), wit (her lively intellect was well known), and music-making.

This conception of the salon has parallels with Schlegel's philosophical system, in which coexisting multiplicity, totality, and unity are distinguished.

---

14 Michael Wise, "Introduction," in Hilde Spiel, *Fanny von Arnstein: Daughter of the Enlightenment* (New York: New Vessel Press, 2013), xi.

15 Ibid.

16 See Matthew Tanner, "Chemistry in Schlegel's Athenaeum Fragments," *Forum for Modern Language Studies* 31, no. 2 (1995): 140–153; and Michel Chaouli, *The Laboratory of Poetry: Chemistry and Poetics in the Work of Friedrich Schlegel* (Baltimore: The Johns Hopkins University Press, 2002).

Moving away from the notion of organic unity, which had dominated his earlier thinking, the later Schlegel speaks metaphorically of a "chemical system," which entails a merging (*Verschmelzung*) of disparate elements. He referred to his own literary fragments in the *Athenaeum*: they were brief, pithy (almost prickly) statements, each exhibiting internal unity ("A fragment, like a small work of art, has to be entirely isolated from the surrounding world and be complete in itself like a hedgehog" [*Athenaeumsfragment* 206]). The "unity" of each fragment reflects Schlegel's view that things do not come together as a totality but constitute a 'chaotic universality' of infinitely opposing forces and positions.[17] Something akin to a critical mass—a plenitude of fragments—would act as a kind of force field of reciprocal pressures and attractions, ultimately combining the fragments to form a whole. The assembling of diverse people at a salon, or indeed musical pieces (*Stücke*) into collections (as in *Salonstücke*), sought to create something greater than, or at least productively different to, the sum of its parts. This did not mean that each piece (or person) was somehow incomplete. Each was self-contained, although there might be commonalities, and it was the diversity of the individuals that ultimately constituted the attraction that bound them together.

Arnstein clearly valued music in the blending of classes, cultures, and disciplines that was a hallmark of her salons. It is not easy to determine how this conception played out in her musical salons, simply because we lack evidence of exactly what was played and how. We know a certain amount about her own musical tastes. She was clearly an admirer of Mozart, who in 1781 moved into a room (servant's quarters) in the Arnstein's centrally located house at 1175 Graben. He lodged there for over eight months before to his marriage to Constanze Weber and it was there that he wrote *Die Entführung aus dem Serail*.[18] Fanny attended the 1781 premier of this opera, and all of Mozart's subscription concerts, and she was also associated with the Bach revival.[19] Cypess investigates music subscriptions and musical collections owned by women of the Itzig Family (Fanny's family), noting that their possession of copies of vocal music demonstrates that "although their collections consist overwhelmingly of

---

17 Allen Spreight, "Friedrich Schlegel," in *The Stanford Encyclopedia of Philosophy* (Center for the Study of Language and Information, Stanford University, 2015), https://plato.stanford.edu/archives/win2016/entries/schlegel/.

18 Spiel, *Fanny von Arnstein: Daughter of the Enlightenment*, 67.

19 Nicholas Temperley and Peter Wollny, "Bach Revival," in *Grove Music Online* (University of Oxford Press, 2001), https://doi.org/10.1093/gmo/9781561592630.article.01708.

instrumental music, they also sang."[20] We know that she frequented the Italian opera. In one unfortunate incident, an argument arose between two of her admirers who wanted to escort her there in December 1795, and in the resulting duel Prince Carl Liechtenstein was killed.

Around 1800 Fanny's salons were open to a regular stream of important guests and literati virtually throughout the afternoon and evening, outside theatre hours. In November 1808, for example, the German composer, writer, and music critic Johann Friedrich Reichardt arrived in Vienna and went immediately to the Hofburgtheater to hear Joseph Weigl's new opera *The Orphanage*. There he met the diplomat and friend of Fanny, Jacob Salomo Bartholdy, who

> assured me [Reichardt] that one could attend the evening assembly at the Arnsteins', which he had left not long since in full swing, even in boots and traveling clothes; and I gladly hastened thither with him at once. There, too, I found quite a new Vienna; for perhaps half of the very imposing and numerous assembly were indeed wearing boots. The noble, splendid lady of the house, the most interesting friend of my youth from Berlin, and her excellent sister, Frau von Eskeles, received me.[21]

No musical performance is mentioned on this occasion, which was apparently mostly given over to gaming and was, we learn from this description, relatively informal. But Reichardt met Vienna's most popular amateur pianist, Magdalene von Kurzböck, whose playing, according to Mosel's account of the same year "is most similar to the late Mozart, and who also possessed a very fundamental knowledge of music theory."[22] Such performers were well able to create arrangements at sight from orchestral scores, as was the Italian writer and composer Carpani, whom Reichardt met shortly thereafter at "a pleasant dinner of Herr von Pereira's" (the husband of Fanny's daughter), with whom he spent "a pleasant half hour at the fortepiano."[23]

---

20 See Rebecca Cypess, "Ancient Poetry, Modern Music": 21–65.
21 Reichardt, *Vertraute Briefe geschrieben auf einer Reisen nach Wien und den Österreichischen Staaten zu Ende des Jahres 1808 und zu Anfang 1809*, vol. 1 (Amsterdam: Kunst und Industrie-Comtoir, 1810), 145; translated in Spiel, *Fanny von Arnstein: Daughter of the Enlightenment*, 211.
22 Ignaz von Mosel, "Übersicht des gegenwärtigen Zustandes der Tonkunst in Wien," *Vaterländische Blätter für den österreichischen Kaiserstaat* 1, no. 6 (1808): 52.
23 Spiel, *Fanny von Arnstein: Daughter of the Enlightenment*, 212.

By the time of the Congress of Vienna, Arnstein's salons had reached their peak, and the role of music in them was more formalized, if still thoroughly integrated with the other elements. Every Tuesday Arnstein presented musical salons, in addition to her other salons, taking a leading role herself in the music-making, as amateur pianist and singer. Formerly she had regularly invited young women amateurs as well as professional virtuosi to perform in her home.[24] Later, at the time of the Congress of Vienna, there were lavish dinners, *tableaux vivants*, and piano performances by the likes of the young opera composer Giacomo Meyerbeer, who could also be counted on to deliver effective piano arrangements. Hilde Spiel reports:

> At another soirée in 1815, Carl Bertuch, a well-known publisher, recalled having heard the piano virtuoso, Ignaz Moscheles, play the overture to *Fidelio*, in addition to vocal duets and other chamber music. Another time he heard the opera composer, Giacomo Meyerbeer, play piano variations and choruses from the oratorio *Timotheus* or *die Gewalt der Musik*.[25]

This particular Handel oratorio seems to have been a favorite. In 1812 Arnstein combined forces with Joseph Ferdinand Sonnleithner, secretary at the Hofburgtheater (uncle of Leopold von Sonnleithner, and librettist of Beethoven's *Fidelio*), Prince Lobkowitz, Count Moritz Fries and Countess Marianne Dietrichstein, to help organize a public performance of it, in an arrangement by Mozart. The event, which was suggested by Arnstein and supported by Sonnleithner, was a success and immediate precursor to the formation of the Gesellschaft der Musikfreunde in 1812. Directly behind this event was a sequence of private precursor events organized by a group of twelve noble women, Arnstein among them. In 1811 she was elected to their newly formed charitable society, known as the Society of Ladies of the Nobility for the Promotion of the Good and the Useful.[26]

In salon performance, as well as public settings, Arnstein tended to retreat into the background to let others shine in music-making. Schönfeld reported in 1796:

---

24   Dorothea Link, "Vienna's Private Theatrical and Musical Life, 1783–92, as Reported by Count Karl Zinzendorf," *Journal of the Royal Musical Association* 122, no. 2 (1997): 115.
25   Spiel, *Fanny von Arnstein*, 426–27.
26   Ibid.

> Frau von Arnstein: the most instructive and difficult compositions are her favorite pieces. She reads very well, has a light touch and masterly attack. She excels in pieces requiring rapidity. It is to be regretted that for some years she seems to have lost her taste for playing, for she hardly touches the fortepiano any longer. Persons of her powers should not desert their necessitous art, which always, more and more, is in need of encouragement. She also has a very pleasant voice and fluent throat. Her little daughter likewise shows promise of many musical talents.[27]

Reichardt's account of a performance by Arnstein's daughter Henriette in 1808 allows us a glimpse into the performance of musical arrangements at this time—it was so ubiquitous that it seldom attracted detailed description. Here we see how musical arrangements, like the social arrangements of Fanny's salon, could inspire and promote the people involved, leading to something greater than the sum of the parts, and perhaps to transformation. Reichardt was invited to a Sunday concert at the home of Henriette's tutor, the piano maker Andreas Streicher (1761–1833). Streicher had arranged for two pianos (four hands) the Piano Quartet in F Minor, op. 6, by Prince Frederick Louis Ferdinand of Prussia (1806) for Madam Comtesse de Majan (née Franziska von Spielmann). Mosel listed her under his chosen amateurs in 1808 and described her as "a pupil of Streicher admired as a very excellent performer."[28] The arrangement was published in 1814 by the firm Riedl in Vienna. Of the performance involving Henriette and Kurzböck, Reichardt reports:

> Thus, on a beautiful bright morning in Streicher's apartment, on two of the most beautiful fortepianos of this master, we heard beautiful artistic hands perform this highly ingenious composition with such perfection as one rarely hears. The tender artistic souls entered with so much spirit and feeling into the sublime and beautiful thoughts and fantasies of the composer, and exercised the greatest difficulties with so much precision and roundness, that they truly conjured up a whole world of music around us.[29]

---

27 Johann Ferdinand von Schönfeld, *Jahrbuch Der Tonkunst von Wien und Prag* (Vienna: Schönfeld, 1796; repr. Munich: Katzbichler, 1976), 5.

28 Mosel, "Übersicht des gegenwärtigen Zustandes der Tonkunst in Wien": 52.

29 Johann Friedrich Reichardt, *Vertraute Briefe geschrieben auf einer Reisen nach Wien und den Österreichischen Staaten zu Ende des Jahres 1808 und zu Anfang 1809*, vol. 1 (Amsterdam: Kunst und Industrie-Comtoir, 1810), 346–7 (my translation).

Reichardt opens a window on the perception of female performers in the Viennese private sphere at the time. The performance of this arrangement shows off the prowess of Streicher as arranger and instrument maker. It also displays the two performers to best advantage as women: they are seen to be both beautiful and accomplished, crucial attributes for women wishing to climb the social ladder in early nineteenth-century Vienna. However, we are told, the performance approaches a transformative experience for the listeners, thanks to the highly skilled performers. The listener comes to believe that he or she is listening to an original composition, as it is being composed ("delicate artistic souls entered into the composer's sublime"). Several other reviews of arrangements from this time also suggest that a transformation or "change of state" was brought about: a good arrangement was capable of allowing the listener to "complete the work: or enter into the composer's imagination. For example, an 1807 review of a piano arrangement of Beethoven's *Eroica* Symphony by Müller claimed that "the listener's imagination" (die Phantasie des Zuhörers) is set in "sublime flight" (erhabener Schwung) by the work, and that the piano arrangement allowed a listener repeated experiences of this phenomenon.[30]

Politics in Arnstein's Musical Salons

An account of a salon in the Arnstein home helps us see how music-making in private, and especially opera, could evade censorious political scrutiny but still talk politics in the wider sense.[31] This gathering, held on 20 November 1814, was at the upper end of the social spectrum, with international guests including Lord Castlereagh, leading the British delegation; Hardenberg, chief representative of Prussia; and Talleyrand, representing French foreign affairs. The programming choices spoke subtly against the politics of Emperor Francis I, implying a perception of him a tyrannical dictator.

The operas in the Arnstein salon were performed by excellent singers, on this occasion with accompaniments from piano arrangements. They were probably chosen strategically, foregrounding the German language, and more significantly the triumph of good, rational people over evil dictators: Mozart's *Die*

---

30 For further discussion, see my *Beethoven's Symphonies Arranged for the Chamber* (Cambridge: Cambridge University Press, 2021), 163.

31 Fully reported in Peter Gradenwitz, *Literatur und Musik in Geselligem Kreise: Geschmacksbildung, Gesprächsstoff und musikalische Unterhaltung in der bürgerlichen Salongesellschaft* (Stuttgart: Steiner, 1991), pp. 258–67.

Zauberflöte, Weigl's *Die Schweizer Familie*, and Gluck *Iphigénie en Tauride*.[32] The last is pointedly relevant in terms of plot—a family drama about the tragic aftermath of war; but *Die Zauberflöte* speaks most explicitly to Enlightenment values of reason and freedom. These excerpts from earlier operas framed a program that otherwise foregrounded local talent, in its performers and composers:

1. Aria of the Queen of the Night from *Die Zauberflöte*, performed by court opera singer Sophie Schröder accompanied by Ignaz Möscheles.
2. Recitation: scene from *MacBeth*.
3. Piano Concerto by Johann Nepomuk Hummel played on a Conrad Graf piano.
4. Recitation: Idylls (Count Bindemonte).
5. Franz Clement playing his own violin concerto.
6. Peter Hänsel ("Haydn's student"; violin) playing his own trio together with Hummel (piano) and Ferdinand Kauer (flute).

—Intermission for conversation—

7. Weinmüller sings Sarastro's aria and recitative from *Die Zauberflöte*.
8. Recitation: from *Phädra* (Frau von Weißenthurn).
9. Aria from *Die Schweizer Familie* ("an opera, which, although already five years old still disperses its magic").
10. Maria Theresa von Paradis playing a piano sonata dedicated to her by Leopold Koželuh.
11. Franz Wild "incites a Furore" with his performance of Orestes's aria from *Iphigénie en Tauride*.

In the Arnstein salon, the conversation was witty, intellectual, but lighthearted. The musical repertoire and dramatic readings (declamations) were apparently intended mainly to show off local virtuosity and skill. But by playing off Sarastro against the Queen of the Night, Arnstein could contrive to remind listeners of the triumph of reason and good over irrationality and evil. A magical subject in an opera like *Die Zauberflöte* was not only safe but useful. *Die Zauberflöte* could attest to the powers of German composers and musicians, and also speak in veiled language about Enlightenment ideals, notably that of freedom through wisdom. Of course, salon hosts' political intentions cannot be precisely

---

32 Gluck's French opera might seem to be the outlier in terms of the emphasis on German. But the revised version was the only opera Gluck wrote in German—Gluck's "tragic Singspiel," according to modern scholars. See, for example, Amanda Holden, *The New Penguin Opera Guide* (New York: Penguin Putnam, 2001), 371.

divined—overt political agendas on their part and that if performers would have been problematic in the climate of surveillance and censorship. But the repertoire of the Viennese musical salons at this time conspicuously includes morally uplifting or instructive music of the recent past, such as Haydn's *Die Schöpfung*, as well as symphonies, concertos, and sonatas, which were "safe" in speaking more abstractly, but still could be suggestive, rousing, and emphatically German.

Conclusion

With Arnstein's salons, the central purpose of these house concerts moves on from the social and educational functions of the salons of the late eighteenth century, towards musical and political ones. One aim was still educational, taking in the intensive study of older, "classical" music, considered to be instructive lay substantial, by composers such as Mozart, Haydn, Beethoven, Schubert, Cimarosa, Cherubini, Paër, Spontini, Rossini, Eberl, Weigl, and so forth. Broadening musical literacy and knowledge, especially by means of the compositions of German composers, countered the political influence of Francis I. His educational policies had led to high levels of illiteracy in Habsburg lands, and a widening gap between the upper and lower middle class.[33]

These private salons performed the vital function of promoting agency for middle-class and amateur musicians, and even enabled covert political commentary. Choosing where and how to perform chamber music gave them a sense of purpose in an era of stifling oppression. Participants—women among them—planned and sometimes arranged the repertoire, dictated the standards, and assessed the results. The piano parts of published arrangements from this time frequently contained much of the original texture (they were often designed to be performed with or without other instruments), and thus offered a chance for female leadership, even virtuosity. Times were changing, though. Viennese salons had once fostered some mixing between the aristocracy and middle classes, at least in critical discourse on art; this parity was already waning in the late eighteenth-century salon, and the spilt between classes widened further in the early nineteenth century. This is one reason why Arnstein's salons, with their diverse participants, were such an important phenomenon.

---

33 Daviau, "Bedermeier: The Happy Face of the Vormärz Era," 17–8.

Parity also declined between the sexes in the salons. In the 1820s the younger generation of writers now tended to meet in inns and coffee houses, without women.[34] Male domination was much more pronounced around 1800 in Viennese salons than in the traditional French salons. In the early nineteenth century, male singers, notably Raphael Kiesewetter and Leopold von Sonnleithner, started to dominate the hosting of salons. Schubert, too, exerted considerable influence on the Viennese musical scene through his Schubertiads (see Figure 1, p. 154). But in the musical salon, leaders like Arnstein had already set a precedent for the exercise of power by women in the Viennese public sphere.

---

34 On this shift see Johann Sonnleitner, "Vom Salon zum Kaffeehaus. Zur literarischen Öffentlichkeit im Österreichischen Biedermeier," in Bernd, Pichl, and Wagner, *The Other Vienna*, 71–83.

Bibliography

Chaouli, Michel. *The Laboratory of Poetry: Chemistry and Poetics in the Work of Friedrich Schlegel.* Baltimore: The Johns Hopkins University Press, 2002.

Cypess, Rebecca and Nancy Sinkoff, eds. *Sara Levy's World: Gender, Judaism, and the Bach Tradition in Enlightenment Berlin.* Rochester: University of Rochester Press, 2018.

———. "Ancient Poetry, Modern Music, and the *Wechselgesang der Mirjam und Debora*: The Meanings of Song in the Itzig Circle." *Bach* 47, no. 1 (2016): 21–65.

———. *Women and Musical Salons in the Enlightenment.* Chicago: University of Chicago Press.

Daviau, Donald G. "Biedermeier. The Happy Face of the Vormärz Era." In *The Other Vienna: The Culture of Biedermeier Austria*, edited by Clifford A. Bernd, Robert Pichl, and Margarete Wagner, 11–27. Vienna: Lehner, 2002.

Gradenwitz, Peter. *Literatur und Musik in Geselligem Kreise: Geschmacksbildung, Gesprächsstoff und musikalische Unterhaltung in der bürgerlichen Salongesellschaft.* Stuttgart: Steiner, 1991.

Hanson, Alice M. *Musical Life in Biedermeier Vienna.* Cambridge: Cambridge University Press, 1985.

Holden, Amanda. *The New Penguin Opera Guide.* New York: Penguin Putnam, 2001.

Link, Dorothea. "Vienna's Private Theatrical and Musical Life, 1783–92, as Reported by Count Karl Zinzendorf." *Journal of the Royal Musical Association* 122, no. 2 (1997): 205–257.

Mosel, Ignaz von. "Übersicht des gegenwärtigen Zustandes der Tonkunst in Wien." *Vaterländische Blätter für den österreichischen Kaiserstaat* 1/6–7 (1808): 39–44 and 49–54.

November, Nancy. *Cultivating String Quartets in Beethoven's Vienna.* Woodbridge: Boydell, 2017.

———. *Beethoven's Symphonies Arranged for the Chamber.* Cambridge: Cambridge University Press, 2021.

Pezzl, Johann. *Skizze von Wien.* Vienna and Leipzig: Krauss, 1786.

Reichardt, Johann Friedrich. *Vertraute Briefe geschrieben auf einer Reisen nach Wien und den Österreichischen Staaten zu Ende des Jahres 1808 und zu Anfang 1809.* Vol. 1. Amsterdam: Kunst und Industrie-Comtoir, 1810.

Schönfeld, Johann Ferdinand von. *Jahrbuch Der Tonkunst von Wien und Prag.* Vienna: Schönfeld, 1796; repr. Munich: Katzbichler, 1976.

Sealsfield, Charles [Karl Postl]. *Austria as it is, or, Sketches of Continental Courts. By an Eyewitness/Österreich, wie es ist oder Skizzen von Fürstenhöfen des Kontinents; von einem Augenzeugen.* London: Hurst, Chance and Co., 1828.

Sonnleithner, Leopold von. "Musikalische Skizzen aus 'Alt-Wien.'" In *Recensionen und Mittheilungen über Theater, Music und bildende Kunst* 7, no. 47 (1861): 737–41 and no. 48, 753–57; 8, no. 1 (1862): 4–7, no. 12 (1862): 177–80, and no. 24 (1862), 369–75; and 9, no. 20 (1863): 305–25.

Sonnleitner, Johann. "Vom Salon zum Kaffeehaus. Zur literarischen Öffentlichkeit im Österreichischen Biedermeier." In *The Other Vienna: The Culture of Biedermeier Austria*, edited by Clifford A. Bernd, Robert Pichl, and Margarete Wagner, 71–94. Vienna: Lehner, 2002.

Spiel, Hilde. *Fanny von Arnstein: Daughter of the Enlightenment*. New York: New Vessel Press, 2013.

Spreight, Allen. Friedrich Schlegel. In *The Stanford Encyclopedia of Philosophy*, Center for the Study of Language and Information, Stanford University, 2015. https://plato.stanford.edu/archives/win2016/entries/schlegel/.

Tanner, Matthew. "Chemistry in Schlegel's Athenaeum Fragments." *Forum for Modern Language Studies* 1, no. 2 (1995): 140–153.

Temperley, Nicholas, and Peter Wollny, "Bach Revival." In *Grove Music Online*, Oxford University Press, 2001. https://doi.org/10.1093/gmo/9781561592630.article.01708.

Thormählen, Wiebke. "Playing with Art: Musical Arrangements as Educational Tools in Van Swieten's Vienna." *Journal of Musicology* 27, no. 3 (2010): 342–376.

Vago, Alexandra A. "Musical Life of Amateur Musicians in Vienna, ca. 1814–1825: A Translated Edition of Leopold von Sonnleithner's 'Musiklaische Skizzen aus "Alt-Wien."'" Master's thesis, Kent State University, 2001.

Vick, Brian. "Salon Networks." In *The Congress of Vienna: Power and Politics after Napoleon*, 112–52. Cambridge, MA: Harvard University Press, 2014.

FIGURE 1. 'A Schubert evening in a Vienna Salon' by Julius Schmid (1897). Centralised women from left to right: Katharina Fröhlich, the actor and singer Sophie Müller (standing), Anna Fröhlich (partly hidden), Barbara Fröhlich, Franz Schubert (at the piano), Josephine Fröhlich (with music in her hands). Courtesy of Alamy Images.

Part Three

Performance and Agency

Reflections on Aladdin's Lamp: Creative Practice Research in-and-through Historically Informed Performance

Imogen Morris

"Authentic" means "just as alive as it ever was." Being authentic is, most of all, Aladdin rubbing his lamp: we rehearse some music, and all of a sudden we have the feeling, "Hey! *This is right*. This is the way it must go." And I guarantee you that in a year's time, when we hear the tape of that, we will agree that it's not how it should go. But it's a wonderful feeling—"*This* is how it should go!"—and *that's* authenticity. And I think it's worthwhile. But it has nothing to do with being historically correct.[1]

—Anner Bylsma

In 1997, Anner Bylsma described the interpretative process used in Historically Informed Performance (HIP) as "Aladdin rubbing his lamp": one of serendipitous discovery with little to do with historical correctness. His comments are noteworthy for revealing more agency on the part of performer in the interpretative process of HIP than the practice is widely believed to offer. In this chapter I investigate this interpretative process, with the goal of developing a rigorous theoretical framework for conducting Creative Practice Research

---

1   Anner Bylsma, interview by Bernard D. Sherman, in *Inside Early Music: Conversations with Performers* (New York: Oxford University Press, 1997), 221.

in-and-through HIP.[2] I take a reflective approach, drawing on my own experience as an HIP musician, supported by evidence from significant performers and critics of the practice.

I begin by discussing the interpretative process used in HIP, including the function of historical evidence. I focus on the agency of the performer and concepts and approaches that shape the practice, such as Bruce Haynes's "serendipity effect." In particular, I explore the ways in which performers assimilate historical information into their work and overcome gaps in knowledge. I define Creative Practice Research (CPR) with reference to recent theoretical scholarship. Then I establish the need for a research framework in this field, explain how such a framework may be developed for CPR in-and-through HIP, and explore the potential challenges involved.

The findings indicate that the performer's experience, expertise, and intuition are crucial to transforming historical evidence into a convincing performance that moves the emotions of a modern-day audience. This conclusion leads me to establish the concept of "artistic values": principles that guide the way a performer interprets, filters, and even manipulates historical information in their decision-making process. Structuring a research framework to facilitate interrogation of these decisions and the artistic values behind them is crucial for CPR in this field. I end the chapter by demonstrating how such a framework might be used, taking my recent doctoral research as an example.

HIP Interpretative Process

During the Early Music movement of the 1960s and '70s, musicians used the term "authentic"—in this context a synonym for "historically accurate"—to describe their performances. Discussion of their practice has been wide-ranging, complex, and long-lived, and the criticisms of their approach at the time are well documented. Richard Taruskin presents perhaps the best known of these critiques. He does not take issue with the notion of using historical evidence to inform performance per se, but rather with the specific approach musicians

---

2   The term "in-and-through" comes from Darla Crispin, "Artistic Research and Music Scholarship: Musings and Models from a Continental European Perspective," in *Artistic Practice as Research in Music: Theory, Criticism, Practice*, ed. Mine Doğantan-Dack (Farnham: Ashgate, 2015), 58. I have taken Crispin's term "artistic research" to be synonymous with CPR. Her descriptors are based on those of Christopher Frayling, "Research in Art and Design," *Royal College of Art Research Papers* 1, no. 1 (1993/4): 5, http://researchonline.rca.ac.uk/384/3/frayling_research_in_art_and_design_1993.pdf.

of the time were taking and the ideals that underpinned it.[3] His critique makes three key points. Firstly, the term "authentic" implies a kind of "cultural elitism,"[4] by suggesting that other approaches are "inauthentic" and therefore inferior.[5] Secondly, Taruskin questions how much of "authentic performance" is truly historical, pointing to the selective application of historical evidence by many musicians, and the way the practice reflects the philosophies of modernism.[6] Finally, he argues that the emphasis on adhering to historical information—and especially relying on historical instruments—reduces the performer's agency in the interpretative process by effectively eliminating their own personality, opinions, and creativity.[7]

As a consequence of the writings of Taruskin and other contemporary critics, HIP musicians today have become more open to admitting that their practice is a combination of historical information and personal invention and taste. Most commonly, this admission results from acknowledging the lack of complete, accurate historical information on which to base our performances. Historical knowledge presents us with speculation, vagueness, gaps, and contradictions. In contrast, an interpretation is deemed successful when the performer is completely certain of, and convincing in, their creative decisions. Therefore, a performer cannot rely wholly on vague or incomplete historical information as the basis for developing their interpretation of a work. While the unknowns encountered in historical research are welcomed by scholars as offering scope for further study, they must somehow be "remedied" by a performer in order to produce a compelling performance.

I would argue that the inevitability of personal invention in HIP is also a symptom of purely modern concerns: the need, as Bruce Haynes describes it, for "a little adaptation ... to fit their music to us."[8] Historical works were not

---

3   See, for instance, Richard Taruskin, "The Limits of Authenticity: A Contribution," in *Text and Act: Essays on Music and Performance* (New York: Oxford University Press, 1995), 67–82.

4   John Butt, "Authenticity," in *Grove Music Online* (Oxford University Press, 2001), DOI:10.1093/gmo/9781561592630.article.46587.

5   See, for instance, Taruskin, "The Pastness of the Present and the Presence of the Past," in *Text and Act*, especially 90–91.

6   See, for instance, ibid., 90–154.

7   For comments on instruments in particular, see Taruskin, "Backslider or Harbinger?," in ibid., especially 305–6.

8   Bruce Haynes, *The End of Early Music: A Period Performer's History of Music for the Twenty-First Century* (New York: Oxford University Press, 2007), 9.

written for us, nor our tastes, expectations, values, or lifestyles. Consequently, performers incline—consciously or not—towards a practice that involves being informed by history, but not bound by it. The way we perform is driven by our personal artistic identities, which are in turn influenced by factors such as education, previous experiences, interactions with other performers, and aesthetic values and preferences. Additionally, performances can be influenced by external demands over which the performer has little to no control—the various expectations or requirements of audiences, critics, and audio engineers, for example, can shape the final result of a performer's work. Consequently, an HIP performer must establish and maintain a sensitive balance between historical fidelity, artistic identity and agency, and external demands and expectations in order to pursue the expressive potential of their performance. This balance is achieved through their interpretative decisions.

There is evidence that performers of the Early Music movement were aware of the personal invention and experimentation that was involved in their performances all along. As Haynes notes, the rhetoric of authenticity at the time was often driven by marketing (as it often still is today): "musicians didn't usually make up the liner notes that went with their recordings, and if they were described as 'authentic' when they were really 'an *attempt* to be authentic,' it seemed like quibbling."[9] In his interview with Bernard D. Sherman, harpsichordist Gustav Leonhardt admits to uncertainty as to whether any of what he and his colleagues—particularly Frans Brüggen, Anner Bylsma, and the Kuijken brothers—were doing was historically accurate, portraying them as motivated by an experimental spirit: "I was investigating all the time.... And maybe it [our style] is all wrong; I don't know, it could be."[10] This suggests that performers' notions of authenticity in the Early Music movement may have been more personal than Taruskin credits—and that the musicians may have been aware of it. Their experiments with incorporating historical information into their practice resulted in a sense of understanding the music "on its terms" that had as much to do with personal opinion and aesthetic taste as fidelity to the historical evidence.

Haynes calls this phenomenon—which has been described by HIP performers and critics alike since the mid-twentieth century—the "serendipity effect."[11] It is defined as the sense of "rightness" that comes from persistent

---

9   Ibid., 10 (italics original).
10   Gustav Leonhardt, interview by Sherman, in *Inside Early Music*, 203 (clarification of "our style" original).
11   Haynes, *The End of Early Music*, 7.

experimentation with applying historical information to performance. According to Taruskin, its success lies in the belief that "we have achieved the identification of performance style with the demands of the music."[12] The serendipity effect is what Bylsma means when he talks about "how it must go" in the epigraph to this chapter. Bylsma's description highlights the fleeting nature of the serendipity effect, an observation reflected by Haynes's statement that "HIP starts in the present and ends in the present."[13] Bylsma's account suggests that our assessment of whether the serendipity effect has been achieved is also based on personal judgements rather than historical fact, noting that "one's view of history changes with the times."[14] However, as Bylsma acknowledges, this is not an indictment on HIP musicians. On the contrary, the convincing achievement of the "right way" to play a piece is arguably what allows performers to uphold a level of artistic identity and agency, and to communicate their ideas to modern audiences.

Crucially, Daniel Leech-Wilkinson observes that HIP performers often forget or overlook the role of their personal ideas and invention because interpretation is an automatic process.[15] Decision-making becomes faster and more imperceptible as the process is repeated over and over, a habit that begins early in education to ensure it is well established by the time the performer reaches professional standard. Such automatic processes are common to all creative practices and come with practical benefits. In terms of music, they include facilitating cohesive rehearsals, thus reducing rehearsal time and promoting unanimity between performers.

This may explain some of the criticism that practitioners of the Early Music movement received: their interpretation and incorporation of historical evidence became such a fast, practiced process that they no longer noticed it happening. In his interview with Sherman, Leonhardt discusses his playing techniques—which he derived from historical evidence and developed through experimentation and experience in the course of his career—as means to an end: tools to be integrated and combined in different ways to achieve a multitude of expressive outcomes as required for each individual work or

---

12   Taruskin, "Limits of Authenticity," 79.
13   Haynes, *The End of Early Music*, 10.
14   Bylsma, interview by Sherman, in *Inside Early Music*, 222.
15   Daniel Leech-Wilkinson, "What We Are Doing with Early Music Is Genuinely Authentic to Such A Small Degree That the Word Loses Most of Its Intended Meaning," *Early Music* 12, no. 1 (1984): 13.

performance situation.[16] Importantly, he notes that the experienced musician does not think consciously about each individual technical skill nor the precise way in which it is combined with other skills, but only about the desired expressive outcome.[17] He elaborates on the difference between this approach and that of the student, saying, "when one is a student one does things consciously, but when one is more experienced one does not play intellectually any more. One doesn't *think*; one *has thought*."[18] This comment implies a blending of historical information with the musician's own creative ideas and expression as they progress, which, coupled with increasingly automatic interpretative processing, is likely to make it very difficult to distinguish the individual contributing parts of the interpretative process of a master performer.

Alongside this progressive integration, I would argue that HIP musicians somewhat repress their awareness of their personal involvement in the interpretative process. Even now, the rhetoric that surrounds HIP still focusses primarily on the role of historical information, despite performers being well aware of the part their own invention plays in their interpretation. This language can be found throughout all facets of HIP practice: rehearsal; teaching; communication with audiences in concerts, CD liner notes, interviews, and marketing; and reviews published in the media. Leech-Wilkinson argues that this attitude is "sustained only by the larger illusion that contemporary performance styles—in contrast to the interpretative excesses of earlier twentieth-century artists—are largely uncolored by personal involvement."[19] Until this illusion is broken down, it is likely that HIP performers will continue to foreground the role of historical information in their practice and minimize their own role in interpreting it.

From this perspective, the personal judgements, expertise, and experiences that drive the transformation of historical fact into performance are—and have been since the Early Music movement—the crux of creativity and innovation in HIP. In order to build a CPR framework that facilitates research in-and-through the HIP interpretative process, it is clear that this personal invention—or, perhaps, intervention—must form the focus of any research design. A research framework should allow the performer-researcher to explore the beliefs and expertise that enable them to interpret historical information and judge

---

16 Leonhardt, interview by Sherman, *Inside Early Music*, 198.
17 Ibid.
18 Ibid (italics original).
19 Leech-Wilkinson, "What We Are Doing with Early Music," 13.

a performance to be "how it must go." This in turn will allow them to reach valuable insight not only into HIP's interpretative process but also into the historical information on which the practice relies.

Building a Research Framework

As a research methodology, CPR recognizes that knowledge is generated through creative practice, which can provide unique insights and pathways for academic research. However, it also acknowledges that, on its own, the validity of this knowledge in a scholarly context is severely limited. To remedy this, structures are needed to allow the performer-researcher to balance the subjective, intuitive nature of creative practice with the more systematic, objective nature of research. Such a balance would mean that the knowledge intrinsic to creative practice could be used and communicated in a way that held scholarly validity.

As a relatively new method of musicological research, especially in the field of classical performance, CPR raises a number of questions and challenges. To begin with, how do we distinguish between innovative, high-quality performance practice and genuine research in-and-through this practice? And how does the researcher draw performance and research together while still fulfilling the distinct aims and objectives of each?

In "Artistic Research and Music Scholarship: Musings and Models from a Continental European Perspective," Darla Crispin explores the relationship between practice and research, and devises a continuum between practice as a purely creative act and practice as a basis for scholarly research. Along this continuum she identifies four key categories—musical practice, informed musical practice, informed reflective musical practice, and research in-and-through musical practice (CPR).[20] Each of these can be characterized by a specific interaction with research and reflection, and by the way they build and expand on each other.[21]

Crispin defines informed, reflective musical practice (the third category on her continuum) as "reflecting on the musical practice and the contextual information gathered, so as to deepen insight and understanding."[22] This represents

---

20 Crispin, "Artistic Research and Music Scholarship," 58.
21 Ibid.
22 Ibid.

the way innovative musicians at the top of their fields operate. It is noteworthy that an element of information gathering is involved here, but that it is used in a relatively subjective way to inform the performance. This kind of research therefore does not necessarily fulfil scholarly aims, and nor is it required to. In my experience as an HIP musician, this research may involve reading what musicologists have written in order to inform my interpretative decisions. It does not have to involve any scholarly criticism or generation of new knowledge as might be expected in academic circles, nor is there any expectation or demand for objective handling of the research material.

In contrast, Crispin identifies two key features that distinguish research in- and-through musical practice (CPR) from informed, reflective musical practice: the first, "locating the reflection, contextual information and the musical practice within a rigorous methodological framework," and the second, disseminating findings within a scholarly community.[23] The first of these features is key to this chapter. Developing a methodological framework allows the decisions that a performer makes in their interpretative process to be interrogated. While the reasons behind these interpretative decisions are generally not questioned during practice itself—with more value being placed on the success of their outcomes—interrogating them uncovers knowledge and insights into areas that can be examined in a scholarly context. These areas include the performer's interpretative process, the musical work they are playing, the instrument they are using, and—especially in the case of HIP—the historical performance practices they use to inform their playing.

To facilitate these interrogations, Kathleen Coessens has developed a model known as the web of artistic practice. This web provides a framework for a deep understanding of the skills, knowledge, and expertise that musicians use to develop, support, and enrich their creative practice. It consists of five "tacit dimensions": embodied artistic know-how, personal knowledge, cultural-semiotic codes, ecological environment, and interaction.[24] These five dimensions interweave to shape what Coessens identifies as "the musician's act," which sits at the center of the web; in the context of the present study, this musician's act is synonymous with the interpretative process.[25] Coessens calls the dimensions

---

23 Ibid., 58–59.
24 Kathleen Coessens, "The Web of Artistic Practice: A Background for Experimentation," in *Artistic Experimentation in Music: An Anthology*, ed. Darla Crispin and Bob Gilmore (Leuven: Leuven University Press, 2014), 69–70.
25 Ibid., 70.

tacit because they operate in the background of a musician's interpretative process. They can be brought to the fore by the artist through "re-enactment of the background" via theorizing and reflecting on the process.[26] This does not necessarily need to mean reflecting on an entire concert performance; it may simply constitute reflection on the performance of a piece, a single phrase, or even a single note. This means that the performer-researcher can shift relatively quickly between two modes of operating—the act of interpreting and the reflection upon that act—entailed in CPR.

It is important that Coessens places the musician's *act* at the center of the web, not the musician themselves. The research framework is designed to facilitate scrutiny of the act, not the musician; the musician is the "locus for the network of tacit knowledge."[27] However, as Crispin points out, the performer-researcher is likely to develop as a result of engaging with their interpretative process, "both through embodying the tacit network and by asking explicit research questions."[28] Likewise, the web itself represents a dynamic system that supports the musician's act but also changes and adapts with use and interrogation.[29]

CPR in-and-through HIP: Some Challenges

Naturally, designing a research project that operates in-and-through HIP is not without its challenges. A central issue in CPR, regardless of the creative practice involved, is distinguishing between well-informed, reflective creative practice and CPR. This is especially pertinent to using HIP as the basis for research, because the practice in itself already engages with scholarship, albeit of a historical kind. Peter Walls highlights the difficulty encountered in HIP practice alone of distinguishing between the role of the researcher and that of the practitioner—in other words where the historical research leaves off and where the practice, and

---

26   Ibid., 69.
27   Darla Crispin, "From Territories to Transformations: Anton Webern's Piano Variations Op. 27 as a Case Study for Research in-and-through Musical Practice," in *Sound and Score: Essays on Sound, Score and Notation*, ed. Paulo de Assis, William Brooks, and Kathleen Coessens (Leuven: Leuven University Press, 2013), 50.
28   Ibid.
29   Coessens, "Web of Artistic Practice," 70.

related artistic decision-making, begins.[30] When HIP practice is used as a basis for CPR the problem is compounded, creating a real risk of the performer-researcher not recognizing and acknowledging the difference between the historical research they use to inform their practice and the CPR that allows them to conduct research in-and-through their practice. For this reason, a methodological framework needs to clearly distinguish between these two kinds of research.

However, when this distinction is made, CPR methods can be beneficial to historical research. In the field of fine arts, the Hockney-Falco thesis provides a relevant example. Artist David Hockney, with the aid of physicist Charles M. Franco, proposed that Renaissance artists used optical aids such as the camera lucida, camera obscura, and curved mirrors in search of greater accuracy and realism in their paintings than is possible when working by eye alone. In his book *Secret Knowledge: Rediscovering the Lost Techniques of the Old Masters*, Hockney demonstrates that several old masters would have used such devices, pointing to evidence in their works of specific distortions similar to those which these aids produce.[31] Alongside this visual analysis, Hockney conducted practical experiments using optical devices to assist his own drawing, and compared the results with what he could achieve through freehand drawing.[32] His findings supported his conclusion that the kind of realism achieved by certain of the old masters is not possible without the use of optical devices.

As might be expected, Hockney and Falco's work caused a great deal of scrutiny and debate among artists, art historians, and physicists, many being skeptical of their claims or rejecting them outright.[33] Regardless, their work—especially Hockney's experiments—proves the value of CPR methods in creating new avenues for historical research, including the testing of theories in practice, and interrogating and—as Hockney did—potentially even overturning long-held conclusions. Hockney and Falco's work pushed experts in their fields to

---

30 Peter Walls, *History, Imagination and the Performance of Music* (Woodbridge: Boydell Press, 2003), especially 28–52.
31 David Hockey, *Secret Knowledge: Rediscovering the Lost Techniques of the Old Masters* (London: Thames & Hudson, 2001).
32 Ibid., 28–31, 74–77.
33 Sven Dupré, "Introduction. The Hockney-Falco Thesis: Constraints and Opportunities," *Early Science and Medicine* 10, no. 2 (2005): 125–36, DOI:10.1163/1573382054088141; A. Mark Smith, *From Sight to Light: The Passage from Ancient to Modern Optics* (Chicago: University of Chicago Press, 2014), 317–19.

rethink their beliefs and spurred further investigations on the topic.[34] However, Hockney's project differs from those involving HIP in the role and agency of the artists involved. Hockney's research took finished products (historical works of art) and explored the artistic method that might result in them. In contrast, the finished product in HIP (the interpretation of a work) is multiple and repeated, and influenced by both historical and modern methods for producing it. There is no definitive evidence as to how the interpretation of a work may have sounded historically, the composer's notated music providing only one piece of an incomplete puzzle. Furthermore, there is historical evidence that performers exercised a significant level of agency in interpretative decisions, and that, aside from the elusive expectations of "good taste," individual interpretations could often sound very different from each other, meaning performers played a key role in deciding the final sound of a musical work.[35] The patchy historical evidence on what might be considered an "acceptable" interpretation of a work must then be coupled with modern-day tastes, aesthetics, and performance traditions to produce an HIP interpretation. The performer's agency in the interpretative process is thus an extra link in the interpretative chain between the composer's original inspiration and the final performance that has no parallel in Hockney's work. The dynamic nature of performance, lack of evidence of historical interpretations, and temporal distance between the composer, historical performers, and HIP performers make the performer's role in interpretation more complex to scrutinize than the artist's role in Hockney's work.

Unlike other art forms, classical performance is primarily reliant on musical works that have already been created by someone else, who is often long dead and from a different sociocultural context to the performer. Additionally, HIP relies on historical sources to attempt to rebuild an understanding of interpretation contemporaneous with the work. Inherent in all HIP interpretations, therefore, is a temporal and sociocultural distance between the modern performer and the composer, and between their respective contexts.

Coessens identifies a form of distance inherent in the translation and realization of cultural-semiotic codes in describing her web of artistic practice. However, she defines this as the distance that the musician inserts between the

---

34 Of particular note is Francis O'Neill and Sofia Palazzo Corner, "Rembrandt's Self-Portraits," *Journal of Optics* 18, no. 8 (2016), DOI:10.1088/2040-8978/18/8/080401, in which the authors extend Hockney's arguments by applying them to self-portraits.

35 Johann Joachim Quantz, *Versuch einer Anweisung die Flöte traversiere zu spielen* (Berlin: Johann Friedrich Voß, 1752), 61, IMSLP59464.

culturally accepted code system and the musician's individual use of it.[36] While this distance clearly exists in classical performance, we need to recognize a second kind of distance, between the cultural-semiotic code system of the time the composer wrote the work and the musician's own use of what is currently known of that system. Our inability to know with certainty what a composer intended or what past performance practices might have looked and sounded like means that this distance is inherent in all classical performance that involves works by dead composers. HIP performers' attempts to reconstruct performance practices of the past should not be misconstrued as closing this distance, especially because it is impossible to know how historically accurate any particular HIP interpretation is. A research framework should be designed to recognize this distance and allow the interrogation of the way a performer handles it, including any conscious decisions that appear to widen it, for example by rejecting strong historical evidence in pursuit of some other goal.

This point is especially pertinent when we consider the effect of modern performance traditions on the current state of Early Music performance. Around sixty years have now passed since the Early Music movement of the 1960s. In that time, clear traditions of HIP performance have emerged. The experimental, exploratory nature of the Early Music movement—when musicians were still establishing the practice and trying to make sense of historical evidence available to them—has largely disappeared, replaced with well-established "appropriate" (or even "correct") ways to interpret works and historical documents such as musical treatises. With more and more musicians releasing recordings and presenting performances of well-known works, an HIP performance tradition has emerged that must be recognized as distinct from the historical traditions on which it is based. Furthermore, these recordings and performances serve as information or even evidence in their own right. Performers refer to them for inspiration as often as—if not more than—they do treatises and other historical evidence. Among Early Music students, in particular, I find that there is a decreasing need to consult historical sources at all, as the information they supply is being passed on to students—albeit interpreted and therefore plagued with bias and personal opinion—by teachers, performances, and recordings. This is another reason that any methodological framework for CPR in-and-through HIP should demonstrate and allow the interrogation of the historical evidence

---

36 Coessens, "Web of Artistic Practice," 76.

as an element distinct from the HIP performance tradition and from the artistic decisions that are made as part of that interpretative practice.

Artistic Values

To build a framework for CPR in-and-through HIP, we need to establish a model of interpretation that delineates the role of historical source material, including the notated music, which may involve use of facsimiles and/or modern editions. The model should allow close analysis of the way the musician interprets these materials to produce a performance that balances historical fidelity, artistic identity, and external demands and expectations.

In my methodological design, I have re-shaped Coessens's web of artistic practice as a kind of filter through which the notated music and all other historical information is passed. I have repurposed the interactions and exchanges that make up each of Coessens's five tacit dimensions as what I call "artistic values": principles that guide the way a performer interprets, filters, and even manipulates historical information in their decision-making process. Much like the dimensions in Coessens's web of artistic practice, each of these artistic values has an impact on the interpretative process. If they are defined as distinct but inter-connected principles, a researcher can select and investigate those values that afford the information most relevant to the research question, while avoiding the risk of considering the artistic values in an isolated way, producing an incomplete analysis.

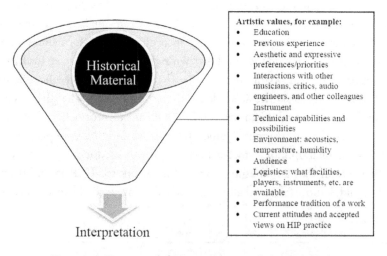

FIGURE 1. Framework for research in-and-through HIP.

While the categories in the model are distinct from each other, it is worth noting that there is no inherent hierarchy in it. In particular, there is no privileging of historical information over the creative response—these are given an equal and distinct role in the process. The model also distinguishes clearly between the historical research and materials that inform HIP practice—represented at the top of the model as an input—and the CPR that occurs as a result of applying the model. It facilitates enquiry into a musician's previous experience of interpreting historical material—which here functions as an artistic value—again without confusing the role of either the historical research or the performer's interpretation of it. This is extremely important when dealing with frequently used sources such as key treatises, where well-trodden paths of interpretation might bias a performer's view of the source's contents.

The Research Framework in Action

This framework formed a part of my recently completed doctoral research. I used the framework to investigate features of a selection of seventeenth- and eighteenth-century works for recorder and in doing so highlighted certain artistic values in play in my interpretative process, which was beneficial to the thesis discussion. My investigation of claims that Vivaldi's chamber concerti in sharp keys were likely to have been originally conceived for alto recorders in g' (G-altos), rather than those in f' (F-altos), deserves particular mention here, to demonstrate how the framework can be used. This theory was originally presented by Federico Maria Sardelli in his research on Vivaldi's use of flute and recorder and has been the basis for an increasing number of performances of these works since its publication.[37] His main reason for believing G-altos should be used to play the chamber concerti in sharp keys is that they simplify the fingerings used in the works, making them easier to play.[38] Sardelli bases his theory partly on an analysis of Vivaldi's writing, partly on historical sources, and to some degree on practical experience, but there is no evidence that his practical observations come from carefully scaffolded CPR.

To investigate Sardelli's claims, I began by slowing down my process of fingering to explore exactly how my fingers move from note to note. I played

---

37 Federico Maria Sardelli, *Vivaldi's Music for Flute and Recorder*, trans. Michael Talbot (Aldershot: Ashgate in association with Istituto Italiano Antonio Vivaldi, Fondazione Giorgio Cini Onlus, 2007), 129–31.
38 Ibid.

a number of eighteenth-century works that are considered technically demanding (including some by composers other than Vivaldi) with the expectation that they would sit closer to the limits of what is considered technically feasible and therefore provide more usable data on where technical boundaries lie.[39] By examining the finger movements in these pieces, I was able to establish theories on why some movements feel more complex than others (those that require fingers to move up and down simultaneously appearing more complex than those that require fingers to move in the same direction), and why some movements feel less comfortable or "embedded" in my technique than others. Such knowledge often informs the education of new players, as easier finger movements are introduced to beginners first. This knowledge remains in the foreground of these players' budding practice as they focus on mastering various patterns of finger movements. As this knowledge becomes familiar, it is shifted to the background and more complex concepts are introduced. I explored what was happening at this fundamental level in order to establish a method for investigating Vivaldi's chamber concerti in sharp keys, consciously shifting the knowledge and skills back into the foreground by reflecting in detail on my practice.

On the basis of the information about fingering complexity established in this initial stage, it became clear to me that, while these works by Vivaldi certainly required less complex finger movements when played on a G-alto, this technical simplification also meant sacrificing the diversity of tone color imparted by the forked fingerings often used in the performance of these works of F-alto.[40] This contradicted the historical information that I was aware of indicating that these "colorful" fingerings were crucial to the perceived character of a piece and that composers used these fingerings for effect.[41]

I explored this contradiction by making observations on my own playing that stepped beyond purely technical and physical concerns and required me to reflect on the artistic values that inform my practice, such as education, previous experience, performance tradition, and instrument capability. Frequently, recorder players today will play eighteenth-century works such as Vivaldi's

---

39 Naturally, fingerings are impacted by other technical skills; skills such as breathing, articulation, and registral changes were also considered in conjunction with the finger movements.
40 Forked fingerings involve a finger-hole or holes being closed beneath an open one. They often (although not always) result in more complicated finger movements and frequently have a shaded or subtle tone color.
41 Bruce Haynes, *A History of Performing Pitch: The Story of "A"* (Lanham: Scarecrow Press, 2002), 188.

concerti on replica Baroque instruments that are designed to use English fingerings—a fingering system developed by Arnold Dolmetsch in the early twentieth century—rather than historical fingerings. English fingerings largely resemble historical ones, but some notable deviations and simplifications were introduced with the intention of making technique simpler. Historical fingerings, on the other hand, were not wholly standardized in the eighteenth century—hardly surprising for an instrument whose pitch and intonation are determined by a combination of fingers and breath—but the surviving fingering charts exhibit enough similarities that a system of historical fingering can be discerned. Like many of my colleagues, I have always used recorders built for the English fingering system for playing eighteenth-century works. I was taught this system as a child and it became embedded in my practice as I continued my education.

Playing through Vivaldi's chamber concerti in sharp keys, it became evident to me that the differences between English and historical fingerings were crucial to understanding these works. I was struck by how often the most uncomfortable passages required English fingerings that differed from the historical fingerings the pieces were written for. When I substituted historical fingerings into my playing—thus adding new historical material into the filter of my research framework—I found that many of these difficult finger movements were eased to a point that there appeared to be little to no difference in technical difficulty between F- and G-altos for the purpose of playing these pieces. Additionally, I found that the F-alto still retained more timbral interest than a G-alto. As a player this disposed me towards using an F-alto with historical fingerings for these works, revealing my preference for maintaining timbral interest—which provides much more expressive potential—especially when little technical difference is perceptible.

Conclusion

A couple of closing remarks remain to be made. The framework developed in this chapter represents a process of mixing, evaluating, and filtering information to arrive at one single interpretation. Naturally, every performance, and indeed every "run-through" during practice, even every test of a bar or two, represents a new cycle through this process, each of which will necessarily be different from the last. Any model of performance must be viewed as a dynamic system, recognizing the modifications and readjustments the performer makes to each playing. Finally, this model does not require a performance on a stage in front of an audience. It can just as easily be applied in the practice room. In fact, it could be argued that, depending on the research question, the practice room is the place most conducive to conducting CPR, as it is where performers often explore and expand their creative thinking the most. In this way, the space where serendipitous discoveries are made becomes a kind of laboratory for new insights and experimentation.

Bibliography

Butt, John. "Authenticity." *Grove Music Online*. Oxford University Press, 2001. DOI:10.1093/gmo/9781561592630.article.46587.

Coessens, Kathleen. "The Web of Artistic Practice: A Background for Experimentation." In *Artistic Experimentation in Music: An Anthology*, edited by Darla Crispin and Bob Gilmore, 69–81. Leuven: Leuven University Press, 2014.

Crispin, Darla. "Artistic Research and Music Scholarship: Musings and Models from a Continental European Perspective." In *Artistic Practice as Research in Music: Theory, Criticism, Practice*, edited by Mine Doğantan-Dack, 53–72. Farnham: Ashgate, 2015.

———. "From Territories to Transformations: Anton Webern's Piano Variations Op. 27 as a Case Study for Research in-and-through Musical Performance." In *Sound and Score: Essays on Sound, Score and Notation*, edited by Paulo de Assis, William Brooks, and Kathleen Coessens, 47–60. Leuven: Leuven University Press, 2013.

Dupré, Sven. "Introduction: The Hockney-Falco Thesis: Constraints and Opportunities." *Early Science and Medicine* 10, no. 2 (2005): 125–36. DOI:10.1163/1573382054088141.

Frayling, Christopher. "Research in Art and Design." *Royal College of Art Research Papers* 1, no. 1 (1993/4). http://researchonline.rca.ac.uk/384/3/frayling_research_in_art_and_design_1993.pdf.

Haynes, Bruce. *The End of Early Music: A Period Performer's History of Music for the Twenty-First Century*. New York: Oxford University Press, 2007.

———. *A History of Performing Pitch: The Story of "A."* Lanham: Scarecrow Press, 2002.

Hockney, David. *Secret Knowledge: Rediscovering the Lost Techniques of the Old Masters*. London: Thames & Hudson, 2001.

Leech-Wilkinson, Daniel. "What We Are Doing with Early Music Is Genuinely Authentic to Such a Small Degree That the Word Loses Most of Its Intended Meaning." *Early Music* 12, no. 1 (1984): 13–16.

O'Neill, Francis, and Sofia Palazzo Corner. "Rembrandt's Self-Portraits." *Journal of Optics* 18, no. 8 (2016). DOI:10.1088/2040-8978/18/8/080401.

Quantz, Johann Joachim. *Versuch einer Anweisung die Flöte traversiere zu spielen.* Berlin: Johann Friedrich Voß, 1752. IMSLP59461–59492.

Sardelli, Federico Maria. *Vivaldi's Music for Flute and Recorder.* Translated by Michael Talbot. Aldershot: Ashgate in Association with Istituto Italiano Antonio Vivaldi, Fondazione Giorgio Cini Onlus, 2007.

Sherman, Bernard D. *Inside Early Music: Conversations with Performers.* New York: Oxford University Press, 1997.

Smith, A. Mark. *From Sight to Light: The Passage from Ancient to Modern Optics.* Chicago: University of Chicago Press, 2014.

Taruskin, Richard. *Text and Act: Essays on Music and Performance.* New York: Oxford University Press, 1995.

Walls, Peter. *History, Imagination and the Performance of Music.* Woodbridge: Boydell Press, 2003.

When Your Heart is Set on Both Broadway and the Met: An Exploration of Vocal Technique in Contemporary Musical Theater

Christopher McRae

Introduction

"They Don't Let You in the Opera (If You're a Country Star)!" So laments Kelli O'Hara in the song of the same name, reflecting the too common belief that contemporary singers are incapable of classical technique and vice versa.[1] But O'Hara defiantly declaims the song with an upper register that would be entirely at home at the Metropolitan Opera. O'Hara's performance reminds us that, while she may be a musical theater star rather than a country star, "they" did let her in the opera, and deservedly. O'Hara demonstrates that these worlds can be traversed in a single song, taking the listener through her country twang, her rocky belt, and her soaring operatic heights. Nor is O'Hara alone in this ability, as many singers now demonstrate a command of this crossover. The skills required are far from trivial, as a comprehensive mastery of the voice is crucial to transitioning with ease between contemporary and classical vocal paradigms. Two questions arise: how do singers achieve the crossover, and what makes this effective?

The voice is a complex, malleable, powerful but fickle instrument. A well-trained voice can move effortlessly through complicated musical passages, breathing life into character, text, imagery, and melody. For centuries, singers

---

[1]   Michael J Moritz Jr., "'They Don't Let You in the Opera,' Kelli O'Hara (Michael J Moriytz Jr-Conductor)," YouTube video, 5:24, September 1, 2017, https://www.youtube.com/watch?v=Q2PBOAbdIcU.

and pedagogues have worked to refine the technical action and development of the voice, while adapting to evolving physical and social expectations. By the nineteenth century, a technique known as bel canto (beautiful singing) was widely agreed upon as the leading technical paradigm for singers and pedagogues. This technique is most evidently dominant in Romantic operatic repertoire of the 1800s and early 1900s.[2] Towards the end of this period a new piece of technology emerged, the phonograph. As it evolved, the fidelity of vocal recordings improved.[3] Recording has allowed musicologists and vocologists to analyze singers' mechanical and artistic vocal choices more accurately and diagnose potential issues, opening pathways to more evidenced exploration of the development of vocal techniques.

As this genre of Romantic opera developed through the late nineteenth century, so did operetta, and then musical theater in the early to mid-twentieth century.[4] Many of the technical and stylistic choices of classical singing were carried over into these genres; although musical styles were changing, singers still needed to project unamplified.[5] This was the case until the 1960s, when two factors shifted a singer's vocal choices: amplification of the voice and amplification of the accompaniment. The electric microphone quickly became standard in popular music, with wired models growing in popularity in the early twentieth century. The turning point for musical theater was the development of wireless body microphones. Lawrence O'Toole says that the first musical to employ wireless body mics was *Funny Girl* in 1964.[6] Mark Grant notes that it was not until the late 1970s that they were used by entire companies of singers.[7] This technological advancement gave musical theater singers a wider range of

---

2 Friedrich Blume, *Classic and Romantic Music: A Comprehensive Survey* (London: Faber, 1972), 95.

3 Hermann Klein and William R. Moran, *Herman Klein and the Gramophone: Being a Series of Essays on the Bel Canto (1923), the Gramophone and the Singer (1924–1934), and Reviews of New Classical Vocal Recordings (1925–1934), and Other Writings from the Gramophone* (Portland: Amadeus Press, 1990), 63.

4 Richard Traubner, *Operetta: A Theatrical History* (New York: Taylor & Francis Group, 2003), 357.

5 Traubner, *Operetta*, ix.

6 Lawrence O'Toole, "THEATER; Musical Theater Is Discovering a New Voice," *New York Times*, January 22, 1995, https://www.nytimes.com/1995/01/22/theater/theater-musical-theater-is-discovering-a-new-voice.html.

7 Mark N. Grant, *The Rise and Fall of the Broadway Musical* (Boston: Northeastern University Press, 2004), 195.

vocal choices. The shift from acoustic to amplified sound meant that a singer no longer needed to prioritize vocal resonance, which could now be achieved via electrical signals and radio waves. Voices became amplified, accompaniments soon followed, and composers and orchestrators began to explore electric instruments as they followed the genre-specific trends of the time. Grant discusses two "watersheds," *Promises, Promises* (1968) and *Jesus Christ Superstar* (1971), the first musicals to establish electronically amplified orchestras.[8] Finally, as the rock idiom was introduced into musical theater during this period, the need for amplification of both instruments and voices grew to match.[9] This project focuses on amplified musical theater of the period.

Three singers who bring elements of operatic technique into their musical theater work are Kristin Chenoweth, Audra McDonald, and Kelli O'Hara, whose ubiquity in the field makes them ideal case studies for exploring these crossovers.

Exploring the Voice

Technical research into the voice as an instrument is a curious task. The voice is arguably the only musical instrument that requires internal major muscular shifts to adapt to different musical styles, largely invisible changes that vary from person to person.[10] Every singer has a different approach; every teacher, a different pedagogy; every author, a different interpretation.[11] This makes analyzing singers' work difficult.

One solution is looking to the discourse around singing. While there are multiple ways of describing vocal postures in different genres, the Estill framework of vocal qualities offers a simple, effective method of categorizing vocal choices and sounds within the voice, and has precedent in research

---

8   Ibid., 195.
9   Larry Stempel, *Showtime: A History of the Broadway Musical Theater* (New York: W. W. Norton & Co. 2010), 509.
10 Kenneth Bozeman, "A Case for Voice Science in the Voice Studio," *Journal of Singing* 63, no. 3 (2007): 265–270.
11 Scott Jeffrey McCoy, *Your Voice: An inside View*, 2nd ed. (Delaware: Inside View Press, 2012), 2.

on vocal pedagogy.[12] Vocal qualities and attributes are described using six terms:[13]

- Speech: Often referred to as modal voice—a singer's base spoken voice, involving a neutral larynx and thick fold phonation.[14]
- Falsetto: An aspirated vocal quality in which the singer purposely allows air to escape through the vocal folds when phonating.[15]
- Sob: A vocal quality in which the larynx is tilted in a neutral position, and the pharynx is widened, creating a crying sound.[16]
- Twang (oral and nasal variations): What for many defines the stereotypical Broadway singer. The larynx is high, and the pharynx is narrow. The sound can be made either orally or nasally resonant by closing or opening the velopharyngeal flap.[17]
- Belt: In contemporary vocology, a mix of speech and twang. The larynx is high and slightly tilted, and the body of the vocal folds is thick.[18]
- Opera: Opera is perhaps the trickiest quality to define, as it is a hybrid one. This is where an understanding of bel canto is beneficial. This beautiful singing involves a similar setup to both belt and sob, the difference being that the larynx is completely lowered, and the vocal folds are thin.[19]

These six terms not only offer aural descriptions of the sound components but align them with what Estill terms an internal anatomical "recipe," easily explaining the combination of physical actions underpinning the sound.[20]

---

12 Lisa Golda, "Deciphering Vocal Technique with Estill Voice Training," *Classical Singer* (2010): 28–29.

13 T. V. Ananthapadmanabha and Jo Estill, "Analysis and Synthesis of Six Voice Qualities," *Journal of the Acoustical Society of America* 86, no.1 (1989): 36, https://doi.org/10.1121/1.2027477.

14 Gillyanne Kayes, *Singing and the Actor*, 2nd ed. (London: A & C Black, 2004), 157.

15 Barb Jungr, "Vocal Expression in the Blues and Gospel," in *The Cambridge Companion to Blues and Gospel Music*, ed Allan Moore (Cambridge: Cambridge University Press, 2002), 105.

16 Tom Harris, Sara Harris, John S. Rubin, et al., *The Voice Clinic Handbook* (London: Whurr Publishers Ltd., 1998), 175.

17 Mary McDonald Klimek, "Using Twang," in *Exercises for Voice Therapy*, ed. Alison Behrman and John Haskell (San Diego: Plural Publishing, 2008), 95.

18 Kayes, *Singing*, 158.

19 Ibid.

20 Kimberly Steinhauer, Mary McDonald Klimek, and Jo Estill, *The Estill Voice Model: Theory & Translation* (n.p.: Estill Voice International, 2017), 213.

There will undoubtedly be vocal moments of which diagnosis could blend two or more of these six vocal qualities. Vocal authorities call this phenomenon "mix."[21] The challenge with mix is that it can be difficult to decipher exactly what qualities are mixed in a particular instance. Frameworks such as Estill are designed to give vocologists and pedagogues the tools to qualify as precisely as possible the vocal choices being addressed, and, for the purposes of this chapter, vocal moments will be categorized according to the most prominent quality. Auditory evidence will be explored to classify certain vocal moments effectively and analyze the singers' vocal choices. Some moments will also be unpacked further, to consider evidence of blended classical and contemporary vocal techniques.

In addressing contemporary vocal techniques, the difficulty of vocal analysis results in a gap in the literature, meaning data must be collected and reviewed by other means. A possible solution is the use of case studies. In a study of belt quality, Johan Sundberg et al. address this lack of literature, observing that the focus of most writing is purely operatic and "as a consequence, vocal techniques used in nonoperatic singing are poorly understood."[22] To examine these physical phenomena, they used case studies.

Case studies lend themselves to this project, allowing the exploration of a singer's voice across this range of repertoire. Chenoweth, McDonald, and O'Hara will be analyzed using two pieces of music each. A critical listening approach will be taken, and, borrowing terminology from the Estill framework, the singers' vocal qualities will be mapped on the corresponding scores. By weaving together analysis of these highlighted moments, I will describe how these sopranos blend classical and contemporary vocal techniques, and to what ends.

Kristin Chenoweth—Glinda, Glitter, and Glee

Kirstin Chenoweth's curriculum vitae as a singing actor is extensive. She is probably best-known for originating the role of Glinda in Stephen Schwartz's *Wicked* in 2003, although she had already won a Tony Award for her 1999 performance

---

21 Christianne Roll, "The Evolution of the Female Broadway Belt Voice: Implications for Teachers and Singers," *Journal of Voice* 30, no. 5 (2016), https://doi.org/10.1016/j.jvoice.2015.07.008.

22 Johan Sundberg, Patricia Gramming, and Jeanette Lovetri, "Comparisons of Pharynx, Source, Formant, and Pressure Characteristics in Operatic and Musical Theatre Singing," *Journal of Voice* 7, no. 4 (1993): 301–310, doi:10.1016/s0892-1997(05)80118-3.

in *You're a Good Man, Charlie Brown*.[23] Her skills as a performer have seen her in roles ranging from the operatic Cunegonde in Bernstein's *Candide*, to wannabe contemporary Broadway actress April in the popular TV show *Glee*. Born in Tulsa, Oklahoma, in 1968, Chenoweth was raised in a musical environment. She was primarily exposed to country and gospel musical stylings, which undoubtedly influenced her vocal choices.[24] Her initial undergraduate training at Oklahoma State University focused on musical theater and would have explored classical technique, but primarily with musical theater outcomes.[25] Through a Master's degree there, she developed the classical side of her vocal technique, studying operatic performance under renowned singing tutor Florence Birdwell.[26] This progression makes Chenoweth a natural choice for exploring the crossover of these vocal techniques, as she is a master of both.

Piece One: "Popular," Schwartz[27]

In choosing recordings to analyze, it would be foolish to ignore the role that made the soprano a household name, Glinda from Schwartz's musical *Wicked*. Through the song "Popular," the audience is given a chance to explore this character deeply, and her relationship with the protagonist, Elphaba (Idina Menzel). Glinda and Elphaba are young witches studying at a high school for the magically gifted in the land of Oz. This character, along with Schwartz's sweet, bubbly score, provides a base for the soloist to explore a range of vocal qualities. In Chenoweth's case, the song offers an ideal playing field for her contemporary and classical skills.

Midway through this performance, Chenoweth shows the caliber of her classical skills by, if briefly, pulling out an operatic top D, as marked in Figure 1. In line with the surrounding dialogue, the natural response from the listener at this moment is amusement. Chenoweth has a talent for exploiting her operatic abilities in a parodic way. Clearly, it works, as evidenced by the audience's laugh-

---

23 Kristin Chenoweth, and Joni Rodgers, *A Little Bit Wicked: Life, Love, and Faith in Stages* (Michigan: Touchstone, 2009),114.
24 Ibid., 34.
25 Ibid., 55.
26 Ibid., 56.
27 A link to Chenoweth's performance of the piece can be found at SMD11036, "WICKED 'Popular' press footage," YouTube video, 4:57, November 15, 2009, https://www.youtube.com/watch?v=LZpeWC_r0oU.

ter in this live recording. Part of Chenoweth's success comes from her comedic skills as a singer and actor. She can use the appropriate sounds, and moreover she can embody them and time them with her action to create moments of full-fledged comedy.

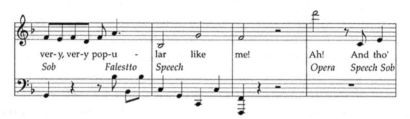

FIGURE 1. "Popular" from Wicked, measures 95–98.

The last note of this performance is worth unpacking on a technical level. Here, Chenoweth demonstrates a complex vocal setup involving multiple qualities of the voice. At the root of the sound there is a belt quality. But, the typical sound created by the thick fold approach of a belt setup is not present; the sound seems to be produced by a thin fold approach.[28] Thus, this moment probably exhibits a mixed quality of belt and sob (see Figure 2). The larynx is high and tilted, and the bodies of the vocal folds are thin. This laryngeal positioning generates a different sound from the typical sob quality we heard earlier in the piece. As the larynx is high, the pharyngeal resonance is lessened. This does not allow the sound as much time to bounce around and darken before leaving the oral cavity. Here, Chenoweth gets both the aural effect of a full belt and the vocal safety of a sob, as thinner folds require less pressure to vibrate at the required pitch.

FIGURE 2. "Popular" from Wicked, measures 114–118.

---

28   Phonation of this manner involves sound generated by the vibration of the thin edge of the vocal fold, rather than a thick mass of the entire fold.

Piece Two: "The Girl in 14G," Tesori[29]

Chenoweth's repertoire also includes pieces where moments of classical technique are more prescribed. "The Girl in 14G" (written by Jeanine Tesori and lyricist Dick Scanlan), was not specifically composed for a musical, but adheres to musical theater style. There are clearly notated moments of classical, contemporary, and blended techniques throughout the score and the text. This piece was written for Chenoweth and based primarily on her own experiences of apartment living in New York City. This is an ideal piece in which to observe these moments of blending.[30]

In this piece, Chenoweth is no longer representing the voice of a single character, but the voices of multiple characters on succession and she must adjust her vocal qualities accordingly. As in Chenoweth's approach to "Popular," the core sound for this performance is her distinct and pleasing twang quality. Unlike the nasal twang quality heard in "Popular," "The Girl in 14G" has a more orally driven tone, as a result of the closure of the velopharyngeal port. This base tone allows more exploration of vocal quality when mimicking other characters.

Early in the piece, Chenoweth imitates a downstairs neighbor who is an opera singer in the familiar operatic passages in Figure 3. Again, the character

FIGURE 3. "The Girl in 14G" by Jeanine Tesori, measures 21–24 and 34–36.

---

29 Catchyyy, "Kristin Chenoweth—The Girl in 14G," YouTube video, 4:41, May 6, 2007, https://www.youtube.com/watch?v=jBJn4BHtqqY.
30 Chenoweth, *A Little Bit Wicked*, 140.

of this operatic singing is comical, largely because of the authenticity of Chenoweth's operatic sound and the speed with which these vocal transitions are made. Unlike the other two sopranos considered in this project, who employ operatic sounds for non-comical purposes, Chenoweth embraces humor using these familiar operatic motifs. The vocal accuracy with which Chenoweth sings these passages is impressive, and, like her operatic moment in "Popular," the characterful representation is more effective than it would be if these moments were faux-operatic.

An upstairs jazz singer is then introduced, requiring of Chenoweth another vocal shift. Here, she mimics the jazz style with a chesty speech quality. The effect is similar to her mimicry of the opera singer: the accuracy with which she can represent these sounds is key to her successful characterization. Verging on a belt, this speech sound lends a contemporary feel to the section, drawing this third character away from the first and highlighting the difference between it and the second. This distinction between styles becomes even more pronounced as Chenoweth shifts between the jazz and operatic characters.

Chenoweth's final note in this piece is similar to the last note of "Popular," as shown in Figure 4. It exhibits the same choice of leading into this note with a full belt and mixing a sob quality in as the phrase becomes more sustained. The effect is similar to the case in "Popular," allowing the greatest sound with the least effort.

FIGURE 4. "The Girl in 14G" by Jeanine Tesori, measures 131–137.

These mixed moments scattered through both pieces show Chenoweth's mastery of her instrument. Chenoweth balances these blended qualities, and produces an exciting and stylistically suitable sound while maintaining vocal safety. A pure belt might better represent the character's intentions but might also be more demanding on the voice. A pure sob might be mechanically undemanding but could lack a level of emotional connection or be less satisfying for a listener. Chenoweth displays a deep understanding of how to balance these considerations.

Audra McDonald—A Master Class in Glamour

For a performer, a Tony Award is the benchmark of success on Broadway. Audra McDonald, with six Tonys to her name, and the only actor to win in all four performing categories, is an ideal candidate for study. In 1996 McDonald featured in Terrance McNally's play *Master Class*, in the role of Sharon, a singer being mentored by the great soprano Maria Callas (played by Zoe Caldwell). She was given the chance to show her skills in legitimate operatic repertoire, such as "Vieni, t'affretta" from Verdi's *Macbeth*. Already noted for her performance in *Carousel* (1994), McDonald could now show wider audiences her classical nous. Born in Berlin in 1970 and raised in California, McDonald had an education with a classical voice focus. Unlike Chenoweth, she completed her training at Juilliard in New York in both the musical theater and opera streams.[31] The result is noticeable in the following analysis, as a straightforward classical setup underpins much of McDonald's vocal arsenal.

Piece One: "The Glamourous Life," Sondheim[32]

As McDonald is known especially for her performances of works by leading musical theater composer Stephen Sondheim, it seems fitting to begin this case study with one of her finest performances of a song by this composer. Sondheim's 1973 musical *A Little Night Music* revolves around the romantic involvements of various couples. McDonald sang this stage version of the son at

---

31 Blake Green, "Never Short of Breath," *San Francisco Chronicle*, July 16, 2000, https://www.sfgate.com/entertainment/article/Never-Short-of-Breath-Taking-a-break-from-2748694.php.
32 Broadway Plus, "Audra McDonald—The Glamorous Life (Sondheim's 80th)," YouTube video, 4:15, January 2, 2011, https://www.youtube.com/watch?v=Z3HYCahNx7U.

a concert celebrating the composer's eightieth birthday in 2010, accompanied by the New York Philharmonic. An extended solo version of "The Glamorous Life," originally composed for chorus, was added to the 1977 film adaptation.[33] Within the musical, this piece would be sung by thirteen-year-old Fredrika, lamenting her absent mother, Desiree; however, in the concert setting of this performance, McDonald could create her own context for telling a story through this song.

The first difference to be heard between the vocal choices of McDonald and Chenoweth is their approach to building classical techniques into their performances. Chenoweth tends to sing from a contemporary space and layers moments of classical expression on top; McDonald does the opposite. Immediately, McDonald's vocal mechanism is aligned in a classical space, with a sob quality at the core of her sound. She creates drama using modern techniques, which will be explored below; however, she often does so by shifting qualities from sob to opera. This full operatic quality reinforces both lower and upper harmonics within the voice by increasing the space in the pharynx from the fully lowered larynx, generating a richer tone with a more profound vibrancy. In the previous case study, Chenoweth's use of this quality was for comical effect; McDonald's is not. Here it is reserved for moments of heightened emotion, especially towards the end of the piece.

One challenge encountered in analyzing McDonald's performance is the distinction between sob quality and opera. Generally, the setup of the vocal mechanism is similar in both, so it is easy to blend the two. In the case of "The Glamorous Life," moments where the larynx releases downwards fully and the pharynx expands are identifiable as opera quality, for example, on the word "life" in Figure 5.

Most frequently, these moments occur on more sustained notes, where McDonald is not having to pay as much attention to consonants, which can disturb the laryngeal placement. Were McDonald to attempt to maintain this operatic quality through phrases of intricate text, clarity would be likely to be lost, and some of the performance's conversational character would be sacrificed.

Finally, the last phrase of this piece contains a similar effect. McDonald mixes one final moment of belt into her operatic quality, as she almost cries through the word "glamorous" (see Figure 6). McDonald's final note shows her full

---

33 Paul M. Puccio, "Sondheim 101: A Little Night Music," *Sondheim Review* (Fall 2013): 8–11, http://ezproxy.auckland.ac.nz/login?url=https://search-proquest.com.ezproxy.auckland.ac.nz/docview/1444146372?accountid=8424.

When Your Heart is Set on Both Broadway and the Met | 185

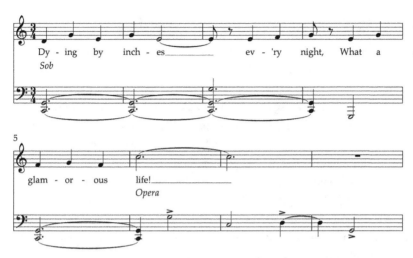

FIGURE 5. "The Glamourous Life" from *A Little Night Music*, measures 29–36.

control over the operatic quality, as she contrasts this cried phrase with one last, sustained note full of warmth and beauty, aligned with the love the character feels for the absent mother.

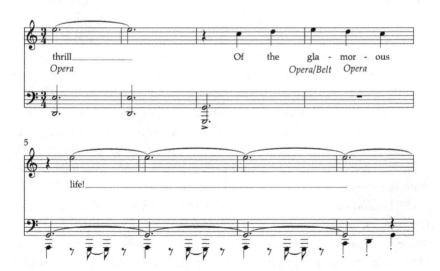

FIGURE 6. "The Glamourous Life" from *A Little Night Music*, measures 235–242.

Piece Two: "The Light in the Piazza," Guettel[34]

Certain shows offer especially suitable arenas for these singers to test their classical mettle. One of these is Adam Guettel's *The Light in the Piazza*, especially its titular song. Here there arises an opportunity to apply McDonald's approach to a character written to be sung with blended classical and contemporary sounds. This show is a well-known crossover piece, borrowing stylistic choices from contemporary and classical musical cultures. John Kenrick describes Guettel's score as "almost operatic."[35] This piece is sung by the character Clara, a young woman with the mind of a ten-year-old in the body of a twenty-six year old due to a childhood incident. Her nature is usually depicted as innocent and naïve. These character elements are often mirrored in the singer's vocal choices. Here, McDonald embodies this character in a concert context. The recording in footnote 34 is a live performance from Carnegie Hall in 2004.

Once again, McDonald sets up this piece from a place of speech and sob. At the beginning of "The Light in the Piazza," unlike the other two pieces, McDonald gently mixes moments of falsetto quality into her speech and sob setups (see Figure 7). When this occurs, the vocal mechanism remains largely unchanged; the larynx and pharynx are not repositioned. However, the stretch of the vocal folds is relaxed slightly, allowing a little air to escape, adding breathiness to the sound. This is an excellent example of a contemporary tweak to a classical sound. A sob setup would be effective in classical singing, but the addition of a falsetto quality would not. Some resonance is lost in letting air escape through the vocal folds, and it would not carry unamplified. McDonald is free to incorporate this quality into her sound as she is using a microphone. Falsetto is often associated with vulnerability and allows the singer to develop an air of intimacy in the text and drama. The effect of this mix contributes to the gentle conversational tone of the opening section, almost a sung stage whisper, which creates a sense of youthful optimism in the character and communicates her childlike nature.

McDonald performs further moments in which vocal qualities transition mid-note, for example on the word "air" in Figure 8. McDonald begins this phrase with a simple speech quality, crescendoing into belt. This is a typical set-up in musical theater singing, serving both to heighten emotion and to navigate

---

34 A recording of the piece can be heard at Justin Pollinger, "Audra McDonald—The Light in the Piazza," YouTube video, 2:58, February 11, 2013, https://www.youtube.com/watch?v=E4Tj-4j9tGU.

35 John Kenrick, *Musical Theatre: A History* (New York: Continuum, 2008), 375.

FIGURE 7. "The Light in the Piazza" from *The Light in the Piazza*, measures 13–21.

into this higher register. However, what is different about McDonald's approach is what occurs in the latter half of the note on "air." Initially, the sound has a clean belt quality, but after the first beat of this note, McDonald lowers her larynx slightly, mixing in a sob quality and allowing the voice to vibrate. Typically, vibrato is a sign of muscular relaxation when the larynx is in a sob position; straightening the voice requires a small amount of extra laryngeal muscle tension. In belt, the opposite is true: vibrato is added to the voice through muscular engagement. These moments can be a compelling clue as to which vocal quality the singer is employing. This effect warms the voice towards the end of the note and provides relief after the tension caused by the straight-toned belt, for singer and listener alike. That is not to say the belt is always straight and sob is vibrated, but they are common symptoms for diagnosing these vocal choices. Generally, a strong vibrato is associated with classical singing, straight-tone singing with musical theater. These singers demonstrate that these boundaries can be productively blurred.

FIGURE 8. "The Light in the Piazza" from *The Light in the Piazza*, measures 25–26.

This piece showcases McDonald's ability to move seamlessly between classical and contemporary vocal techniques and to blend the two. Were she not so adept at this smooth action a listener would probably be distracted from the storytelling of these moments. Her abilities, though, keep a listener engaged. As these techniques are so well blended, distraction from the consideration of the workings of her sound is minimized and the listener is more likely to remain engrossed in the performance.

Unlike Chenoweth, McDonald very rarely uses a twang quality. There are moments where twang is mixed into other vocal qualities, but it is not heard alone, which is possibly due to the classical technique with which McDonald was taught. Classical singers tend to avoid nasality in their sound, as an open velopharyngeal flap may inadvertently raise the larynx or destabilize it due to the imbalance of air pressure around the vocal folds. These symptoms are not as disruptive when singing with a microphone or straight tone; but they cause vocal resonance to be lost in classical music. The vibrato frequency often becomes inconsistent as a result of this destabilized larynx.

Finally, like Chenoweth, McDonald belts sparingly and with mixed qualities. This is a matter of vocal safety, as discussed above regarding Chenoweth. Vocal coach and music director Seth Rudetsky comments on a production of *Dreamgirls*, in which McDonald belted a sustained E^5 with great success. When he phoned the next day to ask her why she did not explore this vocal quality consistently, Rudetsky was answered by a very hoarse McDonald, and the question needed no more discussion.[36] McDonald has a firm grasp of how best to utilize her vocal timbre for both character and dramatic effect, and her ability to blend qualities from contemporary and classical paradigms of singing, grants her great agency in her approaches to a wide range of repertoire.

Kelli O'Hara—Bridging the Gap

The final soprano I will examine is inarguably a master of musical theater and operatic performance and was the initial inspiration for this project; her song "They Don't Let You in the Opera (If You're a Country Star)" sparked my early thoughts about this world of crossover singing. Treading the boards on Broadway and at the Met, Kelli O'Hara is an exemplary explorer of blended classical

---

36   Seth Rudetsky, "Seth Rudetsky Deconstructs Kristin Chenoweth, Audra, Karen Morrow, Joan Diener and Patti Lupone," YouTube video, 8:22, April 30, 2009, https://www.youtube.com/watch?v=fMS4wuO6RLQ.

and contemporary vocal techniques. Born in Oklahoma in 1976, O'Hara had an education as a singer very similar to Chenoweth's, studying opera at the same university under the same vocal tutor, Birdwell, whom both sopranos credit as vital to their success.[37] Her work at the Metropolitan Opera is worth noting, as she has performed with the company in two purely operatic productions, Lehár's *The Merry Widow* and Mozart's *Così fan tutte*.[38]

Piece One: "The Light in the Piazza," Guettel[39]

This piece, having also been sung by McDonald, offers an opportunity to compare two singers' approaches closely. In 2005, O'Hara performed the role of Clara in *The Light in the Piazza* on Broadway, earning a Tony nomination.

As O'Hara is the only one of the three singers who has sung main-stage operatic roles at the Met, her approaches might be expected to be the most purely "classical." However, her vocal qualities are possibly the most blended of the three. There are few moments in "The Light in the Piazza" that exhibit purely one quality or another. O'Hara is a master of underpinning her vocal setup with a sob quality, giving low laryngeal freedom and thin elasticity to the vocal folds, imparting a certain acoustic consistency to her tone.

The opening section of this piece sits mostly in speech quality, but the gentle tilt of the larynx into a slightly sob-like position blends the moments with a fuller sob quality into the phrase. As the vocal line ascends, O'Hara also modernizes these early sob moments with a touch of oral twang. This is, again, unlike McDonald, who embraces the sob quality before moving to a more belt position. The distinction here can be heard early in Figure 9. O'Hara's first C^5 is a full sob. The second is a mix of twang and sob, before transitioning back to full sob on the final B^4. This creates a similar tension/release effect to what was heard from McDonald in the same phrase, the difference here being McDonald's use of belt whereas O'Hara uses twang.

---

37 Beth Stevens, "Kelli O'Hara," broadway.com, September 28, 2004, http://www.broadway.com/buzz/11125/kelli-ohara.

38 Ryan McPhee, "Kelli O'Hara on the Thrills and Challenges of Revisiting Opera After a 20-Year Career on Broadway," playbill.com, Mar 20, 2018, https://www.playbill.com/article/kelli-ohara-on-the-thrills-and-challenges-of-revisiting-opera-after-a-20-year-career-on-broadway

39 MDA Telethon, "Kelli O'Hara—'The Light In The Piazza' (2005)—MDA Telethon," YouTube video, 3:20, July 15, 2017, https://www.youtube.com/watch?v=5ODVHV5W3U0.

FIGURE 9. "The Light in the Piazza" from *The Light in the Piazza*, measures 22–27.

At the climax of the piece, O'Hara again incorporates this mix, blending moments of orally driven twang into sob to add a sharper edge to the voice, calculated to produce an emotional response from the listener. This is similar to what has been observed in McDonald's performances. There are various amounts of each vocal quality mixed into the sound here. There is not a consistent mix throughout this section, O'Hara constantly adjusts this balance. For instance, take the section in Figure 10. Where McDonald mixes belt into these phrases, O'Hara relies on growing vocal intensity using her sob quality. She begins this section with a predominately sob quality with minimal twang. As the phrases move higher, both in pitch and dynamic, enough twang is added for the quality on the word "everywhere" to no longer be labelled only sob. The effect is similar to McDonald's approach to this section in choosing a belt quality, the difference here being O'Hara's favoring of a thinner fold setup in the voice. This sound is, perhaps, the closest to a full belt represented by O'Hara in this piece; her moments of full thick-fold singing are rare.

Following this section, the twang in the voice is reduced, and O'Hara pulls back the intensity to reflect the feeling evoked by the piece's opening, highlighting the simple, gentle nature of the character right to the last sung moments of the piece.

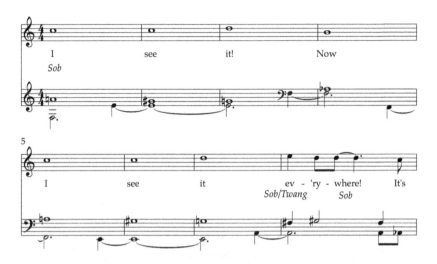

FIGURE 10. "The Light in the Piazza" from *The Light in the Piazza*, measures 58–65.

Piece Two: "Almost Real," Brown[40]

Jason Robert Brown's musical *The Bridges of Madison County* (2014) had a short life on Broadway and a largely mixed reception. However, some individual songs have outlived the show and are frequently performed in various contexts. The song "Almost Real" is one of these. O'Hara's classical approach to this piece offers many moments through which to explore her technical choices. Immediately, it is clear the character influences O'Hara's performance strongly. O'Hara created the role of Francesca, which was tailored for her voice by the composer.[41] Francesca is an Italian woman who has migrated to the United States. Yes, this is clear from her choice of accent and the provision of this information in the first line of the song; however, the essence of the character is reinforced by O'Hara's choice of vocal quality. Her vocal modifications create a sound unlike what was heard in the previous piece examined.

O'Hara begins with an unmistakably full sob quality, which could almost be confused with an operatic quality; were the larynx a little lower, this would be

---

40   Broadwaycom, "Exclusive! Watch Kelli O'Hara Sing the Stunning 'Almost Real' from 'The Bridges of Madison County,'" YouTube video, 5:25, April 15, 2014, https://www.youtube.com/watch?v=apnHOwWuTkQ.
41   Elisabeth Vinentelli, "Kelli O'Hara Makes the Most of 'Bridges of Madison County,'" nypost.com, February 20, 2014, https://nypost.com/2014/02/20/kelli-ohara-makes-the-most-of-bridges-of-madison-county/.

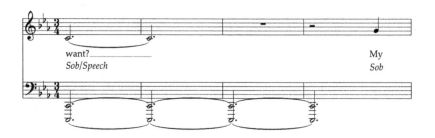

FIGURE 11. "Almost Real" from *The Bridges of Madison County*, measures 47–50.

likely. This sound is maintained exclusively until the first moment, when a very small amount of speech quality is mixed into the sound, as shown in Figure 11, adding a vocal exclamation as the character of the music shifts with the "A tempo." Leading up to this moment, O'Hara can maintain her laryngeal tilt through the low sob quality in the voice, a difficult task due to the low air pressure in that voice range. To vibrate the folds at that lower frequency, it is much easier for the larynx to un-tilt, shortening the vocal folds. Were O'Hara to do this, however, the darker sound from the tilted larynx would be lost. This darkness creates an impression of maturity of character, along with one of Italian-style singing, perhaps evoking the place of origin of the bel canto style.

The final section displays O'Hara's full operatic mastery; there is nothing "faux" about this singing. O'Hara mirrors the rise of the character's passion with her vocal crescendo into these moments of operatic quality, dancing between them and moments of sob reinforced with speech. Whereas earlier in the piece, in similar sections, O'Hara used these opera moments sparingly, they now dominate the vocal line throughout multiple registers of the voice. Having already sung in her voice's lower and middle registers, O'Hara now displays her operatic top (see the G^5 in Figure 12). The sense of character established in the beginning is never lost, as we are teased with these moments throughout the piece. Because sob and opera are not too dissimilar, her adopting this entirely classical approach does not remove the listener from the story's world. The heart of the character is always present in the sound. Finally, as Francesca is brought back from this passionate memory to her reality, O'Hara returns to the same vocal qualities used at the beginning of the piece, moving through a mixed sob-speech quality similar to the approach she took to the final moment in "The Light in the Piazza." The absence of vibrato on this last note confers a simplicity on the sound and, perhaps, hints at the character's vulnerability.

In these two pieces, O'Hara's approach is less about vocal safety than about finding a character's natural voice. Of course, her sounds are never vocally

When Your Heart is Set on Both Broadway and the Met | 193

FIGURE 12. "Almost Real" from *The Bridges of Madison County*, measures 255–271.

unsafe; but in these pieces, the ear is drawn less to the technical decisions than the dramatic choices. Her vocal choices allow qualities to blend easily, make shifts less noticeable, and maintain a smooth sound throughout the piece.

Conclusion

I have examined moments of both classical and contemporary vocal techniques in performances by three professional singers. As a result, a provocative idea suggests itself. In musical theater, vocal technique is hidden; it is on display in opera. Musical theater aims to make singing sound as "normal" as possible, focusing on text, narrative and character. Technical moments in singing should go unnoticed to maintain the listener's involvement in the world of the play. One could argue that classical singing is technically more complex, and as classical singers do not have the luxury of amplification, the margin between "right" and "wrong" is slim, leaving less room for character and dramatic considerations.

Two broad categories represent the reasoning behind blended contemporary and classical vocal techniques: characterful choices (intended to be true to the world of the person being portrayed) and mechanical choices (intended to allow the physically safest sounds, and at times the only realistic vocal choice). All three of the sopranos addressed in this project are storytellers. Even in concert settings and studio recordings, they are playing characters. Their vocal choices are certainly in line with this priority. Some choices may be mechanically informed, but they are never untrue to the voice of the character. However, vocal safety must be considered in order to guarantee the instrument's longevity, especially in a theatrical context where these singers are expected to perform up to eight shows each week. When the vocal folds and muscles in and around the larynx are used, fatigue is unavoidable.[42] To some extent, the singer can control how much their vocal stamina will be depleted. Singers are trained to keep this level of fatigue as low as possible, occasionally choosing to sacrifice some stamina for a given vocal quality. The extent to which they can make such an adjustment is dependent on knowledge of their own instrument. For example, a larynx in a neutral position with thin vocal folds requires little energy to vibrate. When shifting to a belt position, the power needed to vibrate these thicker folds at a higher laryngeal position is much greater but with a very different output in sound.[43] In speech, this would be the difference between speaking and yelling. Speaking may be vocally less draining; but were a passer-by to see that a pedestrian was about to be struck by a car, then a softly spoken "watch out" would be unlikely to help. Similarly, a light sob quality is easy to maintain, but occasionally, the character's world calls for belt.

The mastery of this balance comes with experience, as the three case studies demonstrate. These three singers use a full belt infrequently, as indicated by the annotations on the examples in this chapter. Each of the three knows how to use these qualities, and more importantly how to blend them, to create a similar output in sound. Moments of extended belt from these three singers are almost exclusively mixed with a sob quality. The sound does not lack the intensity of a pure belt quality, but the vocal folds are given a chance to vibrate with less effort. In this setup, a sound similar to belt is created, but this sob quality can clearly be heard underneath. It is unlikely any listener would complain that perhaps the sound was missing a slight vocal edge or cut. The effect of this vocal choice is unarguably similar and would still be classified as a belt. The same can be said of a fully operatic quality, as the two, mechanically, are not too dissimilar.

---

42 Nathan V. Welham and Margaret A. Maclagan, "Vocal Fatigue: Current Knowledge and Future Directions," *Journal of Voice* 17, no. 1 (2003): 21–30.

43 Sundberg, "Comparisons of Pharynx": 304.

Both vocal qualities require moderate to high subglottal pressure and substantial amounts of vocal energy.[44] There is a reason opera singers historically perform every second day, if not less frequently: it is tiring. Even the best-trained singers require rest to keep their voices functioning optimally; this is in no way reflective of poor technical singing.

Perhaps the most important conclusion from this project is that a strand of singing in musical theater borrows techniques from multiple areas; these techniques can be applied individually or blended to expand a singer's arsenal of vocal choices greatly. These three singers have a deep understanding of their instruments and know which techniques to rely on, allowing them a great deal of agency in their vocal performance. While people may think "They don't let you in the opera, if you're a country star!," or indeed a Broadway star, they sometimes do.

---

44   Ibid.: 309.

Bibliography

Ananthapadmanabha, T. V., and Jo Estill. "Analysis and Synthesis of Six Voice Qualities." *The Journal of the Acoustical Society of America* 86, no. 1 (1989): 36. https://doi.org/10.1121/1.2027477.

Blume, Friedrich. *Classic and Romantic Music: A Comprehensive Survey.* London: Faber, 1972.

Bozeman, Kenneth. "A Case for Voice Science in the Voice Studio." *Journal of Singing* 63, no. 3 (2007): 265–270.

Broadwaycom. "Exclusive! Watch Kelli O'Hara Sing the Stunning 'Almost Real' from 'The Bridges of Madison County,'" YouTube video, 5:25. April 15, 2014. https://www.youtube.com/watch?v=apnHOwWuTkQ.

Broadway Plus. "Audra McDonald—The Glamorous Life," YouTube video, 4:15. January 2, 2011. https://www.youtube.com/watch?v=Z3HYCahNx7U.

Catchyyy. "Kristin Chenoweth—The Girl in 14G," YouTube video, 4:41. May 6, 2007. https://www.youtube.com/watch?v=jBJn4BHtqqY.

Chenoweth, Kirstin, and Joni Rodgers. *A Little Bit Wicked: Life, Love, and Faith in Stages.* Michigan: Touchstone, 2009.

Golda, Lisa. "Deciphering Vocal Technique with Estill Voice Training." *Classical Singer* (2010): 28–29.

Grant, Mark N. *The Rise and Fall of the Broadway Musical.* Boston: Northeastern University Press, 2004.

Green, Blake. "Never Short of Breath." *San Francisco Chronicle*, July 16, 2000. https://www.sfgate.com/entertainment/article/Never-Short-of-Breath-Taking-a-break-from-2748694.php.

Harris, Tom, Sara Harris, John S. Rubin, et al. *The Voice Clinic Handbook.* London: Whurr Publishers Ltd., 1998.

Jungr, Barb. "Vocal Expression in the Blues and Gospel." In *The Cambridge Companion to Blues and Gospel Music*, edited by Allan Moore, 102–115. Cambridge: Cambridge University Press, 2002.

Kayes, Gillyanne. *Singing and the Actor.* 2nd ed. London: A & C Black, 2004.

Kenrick, John. *Musical Theatre: A History.* New York: Continuum, 2008.

Klein, Hermann, and William R. Moran. *Herman Klein and the Gramophone: Being a Series of Essays on the Bel Canto (1923), the Gramophone and the Singer (1924–1934), and Reviews of New Classical Vocal Recordings (1925–1934), and Other Writings from the Gramophone.* Portland: Amadeus Press, 1990.

McCoy, Scott Jeffrey. *Your Voice: An Inside View.* 2nd ed. Delaware: Inside View Press, 2012.

McDonald Klimek, Mary. "Using Twang." In *Exercises for Voice Therapy*, edited by Alison Behrman and John Haskell, 176–178. San Diego: Plural Publishing, 2008.

McPhee, Ryan. "Kelli O'Hara on the Thrills and Challenges of Revisiting Opera After a 20-Year Career on Broadway." playbill.com, March 20, 2018. https://www.playbill.

com/article/kelli-ohara-on-the-thrills-and-challenges-of-revisiting-opera-after-a-20-year-career-on-broadway.

MDA Telethon. "Kelli O'Hara—'The Light In The Piazza' (2005)—MDA Telethon," YouTube video, 3:20. July 15, 2017. https://www.youtube.com/watch?v=5ODVHV5W3U0.

Moritz, Michael J., Jr. "'They Don't Let You in the Opera,' Kelli O'Hara (Michael J. Moritz Jr.—Conductor)," YouTube video, 5:24. September 1, 2017. https://www.youtube.com/watch?v=Q2PBOAbdIcU.

O'Toole, Lawrence. "THEATER: Musical Theater Is Discovering a New Voice." *New York Times*, 22 January, 1995. https://www.nytimes.com/1995/01/22/theater/theater-musical-theater-is-discovering-a-new-voice.html.

Pollinger, Justin. "Audra McDonald—The Light in the Piazza," YouTube video, 2:58. February 11, 2013. https://www.youtube.com/watch?v=E4Tj-4j9tGU.

Puccio, Paul M. "Sondheim 101: A Little Night Music." *Sondheim Review* (Fall 2013): 8–11. http://ezproxy.auckland.ac.nz/login?url=https://search-proquest-com.ezproxy.auckland.ac.nz/docview/1444146372?accountid=8424.

Roll, Christianne. "The Evolution of the Female Broadway Belt Voice: Implications for Teachers and Singers." *Journal of Voice* 30, no. 5 (2016): 639.e1-9. https://doi.org/10.1016/j.jvoice.2015.07.008.

Rudetsky, Seth. "Seth Rudetsky Deconstructs Kristin Chenoweth, Audra, Karen Morrow, Joan Diener and Patti Lupone," YouTube video, 8:22. April 30, 2009. https://www.youtube.com/watch?v=fMS4wuO6RLQ.

SMD11036. "WICKED 'Popular' press footage." YouTube video, 4:57. November 15, 2009. https://www.youtube.com/watch?v=LZpeWC_r0oU.

Steinhauer, Kimberly, Mary McDonald Klimek, and Jo Estill. *The Estill Voice Model: Theory & Translation*. n.p.: Estill Voice International, 2017.

Stempel, Larry. *Showtime: A History of the Broadway Musical Theater*. New York: W. W. Norton & Co., 2010.

Stevens, Beth. "Kelli O'Hara." broadway.com, September 28, 2004. http://www.broadway.com/buzz/11125/kelli-ohara.

Sundberg, Johan, Patricia Gramming, and Jeanette Lovetri. "Comparisons of Pharynx, Source, Formant, and Pressure Characteristics in Operatic and Musical Theatre Singing." *Journal of Voice* 7, no. 4 (1993): 301–310. Doi:10.1016/s0892-1997(05)80118-3.

Traubner, Richard. *Operetta: A Theatrical History*. New York: Taylor & Francis Group, 2003.

Vinentelli, Elisabeth. "Kelli O'Hara makes the most of 'Bridges of Madison County.'" nypost.com, February 20, 2014. https://nypost.com/2014/02/20/kelli-ohara-makes-the-most-of-bridges-of-madison-county/.

Welham, Nathan V., and Margaret A. Maclagan. "Vocal Fatigue: Current Knowledge and Future Directions." *Journal of Voice* 17, no. 1 (2003): 21–30.

Part Four

Composition and Agency

Ratner's Topoi and the Cultural Middlebrow in Britten's First Suite for Cello

Eliana Dunford

In 1932, Virginia Woolf wrote an incendiary letter to the *New Statesman* that was to remain unpublished until 1942. The letter responded to a review by J. B. Priestley of Woolf's collection *The Second Common Reader*. Priestley had dismissed Woolf's work as representing a self-congratulatory artistic school of "terrifically sensitive, cultured, invalidish ladies with private means."[1] Priestley intensified this rhetoric in a BBC radio broadcast entitled "To a High-Brow," in which he accused writers such as Woolf of creating their work for a social elite, restricting the domain of high culture to those whose backgrounds allowed them to enter it.[2]

Woolf's riposte was as one-sided as Priestley's accusation. She lambasted Priestley as an adherent of the cultural "middlebrow," who habitually took advantage of the fruits of high culture in order to improve their own standing in society. Middlebrows, she wrote, were people who lived their lives "in pursuit of no single object, neither art nor life itself, but both mixed indistinguishably, and rather nastily, with money, fame, power, or prestige. The middlebrow curries favor with both sides equally."[3] In short, Woolf worried that the middlebrow devalued the pursuit of art for art's sake, and sullied high culture by transforming its consumption into an opportunity for social climbing. Her view was pithily

---

1   J. B. Priestley, "Tell Us More about These Authors," *Evening Standard*, October 13, 1932, 11.
2   J. B. Priestley, "To a High-Brow," BBC Written Archives Centre; reprinted in *John O'London's Weekly*, December 3, 1932.
3   Virginia Woolf, "Middlebrow," in *The Death of the Moth and Other Essays* (London: Hogarth Press, 1947), 113.

summarized by an anonymous contributor to *Punch* magazine, who dismissed the middlebrow as "people who are hoping that someday they will get used to stuff they ought to like."[4]

This spat between Priestley and Woolf did not take place in a vacuum but was symptomatic of rapidly intensifying anxiety about the status of "high culture" during the first half of the twentieth century. Literary theorists Erica Brown and Mary Grover locate the "Battle of the Brows," when these anxieties were at the forefront of cultural discussion, between approximately 1920 and 1960.[5] Musicologist Christopher Chowrimootoo suggests similar dates, noting that the literary critic and historian Van Wyck Brooks bemoaned the existence of a divide between highbrows and lowbrows as early as 1915, while American cultural critic Dwight Macdonald was still dividing culture into binary categories of "High" and "Mass" in 1953.[6] Though this stratification of taste was playing out most obviously in the literary field, it was also beginning to dominate the discourse about Western art music.

A few short years after the publication of Woolf's essay (and on the other side of the Atlantic), Benjamin Britten's operetta *Paul Bunyan* received its 1941 premiere. Early reviews of the work drew on remarkably similar rhetoric to that employed by Woolf, worrying that the piece appropriated (and therefore sullied) elements of high modernism to market itself to a middlebrow audience. Virgil Thomson particularly damned what he saw as a canny incorporation of both high and low elements; he wrote that Britten's "particular blend of melodic 'appeal' with irresponsible counterpoint and semi-acidulous instrumentation is easily recognizable as that considered by the British Broadcasting Corporation to be at once modernistic and safe."[7] While suitably scathing, Thomson's comment says little about the actual language of the music. Rather, it attempts to categorize Britten's place in a perceived artistic hierarchy. The implication is that Britten is shirking a responsibility to be aesthetically "honest," for which we might substitute "easily categorized." The critic Eugene Bonner was marginally more specific in his description of Britten's style. Bonner's frustration focused on Britten's eclecticism; he wrote that in *Paul Bunyan*, "high-flown allegory gives

---

4   "The Middlebrow," *Punch* 169 (December 23, 1925), 673.
5   Erica Brown and Mary Grover eds., *Literary Cultures: The Battle of the Brows, 1920–1960* (London: Palgrave Macmillan, 2011).
6   Christopher Chowrimootoo, *Middlebrow Modernism: Britten's Operas and the Great Divide* (Oakland: University of California Press, 2019), 4.
7   Virgil Thomson, "Musico-Theatrical Flop," *New York Herald Tribune* (May 6, 1941).

way to flat-footed realism with disconcerting suddenness, diatonic writing to chromatic, large chunks of Gilbert and Sullivan being thrown in for good measure while folksy ballads jostle operatic arias."[8] Britten's work, commentators such as Thomson and Bonner maintained, committed a crime: it played up its modernist elements so that it could claim high-art prestige, but also incorporated populist elements that would assure a wide listenership. At the heart of these critics' contempt was a sense that Britten had cannily crafted his musical language for a sort of stylistic Goldilocks zone, where it could capitalize upon others' attempts to push the envelope without having to take the risk of alienating listeners.

Several key questions arise. If critics derided Britten's music as irredeemably middlebrow, which elements of his musical language attracted this description? What social and cultural factors caused critics to so fear middlebrow writing? And how might we account for this cultural climate in our analyses of Britten's music?

If "middlebrow" has been a key term in literary theory for some time, the concept has only recently begun to develop a profile in musicology. Christopher Chowrimootoo's monograph *Middlebrow Modernism: Britten's Operas and the Great Divide* examines the stakes in the use of the term "middlebrow" in the reception of a single genre of Britten's output.[9] Chowrimootoo's work is far-reaching, examining a wide range of written reception and analyzing elements of the libretti of each opera. While he makes passing reference to musical examples, the stylistic makeup of Britten's music is not his primary focus. Taking Chowrimootoo's work as its starting point, this chapter seeks to analyze the way the stylistic language of Britten's music engages with, embraces, and ultimately moves beyond a "middlebrow" modernism.

In 1980, Leonard G. Ratner suggested that eighteenth-century music "developed a thesaurus of characteristic figures" which he termed topics.[10] These topical patterns, which evoked associations, contexts, and physical settings in the external world, became semiotic signifiers whose meaning was clear to a wide range of listeners. The prevalence of such patterns implies that eighteenth-century music was unified by a communicative ethos, in which composers courted listeners' understanding. This chapter investigates specifically

---

8   Eugene Bonner, "Opera in English: Paul Bunyan," *Monthly Musical Record* 2, no. 1 (1941), 12.
9   Chowrimootoo, *Middlebrow Modernism*.
10 Leonard G. Ratner, *Classic Music: Expression, Form, and Style* (New York: Schirmer, 1980), 9.

the relationship between Britten's use of topoi and the cultural phenomenon of the middlebrow, asking how these topical patterns contribute to the communicative ethos of Britten's style. Rather than dismissing Britten's musical language as stylistically disingenuous or overly market-oriented, as his critics did, I read Britten's use of topics as resisting modernism's claims of creative isolation. Close analysis of Britten's use of topics suggests that his eclectic style engages with codified semiotic patterns not just a calculated middlebrow attempt to appeal to a wider audience, but to create and express meaning.

The standard narrative of music history would have us believe that by Britten's time, the communicative ethos that characterized eighteenth-century music had become subjugated to a striving for newness. This reorientation was often depicted as a dramatic break from the style of previous eras, which has often been equated historiographically with tonal writing. For the music semiotician Eero Tarasti, for instance, modernism signified "the dissolution of the traditional tonality and transformation of the very foundations of tonal language, searching for new models in atonalism, polytonalism or other forms of altered tonality."[11] But a second ideal also underpinned conceptions of musical modernism: that works should be as autonomous, and as individual, as possible. Charles Wilson finds that "declarations of creative isolation were always the stock-in-trade of the modernist tradition, whether morbidly self-pitying in tone ([like in Schoenberg's] 'How One Becomes Lonely') or defiantly triumphalist ([as in Milton Babbitt's] 'Who Cares If You Listen?')."[12]

It is no exaggeration that modernists coveted listeners' indifference to a work, since widespread approval almost certainly indicated that the piece was not suitably avant-garde. In such a climate, public approval could sound a death knell for the credibility of a work as evidence of commitment to progress. A prime example of modernism's valuing of indifference can be found in a short 1919 essay by Alban Berg, which sets out the aims of his teacher Schoenberg's Vienna-based Society for Private Musical Performances. One of the society's rules was that "performances must be removed from the corrupting influence of publicity; that is, they must not be directed towards the winning of competitions

---

11   Eero Tarasti, *Myth and Music: A Semiotic Approach to the Aesthetics of Myth in Music, Especially That of Wagner, Sibelius and Stravinsky* (The Hague: Mouton, 1979), 272.

12   Charles Wilson, "György Ligeti and the Rhetoric of Autonomy," *Twentieth-Century Music* 1, no. 1 (July 2004), 5.

and must be unaccompanied by applause, or demonstrations of disapproval."[13] This suggests that even the opinion of a selected and highly discerning audience, as distinct from the public at large, was thought to have a corrupting influence. This climate encouraged Andreas Huyssen to comment in 1986 that "modernism constituted itself through a conscious strategy of exclusion, an anxiety of contamination by its other: an increasingly consuming and engulfing mass culture."[14] Against the backdrop of this aesthetic tradition, middlebrow works of art were unsurprisingly seen to be threatening, rather than merely distasteful. Clement Greenberg agreed, saying in 1948 that middlebrow culture "presents a more serious threat to the genuine article than the old-time pulp, dime-novel... unlike the latter, which has its social limits clearly marked out for it, middlebrow culture attacks distinctions as such and insinuates itself everywhere."[15] No wonder, then, that figures such as Woolf were so quick to denigrate those whose work they saw as middlebrow; for them, the introduction of avant-garde elements into works that simultaneously courted a wide audience was the worst of betrayals.

These two major aesthetic claims of musical modernism—that its style constituted a complete break from what came before, and that it required creative autonomy—have come to underpin much analysis of twentieth-century music. I wish to propose, however, that Britten, along with other post-tonal composers such as Copland, Shostakovich, and Hindemith, was labelled middlebrow precisely because much of his work drew upon the communicative ethos that Ratner has found in eighteenth-century repertoire. Such an ethos can also sometimes be observed in the work of twentieth-century composers who wrote in a neoclassicist idiom, such as Stravinsky and Prokofiev. Britten's stylistic language exhibits this communicative ethos largely by incorporating and developing some of the specific patterns that Ratner originally observed.

Since Ratner, other topic theorists have begun to trace the ways in which these patterns have been carried forward into later music. Kofi Agawu has provided a comprehensive book-length analysis of the use of topics in

---

13 Quoted in Nicolas Slominsky, ed., Stephen Somervelle, trans., *Music Since 1900*, 4th edition (New York: Charles Scribner's Sons, 1971), 1307.

14 Andreas Huyssen, *After the Great Divide: Modernism, Mass Culture, and Postmodernism* (Bloomington: Indiana University Press, 1986), vii.

15 Clement Greenberg, "The State of American Writing" (1948), in *Arrogant Purpose, 1945–1949*, ed. John O'Brian (Chicago: University of Chicago Press, 1986), 257–58.

nineteenth-century music,[16] while scholars such as Wye J. Allanbrook, Robert S. Hatten, and Raymond Monelle have expanded the scope of topic theory in myriad other ways. The usage of topics in the twentieth century, however, has received patchy attention. The dictates of modernism, particularly that individual works should be autonomous, have undoubtedly played a role here. Analysts have often tacitly bought into the rhetoric of modernist composers, assuming that their language shares little with their peers or with composers of earlier eras.

I have chosen to focus on Britten's use of topics in a set of three late works: the Suites for Solo Cello, opuses 72, 80, and 87. Composed between 1964 and 1971, later in Britten's life, these works are rich in topical material: Britten draws heavily on musical patterns with a clear genealogy from those catalogued by Ratner. Furthermore, the titles of the suite's movements allude to topical material, and thus invite a topical reading. In *Classic Music*, Ratner originally proposed that topics appear as either *types* (fully worked-out pieces) or *styles* (figures and progressions within a piece).[17] Thus, a movement can be titled "March" and display march-like characteristics throughout; but equally a march topic can appear as a fleeting stretch of music that does not determine the character of the entire movement. While the titles of each movement suggest established characteristics of styles or genres, such as fugue, march, or chaconne, Britten does not restrict himself to either *types* or *styles* exclusively, drawing on both possibilities throughout. He uses topical material throughout these works, but I will focus on three movements: the Lamento and Marcia from the First Suite, and the Fantastico from the Third Suite.

The First Suite's second movement, the Lamento, draws on, adapts, and transforms signifying musical parameters from an established lament topic. The lament topic's most characteristic feature is its descending bass tetrachord, which generally uses either four diatonic steps (as in Caplin's example [a], shown in figure 1) or a chromatically expanded version thereof (as in example [b]).[18] In most usages of the topic, this bass pattern recurs throughout, so the topic has considerable crossover with the genres of chaconne and passacaglia.

---

16 V. Kofi Agawu, *Music as Discourse: Semiotic Adventures in Romantic Music* (New York: Oxford University Press, 2009).
17 Ratner, *Classic Music*, 9.
18 William E. Caplin, "Topics and Formal Functions: The Case of the Lament," in *The Oxford Handbook of Topic Theory*, ed. Danuta Mirka (Oxford: Oxford University Press, 2014), 417.

FIGURE 1. Caplin's two paradigms for the descending bass tetrachord of a lament.

For Caplin, the lament topic is reasonably unusual in its relationship to *galant* schemata. He finds that despite topics and schemata generally operating independently, the lament topic is "inextricably linked with a single schema."[19] The lament topic's connection with schema theory is pertinent here, since schemas usually comprise two voices, while topics have no such requirement. Therefore, the incorporation of the lament into a work for an instrument with limited polyphonic capabilities—the cello—requires special handling by the composer.

One reason that the lament topic does not necessarily conform to Robert Gjerdingen's conception of a schema is because the lament topic has an older pedigree than many of the other schemata he names.[20] As Ellen Rosand has shown, the descending minor tetrachord became almost exclusively associated with the lament in the fourth and fifth decades of the seventeenth century.[21] This schema is also unusual in that its sole defining feature is its descending stepwise bass line; it does not have a standard melodic component, unlike most schemata. Nonetheless, it is assumed that in most laments some kind of melody will be used over the ground bass. How, then, does Britten treat this schema in a work for solo cello, and how does this treatment compare with other instances of the lament topic in his output?

A small amount of work has already been done on Britten's use of the lament topic. Arnold Whittall holds that in general, the topic is held together by a rather loose set of associations, primarily bass lines that descend chromatically, and

---

19   Caplin, "The Case of the Lament," 416.
20   Whenever Caplin refers to galant schemata, he takes his lead from Robert O. Gjerdingen, *Music in the Galant Style* (New York: Oxford University Press, 2007).
21   Ellen Rosand, "The Descending Tetrachord: An Emblem of Lament," *Musical Quarterly* 65, no. 3 (1979): 246.

also melodic figures analogous to sighing or sobbing.[22] These figures strongly resemble the topic that Monelle has termed the *pianto*, a falling minor second that signifies the act of weeping. Whittall finds that Britten has made generic reference to the lament topic in similar ways in several different pieces, namely the "Lacrymosa" from the *Sinfonia da Requiem*, the "Dies Irae" from the *War Requiem*, and the movement at hand here, the "Lamento" from the First Cello Suite. Whittall's comparison of the three works is as follows:

Ex. a *Sinfonia da Requiem*, 'Lacrymosa', from 7 bars after Fig. 4 (cello line only)

Ex. b *War Requiem*, 'Dies irae', soprano solo, 5th bar after Fig. 54

Ex. c 'Lamento' from First Cello Suite (1965)

FIGURE 2. Melodic sighing in three Britten works, as identified by Whittall.

For Whittall, however, these references to a generic "lament" style are primarily motivic, and he tends to amalgamate the topic's recurring bass tetrachord with the kinds of sighing melodic figures that were often used over it. Thus he does not treat the topic as a two-voiced schema in the way that Caplin does. Since the focus of his article is *Owen Wingrave* and not any of the pieces in the example above, Whittall presents the three lament excerpts together without analyzing them in detail, so it is worth listing their similarities here. Each figure descends in pitch, features a falling third followed by a rising step, and contains either a dotted or an off-beat rhythm. A further similarity between the examples is the use of gap-filling: each instance of a descending pattern is interrupted by one upward step, which fills in the preceding skip.

---

22 Arnold Whittall, "Britten's Lament: The World of Owen Wingrave," *Music Analysis* 19, no. 2 (2000): 145.

While the first two features that Whittall covers—descending pitch and chromaticism—are clearly similar to the chromatic ground bass described in Caplin's version of the lament topic, the offbeat rhythms are more likely to be an idiomatic feature of Britten's language than of the topic as a whole. Since Whittall's reference to the First Suite is so brief, I offer a topical analysis of some parts of the movement here, to demonstrate the way Britten incorporates an established lament topic into his own language.

In general Britten's movement refers to the established practices of the lament pattern in a way that is oblique rather than overt. An immediate difficulty he encounters is that writing for an often-monophonic instrument, he must reconcile the two voices of the schema into a single line, so the cello frequently must imply recurring bass-line motion and melodic motion at the same time. As a result, the distinction between the two elements is often blurred, or almost imperceptible. Here, then, Britten's version of the topic tends to transform the ground bass falling tetrachord into a primarily melodic feature. The movement begins thus:

FIGURE 3. "Lamento" from the First Cello Suite, measures 1–3.

I would submit that the recurring bass line element of the topic is fulfilled by the falling E minor triad at the end of each bar, since it recurs identically and at pitch in each instance. In contrast, the material preceding each instance of the E minor triad can be seen to relate more closely to Whittall's *pianto*-like sigh figures. In these figures, the notes do not fall in order, but are interrupted by gap-filling, as if the lamenter is resisting the inevitable. Also, each individual phrase gets progressively longer as the opening goes on. In this way, Britten augments the topic's affect: it is as if the lamenter repeatedly attempts to overcome the sensation of grief, their efforts intensifying and lasting longer with each phrase. Try as they might, however, they are ultimately unsuccessful, and get sucked back down into the recurring E minor triad, which represents grief's doggedness. Thus, Britten creates a musically mimetic reading of the emotional contour of grief, rather than echoing audible features such as sighs or sobs.

It is worth noting that Britten pairs features of the lament topic with various secondary parameters that enhance the topic's semantic legibility. The sense of structure in this movement, like its intensity of expression, is largely derived from dynamics, register, and the varied length of the phrase units. Structurally, the movement can be split into three parts. The first, from measures 1 to 6, is dynamically soft and serves to introduce the lament topic. The second, from measures 7 to 16, inverts the descending pattern and builds upwards to a clear climax in measure 11. This inverted version of the descending line continues to use the E minor triad at the end of each bar, but adds another note to the figure each time:

FIGURE 4. "Lamento" from the First Cello Suite, measures 7–10.

After the extreme intensity of the climax, the last two lines of the movement ultimately bring the listener back down to earth, with the last four bars resembling the opening material. However, the register has shifted down an octave, perhaps suggesting that the lamenter finishes the movement in an even deeper emotional rut:

FIGURE 5. "Lamento" from the First Cello Suite, measures 11–16.

While drawing on some of the lament topic's short musical features, such as sighing motives, Britten also extends his sonic depiction of the experience of grief by tracing its ebb and flow on the larger timescale of the entire movement. This structure allows him to create a mimetic account of the way that grief tends to come in waves over a protracted period. He ultimately expands the scope of the topic's ability to signify, transforming the lament from a short motivic unit into a musical language that can signal meaning by various semiotic means along the stretch of a whole movement.

While the First Suite's Marcia movement adheres to some of the parameters ascribed to the march topic, it also augments the topic's arsenal of signifiers by setting them alongside various parameters from other topics and adds some musical signifiers that have topical implications but are not yet codified. Used in combination, this range of topics broadly evokes a sense of outdoor spaciousness. This is brought about by mixing several topics related to outdoor activity, infusing much of the movement with a general sense of music imported from elsewhere. The march topic has been surprisingly undertheorized, for several possible reasons. Firstly, since its usage predates the eighteenth century, it has been less discussed than topics that better exemplify eighteenth-century style, such as the pastoral style or various dance types. A further possible reason is that, as Monelle tells us, "even when no title is presented, it is easy to recognize the rhythm and sentiment of the march."[23] Therefore, theorists have all too often assumed that the characteristics of the march style are obvious and require no further analysis.

Analysts have therefore tended to refer freely to the march topic without examining its musical parameters in detail. Ratner's definition therefore remains the canonical one. For Ratner, the march topic's "natural habitats were the parade ground and battlefield, where its moderately quick duple meter, dotted rhythms, and bold manner quickened the spirit."[24] For our twentieth-century purposes, the dotted rhythm clearly belongs at the top of the hierarchy of recognition; as a short rhythmic cell with no particular harmonic or formal implications, it is easily transferable to just about any style of writing. Duple rhythm can be considered fundamentally important for an obvious mimetic reason: the emphatic alternation of left and right steps in the act of marching. However, in a post-tonal idiom this mimetic element can also be evoked simply by any repetitive use of alternation: it need not rely on a duple time signature.

A further point of interest regarding the march topic is its affect. For Ratner, the march represented authority, and especially "cavalier and manly virtues,"[25] but in fact the range of moods the topic has historically been used to evoke is much wider. As Monelle says, marches were used in contexts including

---

23   Monelle, *The Musical Topic*, 113.
24   Ratner, *Classic Music*, 16.
25   Ibid.

weddings, funerals, baptisms, events at court, balls and other dances, as well as various military settings.[26] This history reaches back much farther than the eighteenth century. Monelle contends that the earliest documented use of a march in art music is probably that in the Egerton Manuscript, which dates from about 1590. Even in very early examples of the topic, such as William Byrd's collection of marches for the harpsichord, a range of contexts is evident: Byrd includes marches of footmen, horsemen, the Irish, and the fight, among others.[27] Since the canonical parameters of this topic are almost exclusively rhythmic, it is capable of evoking a wide range of affects and can easily take on an individual composer's stylistic language while retaining its identity. How then does Britten put his stamp on the topic, and what types of affect does his version create?

The movement opens with sparse, bare fifths played on natural harmonics. At the end of the first measure, Britten adds a C♯, thus transforming the fifths into a triad:

FIGURE 6. "Marcia" from the First Cello Suite, measure 1.

I contend that this opening measure, while not drawing on a well-codified topic, is evoking a distant brass call. Traditionally, the established horn call topic has been thought of as encompassing a particular set of descending intervals sounded between two voices: a third, a fifth, and a six.[28] However, Monelle has traced the historical evolution of practical horn calls and has found two distinct historical periods. In the first period, the hunting horn's third register was generally used, so only triadic calls were possible, whereas in the second period the

---

26 Monelle, *The Musical Topic*, 126.
27 Ibid.
28 Ratner includes this musical pattern in the topic he calls Military and Hunt Music, but the throughout the literature this pattern is often referred to simply as a "horn call" topic. See *Classic Music*, 18.

instrument's fourth register became standard, allowing diatonic writing.[29] The four registers are as follows:[30]

FIGURE 7. The four registers of the hunting horn, according to Monelle

Britten's triadic horn call evokes the first of these two historical periods. Here its natural harmonic timbre and *pianissimo* dynamic build a sense of outdoor spaciousness into the topic, as if we are hearing the music float into our ears from afar. Britten's version of the topic thus seems to incorporate some affective elements of the pastoral, rather than evoking a bold, military affect. This is a departure from the topic's generalized affect, which tends to be associated with powerful or noble modes of expression.

The second measure quickly moves on to a contrasting military topic, which here uses the lowest part of the cello's register and a completely different timbral color in the form of *col legno* bowing. Topically, the most important element of the second measure is its rhythm. According to Monelle, there is a straightforward musical formula for evoking a cultural idea of the soldier, or a military affect more broadly. This formula has two elements: the use of notes of the harmonic series, in conjunction with a rhythmic cell that evokes double- or triple-tongued brass playing, with two short notes followed by one longer note.[31] This formula is highly recognizable in many works, the off-stage trumpet solo in Beethoven's *Leonore* Overture no. 3 and the fanfare leading into the final section of Rossini's *William Tell* Overture being prominent examples. Britten clearly follows this formula, drawing on his already-established open fifths and adding the distinctive military rhythmic cell in a much lower, more ominous register. Here, Britten's usage is rather sinister, especially juxtaposed with the first measure; this use of the topic could be read as critiquing the idea of military valor rather than glorifying it.

---

29   Monelle, *The Musical Topic*, 43.
30   Ibid., 44.
31   Ibid., 166.

FIGURE 8. "Marcia" from the First Cello Suite, measure 2.

While this movement clearly invokes elements of established topics, these topical references are not the movement's only instruments of signification. Britten also draws on a range of supplementary features to help communicate semiotic significance the topical elements. The *col legno* bow stroke, for instance, has its own longstanding semiotic tradition, which over time has become codified. There is a remarkable consistency in the contexts in which it has been used, considering that they precede the eighteenth-century origins of many topics and persist well beyond the eighteenth century. An early example is Biber's *Battalia à 10* (1673), which offers a quasi-pictorial description of the elements of battle and uses *col legno* among an arsenal of extended techniques in service of this goal. Another obvious use of *col legno* in a military or warlike context, presumably much more present in the minds of mid-twentieth-century English audiences, is Holst's "Mars, the Bringer of War" from *The Planets*. Here, *col legno* is used in combination with an irregular time signature and chromatic motion to evoke the Roman god of war. One famous instance of *col legno* would seem to depart from this military theme: the final movement of Berlioz's *Symphonie Fantastique*, which uses the technique very late in the fifth movement. Here, it evokes the grotesque character of the witches' sabbath, but the movement's allusion to death via the Dies Irae theme (complete with offstage tubular bells) has at least some crossover with a military theme. In Britten's movement, then, the use of this timbre contributes substantially to our aural recognition of the topic and enriches our understanding of what it signifies.

From measure 10 onwards we hear, for the first time, a march theme proper:

FIGURE 9. "Marcia" from the First Cello Suite, measures 10–11.

The dotted rhythm that Britten employs is a familiar evocation of a march, cited by both Monelle and Ratner as characteristic of this topic. However, here Britten also draws on the simple mimetic aspect of a march topic, whereby musical material mimics the systematic, rhythmic, emphatic alternating of steps. Though they are not thinking in a specifically topical sense, Erich Schwandt and Andrew Lamb have hit upon an element of this rhythmical aspect of the march, without quite noticing its mimetic quality: they characterize the march topic as exhibiting "strong repetitive rhythms and an uncomplicated style."[32] Britten calls upon this quality without using a regular number of beats in each measure, since irregular meter is part of the basic language of the suites, but he still manages to get this mimetic aspect of the topic across clearly.

In the Third Suite's seventh movement, the Fantastico, Britten draws upon certain vestiges of the *ombra* style. Ratner locates the roots of *ombra* in the fantasia style, which is marked by "elaborate figuration, shifting harmonies, chromatic conjunct bass lines, sudden contrasts, full textures or disembodied melodic figures—in short, a sense of improvisation and loose structural links between figures and phrases."[33] The *ombra* effect, Ratner tells us, was used specifically in the domain of eighteenth-century opera[34] to evoke the supernatural, ghosts, the gods, moral values, and punishments, engendering a sense of awe and terror in the listener. Ratner's list of musical parameters for this topic is strikingly nonspecific compared with those he gives for many other topics. "Sudden contrasts," for instance, could refer to just about any musical element one could care to name; in any case, eighteenth-century style tends to exhibit a regularity of contrast more generally. Some of Ratner's other specifications, such as "disembodied melodic figures," give the analyst an abstract, general sense of the *ombra*'s mood, but fail to produce a framework for confident topical recognition.

There is a fairly straightforward explanation for this lack of specificity. While the *ombra* topic portrays ideas that are "real" in the sense that they are cultural constructions with a shared, collective meaning, there is no cultural setting (musical or otherwise) from which they derive. Unlike a march or a gavotte, the

---

32   Erich Schwandt and Andrew Lamb. "March," in *Grove Music Online* (Oxford University Press, 2001), https://doi-org.ezproxy.auckland.ac.nz/10.1093/gmo/9781561592630.article.40080.

33   Ratner, *Classic Music*, 24.

34   Clive McClelland has completed a book-length study on the use of *ombra* in eighteenth-century opera, though the signified elements that he finds in the topic are similar to those of Ratner. See Clive McClelland, *Ombra: Supernatural Music in the Eighteenth Century* (Lanham: Lexington Books, 2012).

supernatural has no musical language of its own. The topic is therefore a further exception to Mirka's principle of importation: its musical style aims to evoke emotional states associated with what it signifies, rather than the character of the signified itself. Frymoyer observes that the *ombra* topic "is remarkable, for unlike many topics built on the abstraction of sounds of 'everyday life', [it] is a purely introversive sign that signifies through the sonic imagination of composers, invoking the supernatural through metonymic—rather than mimetic—means."[35] Frymoyer's phrase "sonic imagination of composers" suggests that this topic might be particularly susceptible to filtration through the idiolect of individual composers, since metonymic interpretation leads to a more varied range of musical parameters than mimetic interpretation.

Despite the *ombra* style's lack of directly mimetic origins, a codified selection of musical signifiers has been added to the topic's arsenal between the eighteenth century and Britten's time. Dickensheets finds that in the nineteenth century, the topic is transformed into what she names the Demonic Style, which is marked by the minor mode, rising chromatic or otherwise altered scalar patterns in the lower register, passages of glissandi, and the frequent use of augmented or diminished chords.[36] Britten's movement cleaves much more closely to this description, drawing on all of those features except for the minor mode.

Alongside the musical parameters noted by Dickensheets, one element of Ratner's definition also accounts for many of Britten's choices in this movement. Sudden contrasts, often of timbre but also of register and dynamic absolutely abound: *sul ponticello* playing, tremolo, glissandi, trills, portamenti, and artificial and natural harmonics all rub shoulders here. This wide range of colors is compacted into a short stretch of time, too: the movement has just twenty-eight measures, so the listener's impression is a fleeting one. All these timbral effects are heard between measures 12 and 19, for instance:

---

35 Johanna Frymoyer, "Rethinking the Sign: Stylistic Competency and Interpretation of Musical Textures, 1890–1920" (PhD diss., Princeton University, 2013), 110.
36 Janice Dickensheets, "The Topical Vocabulary of the Nineteenth Century," *Journal of Musicological Research* 31, nos. 2–3 (2012), 118.

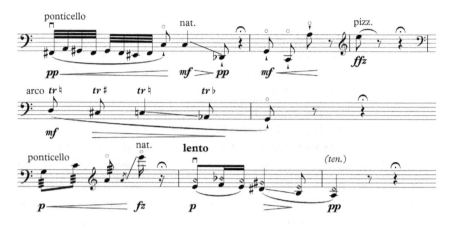

FIGURE 10. "Fantastico (recitativo)" from the Third Cello Suite, measures 12–19.

In the twentieth century, evocations of the supernatural found a particular stylistic vocabulary in Russian music. This relationship may explain Britten's inclusion of the *ombra* topic in the Russian-inflected Third Suite, but not in either of the first two Suites. Richard Taruskin finds that the main marker of a supernatural topic in the Russian music of the early twentieth century was the use of nonstandard scales, and particularly the octatonic scale. In an exploration of the music of Stravinsky, Taruskin posits a habit of "differentiating the human and fantastic worlds by contrast between diatonic and chromatic harmony, the chromatic/fantastic being of a third-related kind (whole-tone or octatonic) to play off against the fifth relations of the human music."[37]

Britten's interpretation of the topic employs such short bursts of melody, in such a restricted range, that it is almost impossible to say definitively whether he draws upon octatonic color. However, some of these fragmented units draw on the octatonic principle of alternating tones with semitones, as in this short segment in measure 2:

FIGURE 11. "Fantastico (recitativo)" from the Third Cello Suite, measure 2.

---

37 Richard Taruskin, "Chernomor to Kashchei: Harmonic Sorcery; Or, Stravinsky's 'Angle,'" *Journal of the American Musicological Society* 38, no. 1 (1985): 103.

For the octatonic principle to work properly here, the listener must mentally supply the missing step in the scale pattern, which here is C natural, to call up the descending octatonic sequence: Db–C–Bb–A–G.

This short scalar excerpt is also governed by a tritone, which Britten returns to later in the movement. While the tritone's immediate impression is of resistance to the standard major or minor scale, it also has a long-standing demonic association which derives from music much earlier than the nineteenth or twentieth centuries. While this is a separate concern from the octatonic tendencies observed by Taruskin, the tritone's usage clearly contributes to the overall topical effect, as at measure 7:

FIGURE 12. "Fantastico (recitativo)" from the Third Cello Suite, measure 7.

Indeed, this bar bears some resemblance to the tritone articulated by the celli and basses at the opening of the fifth movement of Berlioz's *Symphonie Fantastique*, which also follows the octatonic pattern mentioned by Taruskin:

FIGURE 13. "Songe d'une Nuit du Sabbat" from Berlioz's *Symphonie Fantastique*, measure 1.

Dickensheets notes that in the nineteenth century, these rising scalar patterns become associated with the celli and basses because they are the instruments best equipped to mimic "specters arising out of the deep."[38] Britten picks up on this pattern and takes it to new heights in measures

---

38 Dickensheets, "Topical Vocabulary": 118.

10 and 11. Instead of restricting the register of the pattern, as Berlioz does, Britten extends it across most of the cello's range, using very short note values to exaggerate the effect:

FIGURE 14. "Fantastico (recitativo)" from the Third Cello Suite, measures 10–11.

Another of Dickensheets's insights is that in nineteenth-century music, the demonic style is often enhanced by symbolic use of elements from sacred music, such as plainchant or chorales. Positioned among signifiers of ghostly and supernatural affects, these elements "are destabilized by the surrounding musical gestures, which, in effect, invert their sanctity."[39] Once again, the fifth movement of *Symphonie Fantastique* provides the archetypical example: partway through the movement, the low brass sound the Dies Irae, initially as a single line of plainchant and then subsequently in chorale style. While Britten does not explicitly utilize a sacred symbol in this movement, the first strains of the Kontakion will appear for the first time at the beginning of the ninth movement. Since the suite as a whole operates as a kind of theme and variations in reverse, the Kontakion could therefore be said to retrospectively contribute to the articulation of the *ombra* topic.

Another possibly Russian element in this movement is a reference to his friend and colleague Shostakovich. Arnold Whittall has proposed that in this suite, Britten frequently alludes to Shostakovich's DSCH cryptogram.[40] To this suggestion, I would add that in this movement, Britten has also repeatedly employed a rhythmic cell which is a hallmark of Shostakovich's style. It is the anapestic figure that we hear from measure 20 onwards:

FIGURE 15. "Fantastico (recitativo)" from the Third Cello Suite, measures 20–21.

---

39 Ibid.: 120.
40 Arnold Whittall, "Britten's Rhetoric of Resistance: The Works for Rostropovich," in *Rethinking Britten*, ed. Philip Rupprecht (New York: Oxford University Press, 2013), 181.

Although here rendered as long-short-short rather than the usual short-short-long, this effect is clearly recognizable as a rhythm to which Shostakovich returns again and again. In fact, one could argue that this figure is linked not only to Shostakovich but also to his cello writing specifically, since the figure always appears right after an instance of the DSCH cipher in Shostakovich's Cello Concerto no. 1. This rhythm is also clearly derived and excerpted from the third folk song quoted at the end of the suite, titled "Street song—the grey eagle":

FIGURE 16. "Street Song—The Grey Eagle", excerpted from "Passacaglia: Lento solenne", from the Third Cello Suite.

In combination, these two references to Russia strengthen the *ombra* topic, and expand its scope to include some elements of Britten's own stylistic language.

One topical element of this movement I have not yet touched on is the second, parenthetical stylistic designation in the title: Recitativo. Since the main musical function of a recitativo is to mimic the sound of speech, I find this designation an odd one. Recitative is typically accompanied, and therefore the idea is not well aligned with a monophonic movement like this one. It is also typically rather arhythmical; however, many movements of the suites are without regular pulse, and so this movement does not stand out in this respect, either. The only real musical similarity in evidence is that the speechlike construction of recitatives mean that their phrase units are typically delivered in short bursts, and this is indeed how Britten treats phrasing in this movement. It is also possible that Britten intends the movement to function in the same way as a recitative on a large scale: by supplying a sense of contrast and some breathing space between two more musically involved movements such as arias. But in general this recitativo designation is a rare topical descriptor that does not readily come through in Britten's writing.

It is apparent by now that the suites are replete with topical material. Britten's use of topics shows that he had not in fact "adjusted to mass culture by means of calculated feeble-mindedness" but had made a deliberate artistic decision to draw on established modes of musical communication. The communicative ethos that underpins such a choice shows that rather than surrendering his agency, Britten actively resisted the creative isolationism of many mid-century composers.

Bibliography

Agawu, V. Kofi. *Music as Discourse*. New York: Oxford University Press, 2009.

Berlioz, Hector. *New Edition of the Complete Works*. Vol. 16. Edited by Nicholas Temperley. Kassel: Bärenreiter-Verlag, 1971.

Bonner, Eugene. "Opera in English: *Paul Bunyan.*" *Monthly Musical Record* 2, no. 1 (1941): 12.

Britten, Benjamin. *Suite for Cello*, Op. 72. London: Faber Music Ltd., 1966.

———. *Third Suite for Cello*, Op. 87. London: Faber Music Ltd., 1976.

Brown, Erica, and Grover, Mary, eds. *Literary Cultures: The Battle of the Brows, 1920–1960*. London: Palgrave Macmillan, 2011.

Caplin, William E. "Topics and Formal Functions: The Case of the Lament." In *The Oxford Handbook of Topic Theory*, edited by Danuta Mirka, 415–452. New York: Oxford University Press, 2014.

Chowrimootoo, Christopher. *Middlebrow Modernism: Britten's Operas and the Great Divide*. Oakland: University of California Press, 2019.

Dickensheets, Janice. "The Topical Vocabulary of the Nineteenth Century." *Journal of Musicological Research* 31, nos. 2–3 (2012): 97–137.

Frymoyer, Johanna. "Rethinking the Sign: Stylistic Competency and Interpretation of Musical Textures, 1890–1920. PhD diss., Princeton University, 2013.

Gjerdingen, Robert O. *Music in the Galant Style*. New York: Oxford University Press, 2007.

Greenberg, Clement. "The State of American Writing." In *Arrogant Purpose, 1945–1949*, edited by John O'Brian, 254–258. Chicago: University of Chicago Press, 1986.

Huyssen, Andreas. *After the Great Divide: Modernism, Mass Culture, Postmodernism*. Bloomington: Indiana University Press, 1986.

McClelland, Clive. *Ombra: Supernatural Music in the Eighteenth Century*. Lanham: Lexington Books, 2012.

"The Middlebrow." *Punch*, no, 169 (December 23, 1925), 673.

Monelle, Raymond. *The Musical Topic: Hunt, Military, and Pastoral*. Bloomington: Indiana University Press, 2006.

Priestley, John Boynton. "Tell Us More about These Authors." *Evening Standard*, October 13, 1932.

———. "To a High-Brow." BBC Written Archives, October 17, 1932. Reprinted in *John O'London's Weekly*, December 3, 1932.

Ratner, Leonard G. *Classic Music: Expression, Form, and Style*. New York: Schirmer, 1980.

Rosand, Ellen. "The Descending Tetrachord: An Emblem of Lament." *Musical Quarterly* 65, no. 3 (1979): 346–359.

Schwandt, Erich, and Andrew Lamb. "March." In *Grove Music Online*. Oxford University Press, 2001. https://www.oxfordmusiconline.com/grovemusic.

Slominsky, Nicholas, ed. *Music Since 1900*, 4th ed. New York: Charles Scribner's Sons, 1971.

Tarasti, Eero. *Myth and Music: A Semiotic Approach to the Aesthetics of Myth in Music, Especially That of Wagner, Sibelius and Stravinsky*. The Hague: Mouton, 1979.

Taruskin, Richard. "Chernomor to Kashchei: Harmonic Sorcery; Or, Stravinsky's 'AnO gle.'" *Journal of the American Musicological Society* 38, no. 1 (1985): 72–142.

Thomson, Virgil. "Musico-Theatrical Flop." *New York Herald Tribune*, 6 May 1941.

Whittall, Arnold. "Britten's Lament: The World of *Owen Wingrave*." *Music Analysis* 19, no. 2 (2000): 145–166.

———. "Brittten's Rhetoric of Resistance: The Works for Rostropovich." In *Rethinking Britten*, edited by Philip Rupprecht, 181–205. New York: Oxford University Press, 2013.

Wilson, Charles. "György Ligeti and the Rhetoric of Autonomy." *Twentieth-Century Music* 1, no. 1 (2004): 5–28.

Woolf, Virginia. *The Death of the Moth and Other Essays*. 5th edition. London: Hogarth Press, 1947.

Provincializing Practice: Agency and Positionality in Cross-Cultural Music in Aotearoa New Zealand

Celeste Oram

In 1946, New Zealand composer Douglas Lilburn delivered his famous lecture "The Search for Tradition." It was penned and received as a manifesto for a postwar musical modernity in New Zealand that sloughed off European influence and sought out "endemic" musical utterances. In a passage that has since been quoted with almost sacramental frequency, Lilburn describes a scenic train journey through Tongariro National Park:

> I was so excited... that I hung out of the door of the carriage as we came from National Park down to Raurimu at the foot of the Spiral. There was something very strange about that experience of speeding through the night with the vivid night smell of the bush country all around me. At that moment the world that Mozart lived in seemed about as remote as the moon, and in no way related to my experience.[1]

By contrast, New Zealand composer Robin Maconie (a generation younger than Lilburn) opens his essay "On the Prehistory of New Zealand Music" with Mozart, as a boy. The scene: London, 1764, where Daines Barrington, a fellow of the Royal Society, is systematically asking the seven-year-old wunderkind to put his improvisational fluency to work in expressing through music "a range of classic emotions such as rage, fear, hope, and joy."[2] Undergirding Barrington's

---

1   Douglas Lilburn, *A Search for Tradition & a Search for Language* (Wellington: Victoria University Press, 2011), 20.
2   Robin Maconie, "On the Prehistory of Music in New Zealand," *Musical Times* 151, no. 1910 (2010): 23.

examination is an interest in determining what these "essential" human impulses might sound like coming from a genius child, dazzlingly eloquent yet relatively "uncontaminated by adult learning."[3] Presumably Mozart Senior did not spoil Barrington's fun by letting on that, in fact, Junior had already had a considerable amount of learning stuffed into him. From here, Maconie jump-cuts through episodes in which other eighteenth-century European philosophers and scientists similarly probed the capacity of music to express "universal emotional states and temperaments."[4] Maconie then pivots back to the Royal Society, where James Cook's first Pacific voyage is being planned. "Protocols of engagement" are being drawn up for interactions with the Pacific peoples Cook is expected to meet and subsequently establish economic and political ties with. Deciphering Pacific languages was a key concern: the lessons to be learned from music were "considered essential for interpreting natural temperament and state of mind from the gestures and modes of oral communication and alien speech."[5] Barrington's reports on the expressive facility of a child prodigy from Salzburg, along with prevailing beliefs about music's agency, fed into a broader project: preparing for the negotiations of cultural difference in the process of colonial expansion—and thus the establishment of New Zealand the settler-nation state.

These snippets from two Pākehā/settler composers emblemize two different approaches to thinking about musical agency in New Zealand. Lilburn, representing one approach, hedges his affiliations with the metropole by seeking deliberate expression of New Zealand's cultural exceptionalism. However, as literature scholar Susan Najita observes, cultural constructions of settler identity as independent of its imperial past depend on and reinforce "the exclusion or repression of certain aspects of that past."[6] By contrast, Maconie begins his "prehistory of New Zealand music" firmly in Europe—and a bygone Europe at that, five years before Cook's first voyage. Thus he raises the question of how musical agents have activated intellectual and political resources to rationalize the colonial occupation of Aotearoa, historically and in the present day. Even if the world

---

3   Ibid.
4   Ibid.
5   Ibid.: 24.
6   Susan Najita, "Resemblances and Complicity: The Construction of Pakeha History in 'The Piano,'" in *Complicities: Connections & Divisions: Perspectives on Literatures and Cultures of the Asia-Pacific Region*, ed. Chitra Sankaran, Rajeev Patke, and Liew Geok Leong (New York: Peter Lang, 2003), 83.

of Mozart seemed to Lilburn as remote as the moon, it is surely a moon that still governs the tides.

Such long views of cultural history have proved instructive for understanding my own agency as a Pākehā/settler composer, and thus a cultural contributor in Aotearoa New Zealand. In this chapter I survey some critical tools I have found useful in situating the musical practices and environments in which I participate. In particular I focus on the fast-growing genre of concert music in New Zealand involving classically trained musicians performing with practitioners of taonga pūoro, a term referring to precolonial Māori musical instruments and practices, in the context of their revival and contemporary innovation.

My discussion is limited to just one facet of contemporary taonga pūoro practice: in concert settings, together with Western musical instruments and practices. This is a well-established genre in New Zealand music; as a case in point, "taonga pūoro" is now a category in the catalogue of SOUNZ (the Centre for New Zealand Music), alongside, for instance, "orchestra," "choral music," or "jazz." Later in this chapter I unpack the apparent ease with which taonga pūoro has been adopted into the concert music setting. But it is important to note the vitality of taonga pūoro practices extending far beyond this setting. Taonga pūoro practitioners are equally active in free and experimental improvisation; in electronic music, in contemporary Māori waiata and in composer-scholar Te Ahukaramū Charles Royal's revivals of the Whare Tapere (precolonial Māori spaces for entertainment, games, and community gathering). They are also active in music for dance and theatre; in traditional, nonperformance contexts such as therapeutic and spiritual practices, and education; and in music for film, television, and advertising (where existing recordings of taonga pūoro are frequently used without the requisite permissions). Valance Smith, Awhina Tamarapa, and Ariana Tikao have published valuable commentary on the landscape of taonga pūoro practices in relation to Māori cultural revival generally.[7]

While my own creative work in taonga pūoro/classical collaborations, (with taonga pūoro practitioner Rob Thorne) has required me to learn about taonga pūoro, it has equally compelled me to deepen my critical engagement with the Eurological cultures whose influence I regularly negotiate in this

---

[7] See Valance Smith, "Whāia te Māramatanga: The Search for Enlightenment" and Awhina Tamarapa and Ariana Tikao, "Mai te Pō, ki te Ao: The reclamation of Taonga Puoro as a Living Treasure," both in *Searches for Tradition: Essays on New Zealand Music, Past and Present*, ed. Michael Brown and Samantha Owens (Wellington: Victoria University Press, 2017).

settler society.[8] This critical engagement, I argue, is akin to what composer-scholar Sandeep Bhagwati seeks in calling for us to "provincialize" hegemonic cultures: to recognize (rather than to ignore or make invisible) the particular conditions that produce cultural norms.[9] This means tracing the historical factors that variously influence, enable, and inhibit the agency of contemporary musicians. In using the term "provincial," Bhagwati does not invoke its pejorative sense of narrow-minded parochialism. Rather, drawing from postcolonial historian Dipesh Chakrabarty,[10] Bhagwati defines "provincializing" as looking at "everything that you think is central and dominant—and rethink[ing] it as one of many possibilities." This does not mean, Bhagwati goes on to say, "abolishing or despising your own tradition—just coming to the insight that it is but one of many traditions, and that what we think of as the norm . . . is in truth only the product of particular contexts. A change in these contexts might require us to change our opinion."[11]

I see the task of "provincializing" as building on the substantial global project amongst music scholars and practitioners of recognizing the various symbioses between Eurological musical practices and European imperialism.[12] Edward Said argues that the "affiliations" between aesthetic forms and their socio-political agency can easily be forgotten, or deliberately obscured. Making these affiliations "explicit and even dramatic" is, according to Said, a precondition for any

---

8 I adopt the term "Eurological" from composer-scholar George Lewis for its framing of social and cultural practices as "historically emergent, rather than ethnically essential or geographically bounded." George Lewis, "Improvised Music after 1950: Afrological and Eurological Perspectives," *Black Music Research Journal* 22 (2002): 93.

9 Sandeep Bhagwati, 'Curating Musicking as a Mode of Wakefulness in Interesting Times,' Akademie der Künste, YouTube video, 1:00:25, October 15, 2020, https://www.youtube.com/watch?v=NAZ3Cpn8mK8.

10 See Dipesh Chakrabarty, *Provincializing Europe: Postcolonial Thought and Historical Difference* (Princeton: Princeton University Press, 2000).

11 Bhagwati, "Curating Musicking as a Mode of Wakefulness in Interesting Times."

12 See Georgina Born and David Hesmondhalgh, *Western Music and Its Others: Difference, Representation, and Appropriation in Music* (Berkeley: University of California Press, 2007); Loren Kajikawa, "The Possessive Investment in Classical Music: Confronting Legacies of White Supremacy in U. S. Schools and Departments of Music," in *Seeing Race Again: Countering Colorblindness across the Disciplines*, ed. Kimberlé Williams Crenshaw et al. (University of California Press, 2019); George E. Lewis, *A Power Stronger than Itself: The AACM and American Experimental Music* (Chicago: University of Chicago Press, 2008); Timothy D. Taylor, *Beyond Exoticism: Western Music and the World* (Durham: Duke University Press, 2007).

transformation of the balance of agential power.[13] I likewise argue the necessity of recognizing the full extent of the cultural genealogies shaping current creative practice—rather than treating colonial disjunctions as a trail gone cold.

This chapter addresses two main subjects of historical analysis and considers their bearing on the agency of contemporary musicians. One is the continuing legacy of Enlightenment thought, especially its intellectual convergence in the latter half of the eighteenth century with colonial voyaging—and specifically with the Pacific expeditions of James Cook. Drawing from Vanessa Agnew's cultural studies scholarship, I consider the persistence in contemporary musical discourse of the Enlightenment's Orphic rhetoric about music's agential power to negotiate difference and to circumscribe communities. Second, I consider the enduring tenets of Eurological musical modernisms in New Zealand contemporary art music and relate them to Dylan Robinson's critical appraisals of art music's "inclusionary" models for engaging with cultural difference. Particularly at stake here is the support of taonga pūoro practices—and the shaping of discourse around them—by institutions affiliated with the colonial state, which have a vested interest in imagining the kinds of "settler futurity" that Eve Tuck and K. Wayne Yang argue are "incommensurable" with decolonization.[14]

Ultimately, I stop short of making recommendations for collaborative practice, acknowledging the value of developing cross-disciplinary projects from the specific terms of their particular participants, contexts, and constitutive relationships. Nor do I refer to specific musical works or performances, or presume to analyze their efficacy as cross-cultural works. One reason for not doing so is to avoid prematurely canonizing a still-nascent artistic field. Moreover, it is unfair for an outsider to judge a given creative project whose in situ relationship-building might have a value separate from what is visible and audible in a musical performance. Rather, I hope the historical contexts set out in this chapter have value as models for Eurologically trained musicians (like myself) seeking to critically appraise the cultural lineages of their practices, language, thinking, and decisions, and thus define their complex and compromised position as postcolonial agents.

---

13   Edward Said, *Power, Politics, and Culture: Interviews with Edward W. Said*, ed. Gauri Viswanathan (New York: Vintage, 2001), 336.
14   Eve Tuck and K. Wayne Yang, "Decolonisation is not a Metaphor," *Decolonization: Indigeneity, Education & Society* 1, no. 1 (2012): 14, 31.

Orphic Agencies:
Enlightenment and the Colonial Voyage

The popular attention of Europeans in the later eighteenth century was gripped by the "South Seas." The profits of colonial voyaging were not only economic and political, but also imaginative. Robin Maconie's "prehistory" of New Zealand music elaborates on many connections between European high art and colonial voyaging in the Pacific. A crucial figure in this nexus is Georg Forster, the teenage son of Johann Reinhold Forster, the German naturalist engaged to replace Joseph Banks on Cook's second Pacific voyage. As Maconie narrates it,

> Georg Forster's reputation as a new age advocate who had actually encountered Māori and witnessed the haka being performed on the deck of the *Resolution* endeared him to an intellectual elite including Goethe, Herder, and readers of his books and translations. During the 1780s he was a guest in Vienna of Countess Wilhelmine . . . [daughter-in-law] of Mozart's patron in Linz, and eventual patroness of Beethoven. Around 1785 Forster was inducted into the same Masonic Lodge, "Zur Wohltätigkeit", as [Mozart]. . . . Forster's fame spread throughout Europe, as far east as the Ukraine. His translations [which included Cook's diaries and other travelogues] are mentioned in Beethoven's notebooks. The slow movement theme of the Seventh Symphony is cited by Johannes Andersen as a lament modelled on Māori chant. Listening to the repetitive stamping rhythms of the *Coriolan* overture, it is not hard to visualise a red-faced Forster demonstrating the haka in front of a slightly apprehensive salon gathering in Paris or Prague.[15]

Maconie also points out the remarkable similarity between Papageno's costume in the original production of *The Magic Flute*—a fully feathered costume, with feathers also in his hair—and Sydney Parkinson's 1773 sketch of "A New Zealand Warrior in his Proper Dress."[16] Perhaps news had reached Vienna of Omai, a man from Ra'iatea who in 1773 hitched a ride to London on the HMS *Adventure*, and became the subject of an eponymous operetta at Covent Garden. Omai's portrait by Sir Joshua Reynolds remains on display in London's National Gallery as a reminder that European intellectual and cultural currents have long been influenced by interactions with Pacific cultures. If, like Maconie, we entertain the resemblance between Papageno and Parkinson's sketch, we might then

---

15 Maconie, "On the Prehistory of New Zealand Music": 27.
16 Ibid.

consider *The Magic Flute* to be (despite time and distance) of a piece with more recent "New Zealand" music—the operas of Alfred Hill, perhaps, or even contemporary musical works by Pākehā composers on Māori subjects—the common thread being their aesthetic expression of how Eurological world views have negotiated, and been shaped by, interactions with Pacific Indigeneity. As literature and Indigenous studies scholar Alice Te Punga Somerville asserts, the Pacific "is not a colonial place that things happen to: it is a place that makes things happen."[17]

Maconie traces a "prehistory" of "biculturalism"—in the abstract sense of ways two cultures might productively co-exist—in the various "protocols of encounter" drawn up by the Royal Society to guide the behavior of Cook and his crew in dealing with Pacific peoples.[18] Recall Daines Barrington, examining young Mozart's musical paraphrases of, for instance, "rage" versus "hope." Then consider the recommendations to Cook by Lord Morton, one of the voyage's financiers, that the Indigenous people they encounter "should not at first be alarmed with the report of Guns, Drums, or even a trumpet.... But if there are other Instruments of Music on board they should be first entertained near the Shore with a soft Air."[19] The role of music in political conciliation was thus cemented into understanding, in the "Enlightened" eighteenth century, of music's social utility.

Vanessa Agnew explores this utilitarian musical logic via the myth of Orpheus, which she describes as not only the "foundational, self-reflexive gesture for music scholarship in the late 18th century," but "arguably the most tenacious idea in the history of musical thought."[20] Orpheus, the musician-lover, plays his lyre so exquisitely that anybody or anything hearing it—animal, vegetable, or mineral—is entranced. Orpheus's music gets him past Charon, over the River Styx, and into the underworld in his attempt to rescue his beloved Eurydice. In this sense, Agnew underlines, "it was his music that rendered travel possible by overcoming natural obstacles, negotiating forbidden boundaries, taming beasts, and persuading gods."[21] Among all these far-flung encounters, Orpheus's "new

---

17 Ibid.: 26.
18 Ibid.: 23.
19 Quoted in Anne Salmond, *Two Worlds: First Meetings Between Maori and Europeans, 1642–1772* (Honolulu: University of Hawai'i Press, 1991), 113.
20 Vanessa Agnew, *Enlightenment Orpheus: The Power of Music in Other Worlds* (New York: Oxford University Press, 2008), 9, 7.
21 Ibid., 11.

listeners are the ones we remember him for—trees and plants, beasts, birds, rocks, and rivers,"[22] and even beyond-human beings. The Orphic myth therefore stands for the idea that efficacious social relationships—even those impossible by all other logics—can be made possible by the privileged medium of music.

It is Orphic logic, we might recall, which animates Mozart's *Magic Flute*: Tamino is promised, upon receiving the magic flute, that "with it you may act all-powerfully, and transform the passions of men."[23] And he does! The opera's dramaturgical agglomeration of kings, queens, lovers, servants, spirits, a (possibly Polynesian) bird-hunter and the "Moor" Monostatos relies on music to resolve social difference. Musicologist Rose Rosengard Subotnik argues that the heterogeneity of the *Magic Flute*'s social ranks is audible: its eclecticism of musical styles, which nevertheless cohere as satisfying music-theatre, "makes a persuasive claim that the unified world constructed within it is large enough for everyone and thereby establishes the opera as a powerful metaphor for a conception of a humanity bound by universal principles."[24] On account of this social optimism, the opera has been held up as a beacon of Enlightenment humanism, by thinkers from Kierkegaard to Einstein. This humanist ethos is also a persuasive a priori rationale for political structures founded on proposed "universal principles" that bind together a heterogeneous humanity: colonial empires, for instance, or democratic nation-states.

The colonial implications of Orphic rhetoric lie in the value it places on music to assist in efficiently and productively getting on with colonial affairs. In the Age of Enlightenment, cultural learning and exchange are valued for their enrichment of one's own social fluency, and thus one's powers of cross-cultural persuasion. After all, ultimately, it is Orpheus who draws his listeners to him. Orphic listening is a model "whereby others can be proximated to hegemonic society";[25] it is an ethic of belonging, Agnew notes, in which "music—more powerfully than blood or territory—is the mechanism for managing the boundaries of the societies in which we live."[26] In short, "the mere act of listening . . . is what qualifies the listener for membership."[27] In this way, Orphic listening is

---

22 Ibid., 9.
23 Author's translation.
24 Rose Rosenbard Subotnik, "Whose 'Magic Flute?' Intimations of Reality at the Gates of the Enlightenment," *19th-Century Music* 15, no. 2 (1991): 133.
25 Agnew, *Enlightenment Orpheus*, 9–10.
26 Ibid., 10.
27 Ibid., 9.

akin to what Diana Taylor terms a performative act of transfer; it transfers "the not-ours to the ours, translates the Other's systems of communication into ones we claim to understand."[28] Orphic listening is therefore deeply ambivalent: it powerfully facilitates belonging, but, as Dylan Robinson cautions, it can also engender a mis-audiation of belonging that covers over historical and political realities.[29]

Once, at a question time after a chamber music concert involving taonga pūoro, I heard a Pākehā musician speak of the collaboration as a way for two cultures to "take a few steps towards each other." This comment is understandably modest in its claim, and commendable in aspiring to a dynamic of mutuality but stopping short of insisting on it, and carefully limiting hopes and expectations. Habits of Orphic listening are indeed tenacious. And, given the colonial entanglements of Orphic listening, it is crucial for musicians to critically examine rhetoric around music's utility in "coming together." This is especially important where such rhetoric accompanies intercultural musicking supported by institutions affiliated with the settler state—and thus with the ongoing occupation of stolen land and majoritarian governance over Indigenous peoples. If one musical project can amount to "a few steps," the implicit endpoint of the trajectory remains unexplained. Would several more such musical projects bring those cultures face to face, or even fuse them? What then? What political reality do we imagine to lie at that asymptote?

To be sure, belief in music's capacity for facilitating cultural commingling does not stem only from Eurological thought. But, where musicians working from a kaupapa Māori perspective express an interest in music's conciliatory properties, their motives for doing so can differ notably from the settler's. Songwriter Tiki Taane has commented that in his album *With Strings Attached: Alive & Orchestrated*, involving members of the New Zealand Symphony Orchestra and of the kapa haka group Te Pou o Mangatāwhiri, the "orchestra represents the colonial, and the kapa haka represents the very traditional and indigenous aspect of my whakapapa. Bringing those two together is also something that I really try to do with my music—trying to bridge the gap between Māori and

---

28 Diana Taylor, *The Archive and the Repertoire: Performing Cultural Memory in the Americas* (Durham: Duke University Press, 2003), 54.
29 Dylan Robinson, *Hungry Listening: Resonant Theory for Indigenous Sound Studies* (Minneapolis: University of Minnesota Press, 2020), 13.

non-Māori. It's what I try to achieve with my music and art."[30] For Taane, the stated motive for cultural proximation is therefore less about cohesion of social identity than about cohesion of personal identity: about reconciling strands of one's own historically conflicted whakapapa as a means of self-actualization. In another example, taonga pūoro musician Horomona Horo spoke in a recent public talk of his journey to deepen his personal affinity with his English heritage (in parallel to his Māori whakapapa).[31]

I do not deny that music *does* have a remarkable capacity to offer its participants meaningful shared experiences. Indeed, in my own experience, building camaraderie through creativity is one of the great joys of being a musician. Moreover, scholar and taonga pūoro practitioner Rob Thorne argues that the taonga pūoro revival has come about precisely because of the practice's "ability to work laterally and experimentally with other sources and fields of knowledge and practice."[32] I argue that whenever music is deployed as a tool for cross-culturation, attending frankly to the aspirational differences between participants is crucial. Colonial and Enlightenment thought persist in endorsing the impulse to activate whatever genuinely empathetic powers music might have for their social utility, and their affirmation of "universal" principles that justify majoritarian systems of governance. By contrast, Taane and Horo—though their individual perspectives cannot be taken to represent a Māori consensus—expect different outcomes from music's conciliatory agency: self-understanding and the illumination of complex historical entanglements.

Having thus taken stock of motivations for engaging with taonga pūoro, a Eurologically trained musician might approach such collaborations as an opportunity to come to a more detailed and historically situated understanding of their own creative aspirations and affiliations. In doing so we might find surprising, and perhaps unsettling, affinities with the thinking of historical agents. Might Georg Forster, for instance, be an avatar of the Pākehā drawn to others' cultural knowledge by well-intentioned intellectual curiosity, whose own

---

30   Oli Wilson, "Tiki Taane's with Strings Attached: Alive & Orchestrated," in *Global Perspectives on Orchestras: Collective Creativity and Social Agency*, ed. Tina K. Ramnarine (Oxford: Oxford University Press, 2018), 246.

31   "Arts + Climate Innovation: Co-existence with Our Natural World." Public talk at the Auckland Arts Festival, Herald Theatre, Auckland, 14 March 2021.

32   Rob Thorne, "Jumping the Gap: The Distance between Taonga Pūoro and Experimental Music," *Soundbleed* (October 24, 2013), https://soundbleedjournal.wordpress.com/2013/10/24/jumping-the-gap-the-distance-between-taonga-puoro-and-experimental-music-rob-thorne/.

revolutionary political leanings are compromised by the approval their work wins from the imperial establishment, and who profits professionally and imaginatively from the continuing occupation of invaded territories?

Incommensurable Agencies: Modernism and the Settler State

It is worth pausing for thought on the remark by revivalists Richard Nunns and Allan Thomas that taonga pūoro's

> ubiquitous presence in New Zealand music is astonishing given their earlier decline. They have become a national musical icon played in virtually every musical circumstance including diplomatic and state occasions and also to audiences around the world in cultural exchanges, music festivals and concert tours.[33]

To expand on Nunns's and Thomas's synopsis, recent high-profile classical performances involving taonga pūoro have included concert works presented at international music festivals; works commissioned for civic events like grand openings or commemorations of war; works commissioned by major orchestras; works commissioned with government funding; and works awarded top prizes for contemporary music. Presenting concert pieces involving taonga pūoro is arguably a rite of passage for New Zealand composers and music organizations seeking to establish the national, canonic significance of their work.

Moreover, it is worth considering the conditions under which taonga pūoro have moved with apparent ease into contemporary art music specifically: that is, the aesthetic imperatives of musical modernism to seek out demonstrably new and, often, politically acute musical approaches. This pursuit of novelty serves to evidence narratives of cultural advancement and continuity (which, ironically, is preserved even through antithetical pressures and radical ruptures like that of the avant-garde). Pākehā composers have spoken of taonga pūoro and other (quite old) non-Western traditions as a "means of creating something new," or with the excitement of having "never heard anything like it." Yet if taonga pūoro sound "new," it is because colonization has disrupted the continuity and prevalence of the tradition; it is this disruption that the taonga pūoro revival is responding to.

---

33 Richard Nunns and Allan Thomas, "The Search for the Sound of the Pūtōrino: 'Me te wai e utuutu ana,'" *Yearbook for Traditional Music* 37 (2005): 69.

Rob Thorne notes that, as a result of centuries of warfare, social displacement, disease, Christian conversion, removal of taonga pūoro into museum collections, and the criminalization of Māori cultural practices, "taonga pūoro lacks a consistent, fixed body of instrumental musical learning . . . which a student can engage and study from the 'inside.'"[34] Meanwhile, the same historical factors that disrupted taonga pūoro traditions secured the continuity and proliferation of artforms affiliated with colonial Europe: Western cultural hegemonies were established globally in settler-colonial nations; cultural production was boosted by the gains of colonial expansion. It is therefore a troubling double bind for a composer (specifically, a non-Māori composer) to find creative enrichment in engaging taonga pūoro as an underexplored musical resource; the profits of the exercise are, in a sense, the dividends of colonial violence.

Dylan Robinson is a xwélmexw (Stó:lō) musician and scholar whose work offers valuable tools for critical discourse around musical performances in which classically oriented artists work together with artists in Indigenous traditions. Robinson writes from the position of an Indigenous scholar in Canada—a distinct Indigenous perspective which differs from Māori perspectives. However, Robinson's critique of Canadian nationalism has relevance in a New Zealand context, on account of Commonwealth cultural roots. Robinson questions the "ease" of eliding Indigenous cultural identifiers with identitarian narratives of the settler nation-state, asking "should we not feel some uneasiness with this ease? What are the ethics of coding Canadian values as the internalization of First Nations values . . . under the sign of inclusionary multiculturalism?"[35]

Extrapolating from Robinson's critique, it is important in a New Zealand context to keep in view the dissonances between, on the one hand, formations of national identity affiliated with the multicultural-yet-majoritarian settler state, and, on the other, the assertion of tino rangatiratanga (Māori sovereignty and self-determination) enshrined in Te Tiriti o Waitangi. Writing from a North American perspective, Eve Tuck and K. Wayne Yang, in their influential article "Decolonization is not a Metaphor," address the dissonance between the "progressive" aims of liberal democracy and absolute Indigenous sovereignty via an

---

34   Thorne, "Jumping the Gap."
35   Dylan Robinson, "Listening to the Politics of Aesthetics: Contemporary Encounters between First Nations/Inuit and Early Music Traditions," in *Aboriginal Music in Contemporary Canada: Echoes and Exchanges*, ed. A. Hoefnagels and B. Diamond (Montreal: McGill-Queen's University Press, 2012), 227.

"ethic of incommensurability."[36] Incommensurability "stands in contrast to the aims of reconciliation," which "is about rescuing settler normalcy, about rescuing a settler future.... To fully enact an ethic of incommensurability means relinquishing settler futurity, abandoning the hope that settlers may one day be commensurable to Native peoples."[37]

To apply this ethic to the metaphor cited for music's social utility: though two cultures might each "take a few steps" toward a viable cultural future, those steps might not, in fact, lead "towards each other." Artistic expressions that manifest a future for settler cultures are "incommensurable" with sovereign expressions of Indigenous cultural futures in this conception. And yet, there is a documented sense that taonga pūoro practices are being employed in New Zealand's contemporary classical music scene in a way that presents the cultural futures of each tradition as co-dependent and commensurable. By virtue of their unique signification of Aotearoa, taonga pūoro's presence in contemporary art music has—to apply another of Robinson's terms—"resourced" a way out of the modernist crisis of cultural identity that Lilburn diagnosed in 1946. Rather than scrounging around in European hand-me-downs, settler musicians have taken up taonga pūoro as a resource for establishing a New Zealand musical exceptionalism—for taonga pūoro is a resource on which New Zealand has a monopoly. But Robinson highlights the fallacy of the settler "hearing Indigenous subjectivity existing within an aural domain of 'home', a mis-audiation of Indigenous belonging within—or to—the settler state. Worse, it may guide the listener towards not only hearing belonging but toward naturalising a relationship of ownership."[38] Robinson cautions also against trying to solve this impasse via a modernist, "evolutionary notion ... where the composer needs to simply find new techniques and musical forms to better use the resources that Indigenous music provides."[39] It is not a fait accompli that a *musically satisfying* union of different cultural practices will model a *politically efficacious* cultural pluralism.

At this point I want to offer the caveat that Tuck's and Yang's "ethic of incommensurability" arises from an analysis grounded in uncompromising realpolitik which seeks to make clear distinctions between, on the one hand, the aims of progressivist social justice and critical methodologies, and on the other,

---

36 Tuck and Yang, "Decolonization Is Not a Metaphor": 28.
37 Ibid.: 36.
38 Dylan Robinson, *Hungry Listening*, 13.
39 Ibid.

the aims of decolonization, which "specifically requires the repatriation of Indigenous land and life" to the exclusion of any other metaphorical instantiation.[40] I therefore acknowledge the theoretical leap in applying such a resolutely political analytic to the domain of musical performance, the real political efficacy of which is a subject constantly up for debate. It is my personal contention that, although creative agents are uniquely poised to represent, critique, or reimagine political realities, they are not necessarily beholden to do so. Artistic value is not contingent on political efficacy; and it is the prerogative of an Indigenous artist to establish whether, or how, they intend their creative work to contribute to discourse around decolonization or political sovereignty. However, I would argue that public discussion imagining a multicultural political future for Aotearoa New Zealand is so prevalent that it inevitably inflects modes of listening and discourse on intercultural music projects. It is Orpheus all over again, with his promise that music will ease or expedite the establishment of political relations. It is for this reason I argue for the applicability of Tuck's and Yang's "ethic of incommensurability" to the domain of musical performance: it cautions the politically minded listener by delimiting the political realities that musical agency *can* enact and acknowledging those it *cannot*.

Robinson's analyses clearly illustrate what is at stake politically in intercultural music-making, for the conditions of a musical scenario can either afford or deny its agents autonomy and sovereignty. Robinson coins the term "inclusionary music" to signal:

> how Indigenous performers and artists have been structurally accommodated in ways that "fit" them into classical composition and performance systems. The operational emphasis on "fit" situates Indigenous work and performers as a contribution to—or an enrichment of—art music performance. Such inclusionary efforts bolster an intransigent system of presentation guided by an interest in—and often a fixation upon—Indigenous content, but not Indigenous structure. This apathy toward Indigenous structures of performance and gathering leads to epistemic violence through art music's audiophilic privileging of and adherence to its own values of performance and virtuosity. In this framework, while Indigenous singers, instrumentalists, and other performers and increasingly offered space within a composition or a stage, they are infrequently offered the opportunity to define what venue for a performance might be used, the design of the space and audience-performer relationship, and

---

40   Tuck and Yang, "Decolonization Is Not a Metaphor": 21.

the parameters and protocol for gathering at the site of a performance. Inclusionary music, which on the surface *sounds* like a socially progressive act, performs the very opposite of its enunciation.[41]

It is crucial for any musician entering a Eurological concert space to be aware how such "epistemic violence" can be enacted there. At the same time, the agency of Indigenous musicians is acknowledged whenever they enter that concert space on their own terms. Robinson argues that "it is important not to tell this story of Indigenous participation in classical music as one that is entirely centered on a lack of Indigenous agency, or on loss, or on what Eve Tuck identifies as 'damage-centered' narratives."[42] Similarly, in a public lecture about his own work as a composer, Te Ahukaramū Charles Royal offered an "example of perhaps the simplest kind of encounter possible between Māori elements with so-called Western classical composition—using a Māori-language text in a fairly conventional choral work."[43] Rather than treat this scenario as irrevocably compromised, Royal contends that the "possibilities, challenges and opportunities of this kind of encounter are far more nuanced and ambitious" than the sum of its parts.[44]

The risk of the concert space enacting "epistemic violence" depends, as Sandeep Bhagwati observes, on whether "the loss of contexts translates into a loss of cultural signification."[45] Part of the project of provincializing Eurological music is therefore understanding how "presentation formats and contexts are essential components of a musical experience" which support certain experiences of sound and listening and preclude others; they are by no means a neutral zone. To that end, Bhagwati elaborates, "re-framing alien traditions within a familiar aesthetic and temporality . . . in a denuded Western presentation context cuts off the core aesthetics of the music presented."[46]

Ruby Solly—a musician, composer, taonga pūoro practitioner, and scholar—similarly addresses the epistemic violence of such "denuded" cultural representations in her explanation of how in New Zealand "classical music is

---

41 Ibid.: 6.
42 Ibid.: 9.
43 Te Ahukaramū Charles Royal, "Searching for Voice, Searching for Reo," The Lilburn Lecture, 2 November 2017, MP3 audio file, 50:01, https://www.rnz.co.nz/concert/programmes/appointment/audio/2018622563/the-lilburn-lecture-2017.
44 Ibid.
45 Bhagwati, "Curating Musicking as a Mode of Wakefulness in Interesting Times."
46 Ibid.

colonising our culture without empathy or understanding of the people it represents":[47]

> There have been those from the classical music community who've fronted to say that they're trying to form better relationships with tangata whenua by including elements of te ao Māori in their practice as musicians.
> But culture is a deep and complicated thing. Cross-cultural researcher Edward Hall described culture as being like an iceberg where, from the outside, people can see the top. What's on the surface are things like clothing, food, music, and language.
> But, under the water lie things like child-rearing practices, thought processes, and notions of self. I've had a lot of experiences in recent times where Pākehā musicians have engaged with the top layer, with no interest of delving further.
> When they skim the ice off the top like this, they both claim things they don't fully understand, and exercise an imagined privilege where they feel they're allowed to appropriate our culture because it fits under "Kiwi" culture. And yet, as Māori, I have to fight to do the same things and it's always perceived as a political act, when really, it's just us and our culture trying to survive.[48]

There are two crucial ideas in Solly's diagnosis. One is the symptoms of an epistemic attitude that scholar Dylan Robinson terms "hungry listening": a Eurological, colonial tendency to listen and otherwise engage with culture in a way that "consumes without awareness of how the consumption acts in relationship with those people, the lands, the waters who provide sustenance."[49] Second, Solly points to the privilege of abstraction: the ease a settler artist is afforded to engage with Indigenous practices and establish discourse around their work on purely aesthetic or poetic grounds. As Solly notes, this ease is afforded less frequently to Māori artists, whose engagements with Indigenous cultural practices are "always perceived as a political act." Robinson likewise identifies a key characteristic of "hungry listening" as "depoliticization of musical encounter as the simple coming together of difference."[50]

---

47 Ruby Solly, "Being Māori in Classical Music Is Exhausting," *E-Tangata* (March 1, 2020).
48 Ibid.
49 Robinson, *Hungry Listening*, 53.
50 Ibid., 123.

For example, an orchestral work involving taonga pūoro that recently premiered in New Zealand was described by its Pākehā composer in equivocating language that diffused the political stakes of early encounters between colonial explorers and Māori. In program notes the composer described the English colonists' "intentions" as those of "cultivating friendship" with New Zealand's "inhabitants" and "collecting" artefacts: their motivation as "enraptured" fascination with Indigenous knowledge. The equivocation is especially significant given that this orchestral work was commissioned to mark the 250th anniversary of Cook's arrival in New Zealand; Māori author and activist Tina Ngata (2019) notes that the official "languaging" of these commemorations made "continued reference to the event as a celebration of 'dual heritage' and a way of 'coming together',"[51] which, per Tuck and Yang, attempts to commensurate settler and Indigenous futures. Such rhetorical abstractions are what Tuck and Yang term "settler moves to innocence": a response to the (understandable) discomfort and misery of "settler guilt and haunting."[52] Indeed, there could well have been genuine awe and curiosity on the part of European colonists; this humanizing characterization is arguably useful if it invites contemporary Pākehā to contextualize our own engagements with Māori culture amidst transhistorical lineages of Indigenous Pacific influence on Eurological thought. But, as we have seen, the Enlightenment quest for knowledge was far from politically neutral. The settler's privilege of abstraction thus works against the effort to "provincialize" musical practice, for it renders invisible the historical conditions which have, for example, established a national state-funded orchestra in New Zealand and thus enabled the creation of an orchestral composition.

Moves toward abstraction or innocence—or away from an awareness of relationships of "sustenance"—reduce the meaning of an artwork; as Tuck and Yang characterize them, such equivocating gestures are "a foreclosure, limiting in how it recapitulates dominant theories of social change."[53] Conversely, provincializing and historicizing the relational contexts of a musical practice enriches the significance of the practice, and illuminates its social realities. Indeed, Linda Hutcheon argues that "relativity and provisionality are not causes for despair" but in fact "the very conditions of historical knowledge" and historical

---

51 Tina Ngata, *Kia Mau: Resisting Colonial Fictions* (Wellington: Rebel Press, 2019), 25.
52 Tuck and Yang, "Decolonization is not a Metaphor": 9.
53 Ibid.: 3.

meaning.[54] I return to Edward Said, who takes up this idea as it pertains to literature with the observation that, for example,

> descriptions of the rural mansion ... do not at bottom entail only what is to be admired by way of harmony, repose, and beauty; they should also entail for the modern reader what in fact has been excluded from the poems, the labour that created the mansions, the social processes of which they are the culmination, the dispossessions and theft they actually signified.[55]

A musical work—be it a Mozart opera, or a Beethoven overture, or a more recent work of concert music—might very well testify powerfully to craft, elegance, the tenacity of human willpower, a reverence for the natural world, an expression of the sacred or sublime. At the same time, it should entail for the modern listener an audible encounter with the conditions which have resourced that music's creation: the vast first-world profits reaped from resource extraction in sovereign Indigenous territories; the aesthetic expressions of "hungry listening."

Conclusion: Provincializing in Practice

The task of holding such profound opposites in tension is admittedly confounding. Dylan Robinson offers specific proposals as to how musical performances might productively play out the incommensurability of settler "coalition politics" and Indigenous self-determination.[56] To that end, he coins the term "Indigenous+art music" to describe a performance space which might—in contrast to the coercive politics of "inclusionary" music—"foreground a resistance to integration, and signal the affectively awkward, incompatible, or irreconcilable nature of such meetings ... to disrupt 'intercultural music's' implications of union, hybridity, syncretism, and reconciliation."[57] Tuck and Yang similarly acknowledge the confounding position that their "ethic of incommensurability" lands one in, and suggest that a full apprehension of that position "will not

---

54 Linda Hutcheon, *The Politics of Postmodernism* (London & New York: Routledge, 1989), 64.
55 Edward Said, *The World, the Text, and the Critic* (Cambridge, MA: Harvard University Press, 1983), 23.
56 Tuck and Yang, "Decolonization is not a Metaphor": 35.
57 Robinson, *Hungry Listening*, 9.

emerge from friendly understanding, and indeed require a dangerous understanding of uncommonality that un-coalesces coalition politics."[58]

This is a challenging notion. In my experience, I find it hard to get away from the impulse to simply jam—to feel tuned-in to one's musical partners, to feel as if something is being shared. The simple conciliatory impulse of Anglo manners and sociability is also hard to reprogram; it does not come naturally to resist compatibility, or attend to awkwardness, in a collegial setting. Indeed, as performer-composers Horomona Horo and Jeremy Mayall reflect on their more than ten-year collaboration involving taonga pūoro and live electronics, what they cherish about their relationship is that "it's never really been about conflict. It's never really been about finding what friction to build upon to create a conversation."[59]

One helpful proposal, I think, is Sandeep Bhagwati's hypothesis of "co-creative misunderstandings": a "polylogue" in which

> each of the participants actively tries to understand unfamiliar musical phenomena through their own regime of sensations and perceptions, and then respond to them using their familiar or traditional or idiosyncratic artistic responses. This polylogue soon will create a thousand plateaus of understanding, partial understanding, and misunderstanding. At the same time, the participants in the process are asked to always try to find a common ground with each other. In the tension field of such a creative process between different aesthetics, knowledges and musickings and good will to understand the other, I would have hopes for the emergence of coeval relationships between the traditions and musical backgrounds of all participants: because no single participant has decisive control of the result that will emerge from the process, no single participant will have the authority to offer an interpretation either.[60]

This creative scenario potentially dislodges several tenets of Eurological musical practice, especially those associated with modernist aesthetics: hierarchies of creative agency which determine who sets the terms of an artwork's "meaning";

---

58 Ibid., 35.
59 Horomona Horo and Jeremy Mayall, "Kei Tua O Te Arai (Beyond the Veil): Taonga Puoro and Contemporary Technologies in Musical Conversation," in *Indigenous Research Ethics: Claiming Research Sovereignty beyond Deficit and the Colonial Legacy*, Advances in Research Ethics and Integrity, vol. 6, ed. L. George et al. (Bingley: Emerald Publishing Limited, 2020), 225.
60 Bhagwati, "Curating Musicking as a Mode of Wakefulness in Interesting Times."

the conceptual coherence as a marker of artistic quality; the production of discrete, transferable, demonstrably "original" artworks that build an artist's portfolio or professional capital; not to mention the economic imperative of audience or institutional satisfaction. It's a scenario very likely to frustrate Orpheus, who might find himself listening as much as being listened to or sense his powers of persuasion diminishing.

And yet, I argue there is much to be gained in the disorientation from, as Robinson describes them, "anti-relational and non-situated colonial positions of certainty."[61] The presence of taonga pūoro in concert environments in New Zealand has already effected productive shifts in common Eurological practices—shifts which might well be generative within Eurological traditions too. Reflecting on creating chamber music with taonga pūoro, composer Martin Lodge considers the question of "ownership" in a performance involving substantial improvisation, as is the case with taonga pūoro. "Does this mean that compositional credit . . . should be shared?" asks Lodge.[62] "Richard [Nunns] and I have discussed this issue several times, and increasingly I am coming to feel that a shared credit for composition could be right," he concludes, especially owing to the proposition that "all music [is] an improvised dialogue of one sort or another."[63] Even if taonga pūoro were not part of the equation, renovating Eurological musical norms regarding a composer's authorship of a supposedly original, autonomous work might more cogently illuminate the networks of shared creative agency, institutional patronage, accountability to audiences, and historical inheritance that in fact "compose" our musical creations.

Moreover, as compositions with taonga pūoro increasingly call upon classical musical participants to flex their improvisational faculties, these musicians stand to develop a more personal, idiosyncratic instrumental technique, and a heightened sense of creative agency. This stands in contradistinction to many prevailing Eurological musical structures, whose currency is in fact the fungibility of musical labor and the standardization of musical practice. One of the many reasons I appreciate Robinson's term "hungry listening" is that quite frankly the cultures of Eurological music that I inherit do leave me hungry much of the time. Like a feedback loop, Eurological music's prevailing trends of canonization, homogenization, and global standardization are all essentially agendas of scarcity,

---

61 Robinson, *Hungry Listening*, 53.
62 Martin Lodge, "*Hau*: Reflections on some issues encountered when combining traditional Māori and western concert music," *Canzona* 26, no. 49 (2007): 95.
63 Ibid.

which makes their consumers in fact hungrier. By contrast, the more one insists on the value of highly particularized practice, the more agency and power is ceded to the margins.

I see the task of "provincializing practice" to lie in dialogue with a growing initiative in scholarly and creative practices to articulate one's "positionality" as an agent in formations of knowledge and culture. Dylan Robinson invokes the importance of this awareness in musical terms, for one's positionality "guides the way you listen,"[64] and so, in turn, the way you make music, compose music, think and talk about music, and confer value on music. Robinson's critical focus is especially on the ways in which Eurological cultural hegemonies in settler-colonial nations shape musical perception "by generating normative narratocracies of experience, feeling, and the sensible."[65] The effort to denaturalize one's habits of listening and perception, then, might reveal ways in which musical listening can rehearse and reinscribe the "hungry," acquisitive epistemologies which sustain colonial hegemonies. In coining the term "listening positionality," Robinson points towards an extremely fine-grained, personal definition of self that affords "increased potential to acknowledge one's *particular* relationships, responsibilities, and complicity in the continued occupation of Indigenous territories."[66]

This within-arm's-reach perspective yields a different kind of awareness than self-identifying with a more generic term like "settler," "immigrant," "white," or "classical musician": each of which is a "cohesive and essentialist form of subjectivity that does not take into account subtle gradations of relationship, history, and experience."[67] In other words, the finer the grain of attention given to relationships between history, individual, and practice, the more politically efficacious the reflective exercise: for it reveals the particular terms of one's own agency in the networks of cultural power in which one participates.

Though this may sound heady in theory, in practice it might be expressed, as co-composers Jeremy Mayall and Horomona Horo aptly do, in the colloquial terms of

> two people talking together . . . their background, their lineage, their whakapapa, the people they've worked with before. It is all of those

---

64 Robinson, *Hungry Listening*, 1.
65 Ibid., 39.
66 Ibid.
67 Ibid.

things coming together in that point, and I think all of that is present in the musical decisions that you make in each moment.[68]

In my own experience as a composer and musician, I have found my artistic endeavors to be richly energized by this kind of close attention to the "provincial" formations of one's own agency. I therefore anticipate that musicians employing a similarly attentive focus might foster rich musical discourse—in educational settings, in public forums, in guiding artistic programming, or to inform musicians' own creative work and dialogue—in Aotearoa New Zealand and beyond.

Acknowledgements

In addition to those scholars cited, many thanks to the friends, colleagues, and mentors whose interlocutions, and pointers toward resources, have helped shape these ideas: Prof. Amy Cimini, Dr. Keir GoGwilt, Prof. Sarah Hankins, Prof. Vini Olsen-Reeder, Ruby Solly, Rob Thorne, Prof. K. Wayne Yang, Prof. Anthony Davis, Dr. Jeremy Mayall, Dr. Davinia Caddy, Steven Whiteley, and Janet Hughes.

---

68   Horomona Horo and Jeremy Mayall, "Kei Tua O Te Arai (Beyond the Veil)," 228.

Bibliography

Agnew, Vanessa. *Enlightenment Orpheus: The Power of Music in Other Worlds.* New York: Oxford University Press, 2008.

Bhagwati, Sandeep. "Curating Musicking as a Mode of Wakefulness in Interesting Times." Keynote at "Curating Diversity in Europe—Decolonizing Contemporary Music" conference, Akademie der Künste Berlin, September 25, 2020. YouTube Video, 1:00:25. https://www.youtube.com/watch?v=NAZ3Cpn8mK8.

Born, Georgina, and David Hesmondhalgh. *Western Music and Its Others: Difference, Representation, and Appropriation in Music.* Berkeley: University of California Press, 2007.

Chakrabarty, Dipesh. *Provincializing Europe: Postcolonial Thought and Historical Difference.* Princeton: Princeton University Press, 2000.

Horo, H., and J. Mayall. "Kei Tua O Te Arai (Beyond the Veil): Taonga Puoro and Contemporary Technologies in Musical Conversation." In *Indigenous Research Ethics: Claiming Research Sovereignty Beyond Deficit and the Colonial Legacy.* Advances in Research Ethics and Integrity, vol. 6, edited by L. George, J. Tauri, and L. T. A. o. T MacDonald, 223–235. Bingley: Emerald Publishing Limited, 2020.

Hutcheon, Linda. *The Politics of Postmodernism.* London & New York: Routledge, 1989.

Kajikawa, Loren. "The Possessive Investment in Classical Music: Confronting Legacies of White Supremacy in U. S. Schools and Departments of Music." In *Seeing Race Again: Countering Colorblindness across the Disciplines,* edited by Kimberlé Williams Crenshaw et al., 155–174. Berkeley: University of California Press, 2019.

Lewis, George E. "Improvised Music after 1950: Afrological and Eurological Perspectives." In "Best of *BMRJ* (2002)," *Black Music Research Journal* 22 (2002): 215–246.

———. *A Power Stronger than Itself: The AACM and American Experimental Music.* Chicago: University of Chicago Press, 2008.

Lilburn, Douglas. *A Search for Tradition & A Search for Language.* Wellington: Victoria University Press, 2011.

Lodge, Martin. "*Hau*: Reflections on Some Issues Encountered When Combining Traditional Māori and Western Concert Music." *Canzona* 26, no. 49 (2007): 93–95.

Maconie, Robin. "On the Prehistory of Music in New Zealand." *Musical Times* 151, no. 1910 (2010): 23–30.

Najita, Susan. "Resemblances and Complicity: The Construction of Pakeha History in 'The Piano.'" In *Complicities: Connections & Divisions: Perspectives on Literatures and Cultures of the Asia-Pacific Region,* edited by Chitra Sankaran, Rajeev Patke, and Liew Geok Leong, 81–115. New York: Peter Lang, 2003.

Ngata, Tina. *Kia Mau: Resisting Colonial Fictions.* Wellington: Rebel Press, 2019.

Nunns, Richard, and Thomas, Allan. "The Search for the Sound of the Pūtōrino: 'Me te wai e utuutu ana.'" *Yearbook for Traditional Music* 37 (2005): 69–79.

Royal, Te Ahukaramū Charles. "Searching for Voice, Searching for Reo." The Lilburn Lecture, 2017. MP3 Audio File, 50:01. https://www.rnz.co.nz/concert/programmes/appointment/audio/2018622563/the-lilburn-lecture-2017.

Robinson, Dylan. *Hungry Listening: Resonant Theory for Indigenous Sound Studies*. Minneapolis: University of Minnesota Press, 2020.

———. "Listening to the Politics of Aesthetics: Contemporary Encounters between First Nations/Inuit and Early Music Traditions." In *Aboriginal Music in Contemporary Canada: Echoes and Exchanges*, edited by A. Hoefnagels and B. Diamond, 222–248. Montreal: McGill-Queen's University Press, 2012.

Said, Edward. *The World, the Text, and the Critic*. Cambridge, MA: Harvard University Press, 1983.

———. *Power, Politics, and Culture: Interviews with Edward W. Said*, edited by Gauri Viswanathan. New York: Vintage, 2001.

Salmond, Anne. *Two Worlds: First Meetings Between Maori and Europeans, 1642–1772*. Honolulu: University of Hawai'i Press, 1991.

Smith, Valance. "Whāia te Māramatanga: the search for enlightenment." In *Searches for Tradition: Essays on New Zealand Music, Past and Present*, edited by Michael Brown and Samantha Owens, Wellington: Victoria University Press, 2017.

Solly, Ruby. "Being Māori in Classical Music Is Exhausting." *E-Tangata*, March 1, 2020. https://e-tangata.co.nz/reflections/being-maori-in-classical-music-is-exhausting/.

Subotnik, Rose Rosengard. "Whose 'Magic Flute?' Intimations of Reality at the Gates of the Enlightenment." *19th-Century Music* 15, no. 2 (1991): 132–50.

Tamarapa, Awhina, and Ariana Tikao. "Mai te Pō, ki te Ao: The Reclamation of Taonga Puoro as a Living Treasure." In *Searches for Tradition: Essays on New Zealand Music, Past and Present*, edited by Michael Brown and Samantha Owens, 139–157. Wellington: Victoria University Press, 2017.

Taylor, Diana. *The Archive and the Repertoire: Performing Cultural Memory in the Americas*. Durham: Duke University Press, 2003.

Taylor, Timothy D. *Beyond Exoticism: Western Music and the World*. Durham: Duke University Press, 2007.

Te Punga Somerville, Alice. *Two Hundred and Fifty Ways to Start an Essay about Captain Cook*. Wellington: Bridget Williams Books, 2020.

Thorne, Rob. "Jumping the Gap: The Distance Between Taonga Pūoro and Experimental Music." *Soundbleed*, October 24, 2013. https://soundbleedjournal.wordpress.com/2013/10/24/jumping-the-gap-the-distance-between-taonga-puoro-and-experimental-music-rob-thorne/.

———. "The Vesica Piscis of Past, Present and Future Tradition." In *Writing Around Sound #2—In Whose Tradition?* Lyttleton: Cantabrian Society of Sonic Artists Inc., 2016. http://www.robthorne.co.nz/the-vesica-piscis-of-past-present-and-future-tradition.

Tuck, Eve, and K. Wayne Yang. "Decolonisation is not a Metaphor." *Decolonization: Indigeneity, Education & Society* 1, no. 1 (2012): 1–40.

Wilson, Oli. "Tiki Taane's with Strings Attached: Alive & Orchestrated." In *Global Perspectives on Orchestras: Collective Creativity and Social Agency*, edited by Tina K. Ramnarine, 245–260. Oxford: Oxford University Press, 2018.

Contributors

Allan Badley, Associate Professor in Musicology at the University of Auckland, is a specialist in late eighteenth-century Viennese music. He has published articles on Haydn, Leopold Hofmann, Ignaz Pleyel, Stephen Storace, and Wanhal; recent publications include "Leopold Hofmann – Sechs Konzerte für Tasteninstrumente," in *Denkmäler der Tonkunst Österreich* (Vienna: Hollitzer Verlag, 2019), and *Ferdinand Ries—Three String Quartets, Op.150* (Madison, WI: A-R Editions, 2022). He is a co-founder of the now Hong Kong-based publishing house Artaria Editions, which is widely regarded as one of the leading specialist publishers of eighteenth-century music.

Since 2013, **Gregory Camp** has taught musicology, music theory, and musicianship in the School of Music at the University at Auckland, where he is a Senior Lecturer. He is Artistic Director of the University of Auckland Opera Workshop, where he directs an opera each year, and is the School of Music's Director of Research. His current research is on 1950s film music, linguistics in vocal pedagogy, and Disney music. He has recently published two monographs on film music with Routledge: *Howard Hawks: Sonic Style in Film* (2020) and *Scoring the Hollywood Actor in the 1950s* (2021).

Sandra Crawshaw, a pianist and violinist from Dunedin, New Zealand, is currently completing her PhD. In 1987, she graduated with a BMus (Hons) in piano performance from the University of Auckland. She pursued postgraduate studies in performance at the Royal College of Music, London, and completed a master's thesis at the University of Otago, Dunedin titled "The Reception of the Music of Cécile Chaminade in Colonial New Zealand." She graduated with Distinction in 2015. This sparked an interest in life in Colonial New Zealand, with a focus on entertainment and leisure in Dunedin.

Following an undergraduate degree in violin performance, **Eliana Dunford** is now working on her MMus in research musicology at the University of Auckland. Her research examines the applicability of topic theory to modernist music, with a particular focus on the relationship between aesthetic value judgements and musical syntax in Benjamin Britten's cello suites. Eliana is also a Professional Teaching Fellow at the university, tutoring and grading work for a range of undergraduate theory and musicology papers. In 2019 she was awarded the Drake Medal, Auckland University's highest honor for musicology.

A graduate of the National Academy of Singing and Dramatic Art (NASDA), **Christopher McRae** is a professional opera and music theatre singer. Having performed with numerous companies throughout New Zealand, he is currently completing his doctorate on classical performance at the University of Auckland, with a focus on crossover vocal technique. He was awarded the university's Drake Medal for musicology in 2020.

Lawrence Mays is an independent scholar in Canberra, Australia. At the Australian National University, he completed a bachelor of music in voice performance (2009), an MPhil in Music (2013), and a PhD (2018). He works on eighteenth-century Italian comic opera, in particular the works of Niccolò Piccinni. He has recently published a critical edition of Piccinni's *Il regno della Luna* and a chapter on the historiographic aspects of this opera. He is a student of classical mandolin and chorus member of the National Opera Company. Prior to studying music, he practiced medicine for many years in various capacities, and he has published in the field of health services research.

Recorder player **Imogen Morris** is an instrumental teacher at the University of Auckland, where she recently completed her doctorate. She is active as a soloist in ensembles, and has performed in Germany, Austria, and South Korea, as well as her native New Zealand. Imogen completed a Master of Music in recorder at the Hochschule für Musik und Theater Hamburg in 2017 under the tutelage of Professor Peter Holtslag. Studying with Jessica Shaw at the University of Auckland, she received a bachelor of music with First Class Honors in Classical Performance in 2013.

Richard Moyle has published extensively on Polynesian and Australian Aboriginal music traditions and oral literature. He has held university teaching positions in Hawaii and Auckland. For eight years, he was a Research Fellow at the Australian Institute of Aboriginal Studies; for sixteen years, he was the Director of Auckland University's Archive of Maori and Pacific Music. Now retired, he holds an adjunct chair at the Queensland Conservatorium of Music.

Nancy November is a Professor of Musicology at the University of Auckland. Combining interdisciplinarity and cultural history, her research focuses on historiography, canonization, and genre in late eighteenth and nineteenth-century chamber music. She has received three Marsden Grants from the New Zealand Royal Society and in 2010–12 won a Humboldt Fellowship. She recently published *Beethoven's Symphonies Arranged for the Chamber* (Cambridge University Press, 2021).

Celeste Oram is a composer who grew up in Aotearoa New Zealand and is currently based in the United States. Her creative work engages original and historical music, theatre, ethnographic research, collaborative partnerships, and digital media to illuminate historical and contemporary networks of music, culture, politics, and technology. Her scholarly articles have been published in *Current Musicology*, *TEMPO*, and *Naxos Musicology International*. Celeste completed her PhD in music composition at the University of California San Diego, and is an alumnus of the University of Auckland. She has received major departmental musicology prizes from both UC San Diego and the University of Auckland.

Index

A
Abafi, Ludwig, 113, 118, 119n24
act, 51, 88n28, 77n13, 79, 81–84, 88, 91, 93, 98, 100–1, 103, 105
Adinolfi, Francesco, 59
Adorno, Theodor, 11
adagio, 125–26
aesthetics, 7, 14, 18, 56n1, 59, 134, 166, 236, 240
Africa, 59–60, 66
African culture, 69, 70n33
Agawu, Kofi, 204
Agnew, Vanessa, 226, 228–29
Agricultural Hall.
    See Dunedin, His Majesty's Theater
Ainsley, Irene, 52
alla turca, style, 70n33
Allanbrook, Wye Jamison, 205
allegro, 93, 101, 103, 105–8, 125
alto, 169–71
alto recorder, 169
Anaheim, 57
ancestral spirits, 7, 18, 20–21, 29
andante (andantino), 92, 94, 100–4
Andersen, Johannes, 227
Anderson Sheridan Pantomime Company, 51
Aotearoa, 12, 65, 222–24, 234–35, 243
April (pseud), Broadway actress, 179
aria, 76, 79–91, 93, 98, 100–3, 105–6, 109, 122, 124–25, 130–31, 139, 149, 202, 219
ariki, paramount chief, 22–23, 25, 27, 29–30
Arnstein, Fanny von, 10, 136, 141–42, 144–48, 150
Arnstein, Nathan Adam von, 141–43
artistic values, 11, 157, 168–70
Ashdod, 121–22n29
Asia, 59–60, 66–67, 70
Athenaeum, magazine, 143–44
Auckland, 7, 42, 48, 52
    Opera House, 42n18
Australasia, 45–46
Australia, 25, 36, 42, 44–48, 51
Austria, 75, 113–14, 143
Austria-Este, 76

B
Babbitt, Milton, 203
Bach, Johann Sebastian, 47–48, 144
    Chromatic Fantasy, 48
    Fugue in D Minor, 48
    Toccata and Fugue in D Minor, 47
Baeyertz, Charles, 45, 50, 52
Ballarat, 51
banjo, 51
Banks, Joseph, 227
Barcarolle, 60
baritone, 46, 52
Baroque, style, 171
Barrington, Daines, 222–23, 228
Bartholdy, Jacob Salomo, 145
bass, 44, 46n27, 52, 81, 126, 205–8, 214, 217
Battle of the Brows, 201
Bauchop, Maria, 47
Baxter, Leslie Thompson, 59, 60n10, 61
    Ritual of the Savage, album, 59
BBC, 200–1
Beales, Derek, 115–17
Beethoven, Ludwig van, 46, 48, 137n4, 139, 146, 148, 150, 212, 227, 239
    "Adelaide", 139
    Coriolan, overture, 227
    Eroica Symphony, 148
    Fidelio (Leonore), opera, 146
    "Moonlight" Sonata, 48
    Seventh Symphony, 227
bel canto, 175, 177, 192
Belgium, 115
Bellina, Anna Laura, 76
belt, 174, 177–78, 180, 182–84, 186–90, 194
Benda, Georg, 75, 131
    Ariadne auf Naxos, melodrama, 131
    Medea, melodrama, 131
    Pygmalion, melodrama, 131
Benedictines, 123
Benelli, Antonio, 81, 90, 92, 98
Berg, Alban, 203
Berlin, 139, 141–42, 145, 183
Berlioz, 213, 217–18
    Symphonie Fantastique, 213, 217–18
Bernstein, Leonard, 179
    Candide, operetta, 179

Bertuch, Carl, 146
Bhagwati, Sandeep, 225, 236, 240
Biber, Heinrich, 213
    Battalia à 10, 213
biculturalism, 228
Bindemonte, Count, 149
Birdwell, Florence, 179, 189
Bluff, 36–37
Blumenthal, composer, 47
Bonner, Eugene, 201–2
Born, Ignaz von, 117
Borzoni, Alfredo, 41
Bougainville, island, 19–20, 22, 29, 33
Braithwaite, Warwick, 37, 47
Branscombes, Edward, 51
Brisbane, 36
Britain, 13, 36. *See also* England
Britten, Benjamin, 11–12, 200–9, 211–19
    Owen Wingrave, opera, 207
    Paul Bunyan, operetta, 201
    Sinfonia da Requiem, 207
    Suites for Solo Cello, 205–19
    War Requiem, 207
Brooks, Van Wyck, 201
Broschi, Carlo Maria (pseud. Farinelli), 100
Brown, Erica, 201
Brown, Jason Robert, 191
    Bridges of Madison County, musical, 191–93
Bruch, Max, 47
Brüggen, Frans, 159
Brunetti, Maria, 80
Brydone, Thomas, 39
Buckman, Rosina, 50
Buka, North Bougainville, 20, 29, 33
Burney, Charles, 99
Busoni, Ferrucio, 46, 52
Butt, Clara, 42, 49–50, 52
Bylsma, Anner, 10, 156, 159–60
Byrd, William, 211

C
cadence, 132
Caldwell, Zoe, 183
California, 57, 59–60, 67, 183
Callas, Maria, 183
Calvesi, Vincenzo, 75
Campbell, Margaret, 36, 46, 49–50
Campbell, Robert, 39
Canada, 66n26, 233
Caneen, Jefferey, 65
canoes, 19, 23–25
cantata, 9, 76, 117, 123–24, 133
canzone, 77, 88

canzoncina, 82
Carousel, film, 183
Carpani, Giuseppe, 145
Caplin, William E., 205–8
Carthusians, 119
Casaccia, Antonio, 81, 90, 98–99, 101
Castelli, Ignaz Franz, 118n23
Castlereagh, Robert Stewart, Lord, 148
Castles, Amy, 42
Catholics, 123
cavatina, 79, 81, 86
cello, 11, 46, 140, 200, 205–8, 212, 217–19
cellist, 46, 139
Chakrabarty, Dipesh, 225
chamber music, 8, 35, 140, 146, 150, 169–71, 230, 241
Chaminade, Cécile, 47
Charles Begg and Co., 42
Charles VI of France, Holy Roman Emperor, 114
Charon, mythical figure, 228
Chevalier, Maurice, 61
Chenoweth, Kristin, 11, 176, 178–84, 188–89
Cherubini, Luigi, 140, 150
    Elisa, 140
Chills, The, rock band, 37
Chopin, Frédéric, 46–48, 51
    Ballade, 51
Chowrimootoo, Christopher, 201–2
Christchurch, 45, 49
    Opera House, 49
Cimarosa, Domenico, 79, 150
Cinderella, play, 51
clarinet, 94, 109
Clement, Franz, 149
Clement XII, Pope, 114
climax, 65, 79, 91, 190, 209
coda, 127
Coessens, Kathleen, 163–64, 166, 168
col legno, 212–13
Coltellini, Anna, 75, 80, 90, 103, 105–6
Coltellini, Celeste, 75, 103
Coltellini, Marco, 103
commedia dell'arte, 78
commedia per musica, 79, 81–82, 109–10
Comtesse de Majan (née Franziska von Spielmann), 147
conductor, 37, 44, 47, 51
contralto, 47, 51, 52
Cook, James, 223, 226–28, 238
Coombes, James, 44
Copenhagen, 127
Copland, Aaron, 204

Cravalho, Auli'I, singer, 68
Crawshaw, Sandra, 8, 35
Creative Practice Research (CPR), 10, 156–57, 161–65, 167–72
    need for research framework, 157
    distinguishing research from practice, 161–62, 164, 167, 169, 171
    challenges integrating musical works by deceased composers, 164–67
crescendo, 101, 105, 186, 192
Crispin, Darla, 157n2, 162–64
Cromwell, 44
    Cromwell Argus, The, newspaper, 44
Crosby, Bing, 60–61
cross-cultural music, 7, 12, 222, 226, 229, 231, 237
Crossley, Ada, 47
Cypess, Rebecca, 137, 142n12, 144

D

Da Ponte, Lorenzo, 9, 74–76, 78–80, 84, 86, 89–90, 92–93, 103, 110
    I voti della nazione Napoletana, libretto, 76
    Flora e Minerva, libretto, 76
    Le nozze di Figaro, libretto, 9, 74, 76–77, 80–81, 83–84, 88–91, 93, 98–99, 110
Dagon, Philistine deity, 120–22
Dahlhaus, Carl, 78
Dalgety & Co. Ltd., 39
dance, 7, 14, 18, 20, 22, 23–27, 29–32, 41, 51, 55, 64–66, 210–11, 224
    kapa haka dance, 65, 227, 230
    sau dances, 18–20, 27
declamation. *See* recitation
demonic style, 215, 218
Denny, Martin, 59–60, 67
DePledge, Stephen, 35
despotism, 117, 136
Dickensheets, Janice, 215, 217–18
Dies Irae, chant, 207, 213, 218
Dietrichstein, Marianne, Countess, 146
Disney, Roy, 56
Disney, Walt, 56, 64, 70
Disney Imagineers, 58, 62
Disneyland, 8, 55–59, 60n10, 63–67, 69. *See also* Walt Disney World
Disneyland after Dark, TV film, 64
Disneyland Hotel, 67
Disneyland Theme Parks, 8, 55–69
    Adventureland, park, 8, 55–59
    American Wild West, park, 56
    Animal Kingdom, park, 57, 66
    Disneyland Paris, park, 57
    EPCOT (Experimental Prototype Community of Tomorrow), park, 57, 66, 68
    Fantasyland, park, 56–58
    Frontierland, park, 56–58
    Hong Kong Disneyland, park, 69
    Main Street, USA, park, 57–58, 66
    Magic Kingdom, park, 57
    Pirates of the Caribbean, attraction, 59
    Shanghai Disneyland, park, 57
    Tokyo Disneyland, park, 57, 59, 63, 65
    Tokyo DisneySea, park, 57, 69
    Tomorrowland, park, 56–58, 60n10
    Jungle Cruise, park, 58–59
Dittersdorf, Carl Ditters von, 75n6
Dolmetsch, Arnold, 171
Dolores, Antonia, 44–46
Donaghy and Co., 39
dramma giocoso, 77
Dreamgirls, musical, 188
drums, 61, 64, 69, 228
duet (duetto), 79, 81–84, 86, 88–90, 139–40, 146
Duke of Wellington, 137
Dunedin, 8, 35–40, 42, 44–45, 47, 49, 50–53
    Alhambra Theatre, 45, 49
    Choral Hall, 45
    Choral Society, 44, 47–48, 53
    Competitions Society, 47, 52–53
    Garrison Hall, 39, 45, 50
    His Majesty's Theatre (Agricultural Hall), 8, 35, 37–43, 44–51, 53
    Hocken Library, 40, 43, 45
    Liedertafel (Royal Male Choir), 40, 49
    Operatic Society, 53
    Orchestral Society, 40
    Princess Theatre, 45, 49
Dunford, Eliana, 11–12, 200
Durante, Jimmy, 60–61

E

Early Music, movement, 157, 159–61, 167
Ebenezer, 121n29
Eberl, Anton, 150
Edgcumbe, George, Earl of Mount Edgcumbe, 99
Edward VII, King of the UK, 52
Egerton Manuscript, 211
Einstein, Albert, 229
Elizabeth of Württemberg, Archduchess of Austria, 113
Elizabeth II, Queen of the UK, 29

Index

Elfman, Danny, 69
England, 48, 124. *See also* Britain
Enlightenment, 70n33, 119, 122, 142, 149, 226–29, 231, 238
Ephraim, Rebecca, 142
Eskeles, Bernhard von, 142, 145
Estefan, Gloria, 62
Estill, Jo, 176–78
Ete, Igelese, 68
Eurydice, mythical figure, 228
Europe, 9, 35, 46, 113, 136, 223, 227, 233
Evening Star, The, newspaper, 38, 41, 44, 46, 48, 52
exoticism, 9, 55–56, 58–60, 62–63, 66–67, 69–70
Eybenberg, Mariane von, 142

F
Facebook, 32
falsetto, 77, 102–3, 177, 186–87
Farinelli (pseud), singer. *See* Broschi, Carlo Maria
Ferdinand IV, Bourbon King of Naples, 75
Ferdinand, Archduke of Austria-Este, 76
Ferdinand, Prince of Prussia. *See* Frederick Louis Ferdinand, Prince of Prussia
Fergus, Thomas, 39
Ferrari, Giacomo Gotifredo, 99
Fesca, Friedrich Ernst, 139
    Die Geburt, op. 16, 139
Fiji, archipelago, 36
finale, 79, 82–84, 103, 127, 139
fingering, 169–71
fingering systems (historical and English), 169–71
Finn, Neil, pop musician, 35
Fioravanti, Valentino, 139
    I virtuosi ambulanti, opera, 139
    Le cantarici villane, opera, 139
First Nation, 66, 233
Fjellman, Stephen, 58n7, 64
flautist, 45–46
Fliess, Eleonore, 142
Florida, 57, 66
flute, 132, 149, 169, 229
Föderl, Leopold, 10, 118–19, 121, 123, 131–33
Forsayth, Emma, 22
Forster, Georg, 227, 231
Forster, Johann Reinhold, 227
fortepiano, 10, 42, 46, 52, 123, 139–40, 145–50. *See also* pianist
    Conrad Graf piano, 149
France, 108, 124

Francis I Stephen, Duke of Lorraine, Holy Roman emperor, 114
Francis II or I (Franz II), Holy Roman Emperor, 10, 113–14, 136, 140, 143, 148, 150
Franco, Charles M., 165
Frayling, Christopher, 157n2
Frederick Louis Ferdinand, Prince of Prussia, 147
    Piano Quartet in F Minor, op. 6, 147
Freemasonry, 9, 40, 113–19, 123–27, 130–34, 227
    Grand Master, 118, 127, 132–33
    Joseph II's reforms, 9, 113–23
    masonic symbolism, 10, 124–27, 130–33
French Polynesia. *See* Polynesia
French Revolution, 9, 141
Friedrich II the Great, King of Prussia, 141
Fries, Moritz, Count, 146
Frohberg, Regina, 142
Fröhlichs, Anna, 154
Fröhlichs, Barbara, 154
Fröhlichs, Josephine, 154
Fröhlichs, Katharina, 154
From Here to Eternity, film, 59
Frymoyer, Johanna, 215
fugue, 47–48, 79, 205
Fuller, John, 45, 48–49
Funny Girl, musical, 175

G
Galuppi, Baldassare, 76
Gauguin, Paul, 59
Gebler, Tobias Philipp von, Baron, 131
    Thamos, König von Aegypten, play, 131
Gell, Alfred, 15
Gennawey, Sam, 58n7, 60n12
genre, 7, 12, 14–15, 18, 23, 26n18, 27, 29–30, 56n1, 57, 60–61, 76–77, 79, 109, 175–76, 202, 205, 224
George Frederick Ernest Albert, Prince of Wales, 52
German, Edward, 47
Germany, 48
Gilbert, William Schwenck, 202. *See also* Sullivan, Arthur
Ginguené, Pierre-Louis, 75, 78
Gjerdingen, Robert O., 206
Glee, TV show, 178–79
glissandi, 215
Gluck, Christoph Willibald, 149
    Iphigénie en Tauride, opera, 149
golden age, 9, 18, 27, 32

Goldoni, Carlo, 76
    Il mondo della luna, opera, 76, 77n13, 80n21
Gotha, 131
Götz, Friedrich, 139
Graben, district of Vienna, 144
Grainger, Percy, 47
Grant, Mark, 175–76
Greenberg, Clement, 11, 204
Greiner, Franz Sales von, 116
Grieg, Edvard, 46–47
Griffiths, Frederick, 45
Grover, Mary, 201
Guettel, Adam, 186, 189
    The Light in the Piazza, musical, 186–87, 189–92
Giuliani, Mauro, 140
guitar, 59, 140

H
Habsburg, dynasty, 9–10, 76, 114–15, 150
Hadl, Luise, 118n23
Hadrava, Norbert, 75
Hale, Thomas, 124
Hall, Amalia, 35
Hall, Edward, 237
Hambourg, Boris, 46–47
Hambourg, Mark, 42, 44, 46–47
Handel (Händel), George Frideric, 44, 48, 146
    Messiah, oratorio, 44, 48
    Timotheus oder die Gewalt der Musik, oratorio, 146
Hänsel, Peter, 149
Hardenberg, Karl August, Prince, 137, 148
Hatten, Robert S., 205
Hawaii, 63, 65, 67–68
    Brigham Young University, 64
Hawaiian culture, 59, 61, 63, 65–68
    "Hawaiian War Chant", song, 61, 63
    luau, show, 8, 64–65
Haydn, Joseph, 48, 75n6, 139, 149–50
    Die Schöpfung (Creation), oratorio, 48, 150
    The Seasons, oratorio, 139
Haynes, Bruce, 157–60
Hazlett, James, 39
Heinke, Franz Joseph von, Ritter, 119
Henry, Jacques, 119, 127, 132–33
Hindemith, Paul, 204
Historically Informed Performance (HIP), 10–11, 156–72
    and authentic performance, 158
    and personal invention, 158–61
    interpretation as automatic process, 18, 158, 160–61, 166–69, 171, 176, 215, 240
Hill, Alfred, 50–51, 228
    A Moorish Maid, opera, 50
Hislop, James, 39
Hobart, 36–37
Hochenadl, Joseph, 139
Hochenadl, Katharina, 139
Hochenadl, Thomas, 139
Hockney, David, 165–66
Hockney-Falco thesis, 165
Hodges, Hamilton, 52
Hofburg, 145–46
Hollywood, 57, 67–68n28
Holst, Gustav, 213
    The Planets, suite, 213
Hong Kong, 57, 69
horn call, 211–12
Horo, Horomona, 231, 240, 242
Houston, Michael, 35
Hughes, Pete, 43
humanism, 229
Humarire Taniwha, dramma, 41n14
Humboldt, Wilhelm von, 137
Hummel, Johann Nepomuk, 140, 149
    La Sentinelle, 140
Hungary, 115
Hunter, Mary, 70n33
Hurst, Maurice, 36, 42, 44
Hutcheon, Linda, 238
Huyssen, Andreas, 204

I
Idylls, play, 149
impresario, 9, 78
improvisation, 214, 222, 224, 241
Indigenous cultures, 22, 65–67, 228, 230, 233–39, 242
"In the Tiki Tiki Tiki Room", song, 8, 55, 60
instrumental technique, 160, 170–71, 241
interlude, 77
intermezzo, 77, 110
introduzione, 84–85, 125
Invercargill, 37
    Theatre Royale, 37
Italy, 77, 99, 108

J
Jacob, Jacques, 47
jazz, 61, 182, 224
Jesuits, 117
Jesus Christ Superstar, musical, 176
John Fuller and Sons, Co., 48–49

Joseph II, Holy Roman Emperor, 9, 114–22, 131–33
    attitude to freemasonry, 9, 114–15, 119, 121–22, 133
    dissolution of contemplative religious orders, 9, 119–20, 123
    Toleration Patent, 9, 114–16, 119
    patent on freemasonry, 9, 115, 117, 133
Juvenile Opera Company, 49

K
Kaikorai Band, 40, 51
Kaiposu, Tukuteata, 25
Karl August, Prince of Hardenberg, 137
Kauer, Ferdinand, 149
Kaunitz, 115
Kelly, Michael, 99
Kenrick, John, 186
key (tonality) character, 128-130
Kierkegaard, Søren Aabye, 229
Kiesewetter, Raphael, 151
Kimbra, pop musician, 35
Koželuch, Antonín Tomas, 117n16
Koželuh, Leopold, 9–10, 113, 116–18, 123–34, 149
    and Freemasonry, 9, 113, 116, 119, 123, 132
    Joseph der Menschheit Segen, cantata, 9, 113, 117–18, 120, 123–24, 126–29, 131–34
Kreisler, Fritz, 37
Krufft, Nikolaus von, 140
    "Die Wanderer im Walde", 140
Kuijken brothers, 159
Kurzböck, Magdalene von, 145, 147

L
Laie, Hawaii, 64
Lamb, Andrew, 214
lamento, 103, 174, 184, 205–9, 227
Lantz, Victoria Pettersen, 65–66
Las Vegas, 63
Leech-Wilkinson, Daniel, 160–61
Lehár, Franz, 189
    The Merry Widow, operetta, 189
Leipzig, 131
Lemmoné, John, 46
Leonhardt, Gustav, 159–60
Leopold Wilhelm (Vilém) von Kollowrat-Krakowsky, Count, 115
Leopold II, Holy Roman Emperor, 133
Levy, Sara, 142
Lewis, George, 225n8
Lewis, Ludwig, 118nn20–21

librettist, 9, 75–76, 77n13, 78–80, 90, 103, 110, 146
libretto, 9–10, 74–76, 78–81, 86, 88–89, 92, 101, 103, 109, 133, 202
Liechtenstein, Carl, Prince, 145
Lilburn, Douglas, 222–24, 234, 236n43
Liliputian Opera Company, 49
Linz, 227
Liszt, Franz, 46, 48
    Hungarian Fantasy, 45
Llangollen, 35
Lobkowitz, Joseph Franz, Prince, 146
Lodge, Martin, 241
Lombardy, 115
London, 36, 44, 47, 49–52, 222, 227
    Bechstein Hall, 52
    Covent Garden, 50, 217
    Marlborough House, 52
    National Gallery, 47, 49, 227
    Royal Society, 222–23, 228
Lorde, pop musician, 35
Lorenzi, Giovanni Battista (Giambattista), 9, 74, 76, 78–79, 88–89, 98, 103, 109
    La luna abitata, opera, 76
    La serva onorata, opera, 9, 74, 77–84, 86, 88–90, 98, 108, 110
    Opere teatrali, 79
Low Countries, 114
luau show, 8, 64–65

M
Macbeth, play (Shakespeare), 149
Macdonald, Dwight, 201
Maconie, Robin, 222–23, 227–28
Maione, Paologiovanni, 108
Manauī, Sāre, 23, 30, 32
Mandini, Stefano, 75
Māori culture, 12, 37, 65, 68, 224, 227–28, 230–31, 233, 236–38, 241n62.
    See also dance
    purotu, 18–19, 23, 27, 31
    purotu performance specialist, 18, 23, 27, 31–32
    taonga pūoro, 12, 224, 226, 230–34, 236, 238, 240–41
    Whare Tapere, 224
march, 205, 210–11, 213–14
Maria Carolina of Austria, Queen of Naples and Sicily, 75–76
Maria Theresia, Archduchess of Austria, 75, 114, 140
Maria Theresa von Paradis, 137, 149
Marschel, Barrie, 41
Martinelli, Luigi, 81, 90–91

mass culture, 11, 204, 219
Masonic lodge, 9, 113–17, 118n20, 119n24. *See also* Freemassonry
masonic symbolism, 10, 124–27, 130, 132, 218
Mayr, Simon, 139
    Ginevra di Scozia, opera, 139
Mayseder, Joseph, 140
McDonald, Audra, 11, 176, 178, 183–84, 186–90
McKenzie, John, 40
McNally, Terrance, 183
    Master Class, play, 183
Mayall, Jeremy, 240, 242
Mays, Lawrence, 9, 74, 75n5
Meyerbeer, Giacomo, 146
Mehul, Étienne, 139
    Une folie (Beiden Füchsen), opera, 139
Meissner, August Gottlieb, 133
Melba, Nellie, 36–37, 42, 44–45, 52
Melbourne, 37
melisma, 89, 93, 100
Melk, 123
melodrama, 75n6, 119, 125, 131–32
Mendelssohn, Felix, 46
Menzel, Idina, 179
Mercadante, Saverio, 139
    Elisa e Claudio, drama, 139
Merriam, Alan P., 14
Metternich, Clemens von, 136, 140
mezzo-soprano, 52
middlebrow society, 11–12, 200–4
Miles-Stavordale Quartet, 51
Miller, Mitch, 61
Mills, Watkin, 48
mimesis, 208–215
Mirka, Danuta, 215
moderato, 100, 103
modernism, 12, 158, 201–5, 226, 232
Mōmoa, Pāsia, 24–25
Monelle, Raymond, 205, 207, 210–12, 214
Monza, city in Italy, 76
Moore, Vera, 37, 47
Mortlock, James, 22
Morton, James Douglas, Lord, 228
Moscheles (Möscheles), Ignaz, 140, 146, 149
    "Der Abschied des Troubadours", 140
Mosel, Ignaz von, 145, 147
Moyle, Richard, 7, 14, 15n9, 16n10, 17, 18nn14–15, 19, 21–22, 24, 26, 28–29, 31
Mozart, Leopold, 223
Mozart, Wolfgang Amadeus, 41, 74–75, 78–79, 84, 89n24, 91–93, 99, 103, 109–10, 131, 133, 139, 144–46, 148, 150, 189, 222–24, 227–29, 239

Così fan tutte, opera, 189
Die Entführung aus dem Serail, opera, 131, 144
Die Zauberflöte (Magic Flute), opera, 139, 148–49, 227–29
Don Giovanni, opera, 139, 141
Le nozze di Figaro, opera, 9, 74, 76–77, 80–81, 83–84, 88–91, 93, 98–99, 110
Zaïde, Singspiel, 131
Zerfliesset heut' geliebte Brüder, K. 483, 133
Müller, Georg, publisher, 148
multiculturalism, 233–35
Murphy, Amy, 48, 50
Murphy, Dulcie, 50
Musgrove, George, 44
Musical Comedy Company, 43, 50
musical bar, 131, 171, 208–9, 217
musical modernism/modernity, 203–4, 222, 226, 232
Mystic Manor, 69–70

N
Najita, Susan, 223
Naples, 9, 74–76, 77n13, 78, 99, 101, 108
    Banco di Napoli, 108
    San Carlo Theater, 109
    Teatro dei Fiorentini, 74, 92
    Teatro Nuovo, 76, 92
    Neapolitan *commedia per musica*, 79, 81–82, 109–10. *See also* Lenten opera
Napoleon, Bonaparte, 140
nationalism, 233
Netherlands, the, 124
Nettl, Paul, 116, 127
New Statesman, The, journal, 200
New York, 36, 49, 181, 183–84
    Broadway, 11, 36, 174, 177, 179, 183, 188–89, 191, 195
    Carnegie Hall, 183
    Juilliard School, 183
    Metropolitan Opera, 11, 174, 188–89
    New York Philharmonic Orchestra, 184
    West End, 36
New Zealand, 7–8, 12, 35–39, 41n14, 42, 44–50, 52–53, 65, 68, 222–24, 226–28, 230, 232–35, 237–38, 241, 243
    Chamber Music, 35
    National Youth Choir, 35
    Ōtautau, 44

SOUNZ (the Centre for New
    Zealand Music), 224
  South Island, 37
  Symphony Orchestra, 35, 230
  Tongariro National Park, 222
Newell, Clarance, 46
Ngata, Tina, 238
Nicolini, Ernesto, 139
  Carlo magno, opera, 139
  Quinto Fabio, opera, 139
North East Valley Band, 40
nostalgia, 9, 32, 59, 61–63, 67, 69–70
Nunns, Richard, 232, 241
NZ Truth, The, newspaper, 37

O
octatonic music, 216–17
octave, 209
Oedipus, mythical king, 125
Offenbach, Jacques, 60
  The Tales of Hoffmann, opera, 60
O'Hara, Kelli, 174, 178, 188–92
Oklahoma, 179, 189
Omai, 227
ombra style, 214–16, 218–19
opera, 7–10, 36, 49–53, 74–81, 84–88,
    90–92, 98–101, 103, 108–10, 136–41,
    144–46, 148–49, 174–75, 177, 181–84,
    189, 192–93, 195, 202, 212, 214n34,
    228–29, 239
  comic opera, 74, 76, 78–80, 90–92,
    99, 103, 108, 110, 139
  Lenten opera, 108. See also
    Neapolitan commedia per musica
  opera arrangements, 10, 136, 139
  opera buffa, 74, 77, 79, 98
  opera vis comica, 76–78, 99
operetta, 175, 179, 189, 201, 227
Opetaia Foa'I, singer, 68
Oram, Celeste, 12, 222
oratorio, 44, 48, 139, 146, 150
orchestra, 8, 10, 35, 37, 40–41, 51, 53, 75n6,
    131, 145, 176, 224, 230, 232, 238
Ordonez, Karl von, 113
Orient, 127, 132
Orpheus, mythical figure,
    228–29, 235, 241
Orphic theory, 226–27, 229–30
Otago, 36, 38–39, 41–44, 47–48, 51, 54
  Otago Daily Times, The, newspaper,
    38–39, 41, 43, 48, 51
  Otago Witness, The, newspaper, 38,
    42–43
  Jubilee Anniversary, 41

O'Toole, Lawrence, 175
overture, 41, 128, 146, 212, 227, 239

P
Pacific, 7, 59, 66, 70, 223, 227
Paderewski, Ignacy, 37, 46, 48
  Cracovienne, 48
Paer (Paër), Ferdinando, 139, 150
  Agnese, opera, 139
  Camilla, opera, 139
  Sargino, opera, 139
Paisiello, Giovanni, 76, 77n13, 79, 139–40
  Il credulo deluso, opera, 76
  La Molinara, opera, 139–40
Pākehā, 223–24, 228, 230–32, 237–38
Papua New Guinea, 7, 14–15, 17, 19–33
  Nukumanu, island, 22
  Nukutoa, island, 22
Paradis, Maria Theresia von, 137, 149
Paris, 57, 108, 137, 227
Parkinson, Sydney, 227
passage, 126, 131–32, 171, 174, 181–82, 215,
    222, 232
Pereira-Arnstein, Henriette von, 137, 141, 147
Pergolesi, Giovanni Battista, 110
  La serva padrona, intermezzo, 110
Pezzl, Johann, 142–43
Phädra, tragedy, 149
Phillips, Martin, 37
phonograph, 175
piano (pianissimo), 126, 212
pianist, 37, 46, 47–48, 51–52, 140, 145–46.
    See also fortepiano
pianto, 207–8
Piccinni, Niccolò, 9, 74–75, 78–79, 89, 91,
    99–101, 103, 105–6, 108–9
  Gelosia per gelosia, opera, 99
  Gionata, opera, 108
  La serva onorata, opera, 9, 74, 77–84,
    86, 88–90, 98, 108, 110
piccolo, 60
Pichler, Caroline, 116, 137
Piticchio, Francesco, 76
  I voti della nazione Napoletana,
    cantata, 76
Pixis, Johann Peter, 140
  Almazinde, opera, 140
plainchant, 218
Pollard, Tom, 49
Pollinger, Justin, 186n34
Polynesia, 63, 66, 68
  Ra'iatea, island, 227
Polynesian Cultural Center
    (PCC), 64–85

Posongat, Nūnua, 24–25, 27
Prague, 113, 133–34, 227
Priestley, John Boynton, 200–1
prima buffa, 79–80, 82
primo buffo, 79, 81–82, 90, 98
primo buffo Toscano, 81, 90
primo mezzo carattere, 81, 92–93, 98
primo uomo, 100
Prokofiev, Sergei, 204
Promises, Promises, musical, 176
Prouse, John, 46
Puccini, Giacomo, 36
Pucitta, Vincenzo, 140
Punch, The, magazine, 201

Q
quartet (quartetto), 51, 79, 81–83, 147
quatrain, 89, 100, 106
quintet (quintetto), 79, 82, 84, 139, 149
Queree, Mrs. Ernest, 52

R
Ratner, Leonard G., 202, 204–5, 210, 211n28, 214–15
recitation, 138, 149
recitative, 79, 82, 85–86, 91, 93, 100, 109, 131, 149, 216–19
recorder, 169–71
    baroque altos in g' and f', 169–71
refrain, 127
Regensburg, 113
register, 52, 91, 93, 174, 187, 192, 209, 211–12, 215, 218
    lower, 215
    upper, 91, 93, 174
Reichardt, Johann Friedrich, 145, 147–48
repertoire, 7, 11, 18, 26–27, 46, 51, 106, 139, 149–50, 175, 178, 181, 183, 188, 204
Reynolds, Joshua, 227
rhythmic cell, 210, 212, 218
Rickard's Vaudeville Company, 51
Riedl, publishing house, 147
ritornello, 106
Robinson, Dylan, 226, 230, 233–37, 239, 241–42
Robson, Clara, 51
Rode, Pierre, 140
Romantic, style, 46, 175
Romberg, Andreas, 140
    'Die Macht des Gesanges', 140
Rosand, Ellen, 206
Rossini, Gioachino, 139, 150, 212
    L'Italiana in Algeri, opera, 139
    William Tell, opera, 212
    Semiramide, opera, 139
    Sigismondo, opera, 139
    Zelmira, opera, 139
Royal, Te Ahukaramū Charles, 224, 236
Royle, Bert, 42
Rubenstein, Arthur, 46
Rudetsky, Seth, 188
Rumford, Kennerly, 49–50
Russian music, 46, 216, 218
rhythm, 60, 125, 207–8, 210–14, 218–19, 227

S
Saaling, Marianne, 142
Said, Edward, 225, 239
Saint-Saëns, Charles-Camille, 47
Sala, Anna, 80
Salonmusik, 138
salon, 10, 116, 137–51, 227
Salzburg, 223
Sámi culture, 67
Samoan culture, 65, 68
Sarasate, Pablo de, 47
Sardelli, Federico Maria, 169
Saunders, Charles, 51
scale, 133–34, 139, 216–17, 219
Scarlet Troubadours, band, 51
scene buffe, 77
Schatz, Thomas, 56n1
Schereck, Max, 51
Schittlersberg, Augustin Veith Edler von, 133
Schlegel, August Wilhelm, 137
Schlegel, Dorothea, 142
Schlegel, Friedrich, 137, 142–44
Schmid, Julius, 154
Schoenberg, Arnold, 203
Schönfeld, Johann Ferdinand von, 146–47
Schröder, Sophie, 149
Schubart, Christian Daniel Friedrich, 130n39
Schubert, Franz, 139, 150–51, 154
    "Das Erlkönig," song, 139
    "Gretchen am Spinnrade," song, 139
Schumann, Robert, 48
    Carnival, song, 48
Schwandt, Erich, 214
Schwartz, Stephen, 178–79
    Wicked, musical, 178–79
Seddon, Richard, 39
serendipity effect, 157, 159–60
settler colonialism, 37, 39, 223–26, 230, 232–34, 237–39, 242
Shanghai, 57
Sherman, Bernard D., 156n1, 159–60, 161n16

Sherman, Richard M., 55, 60
Sherman, Robert B., 55, 60
Sherwin, Amy, 41–42
Shostakovich, Dmitri, 204, 218–19
    Cello Concerto No. 1, 219
Sini, Avo, 17, 25
Smith, Valance, 224
sob, 177, 180, 182–84, 186–87, 189–94, 208
sobbing, 77, 207
Society of Explorers and Adventurers (SEA), 69–70
Solly, Ruby, 236–37
solo, 41, 46, 60, 99, 103, 184, 205–6, 212
soloist, 46, 48, 52, 126–27, 179
Sondheim, Stephen, 183
    A Little Night Music, musical, 183–85
Sonnenfels, Baron Joseph von, 117–18
Sonnleithner, Joseph Ferdinand, 146
Sonnleithner, Leopold von, 138, 146, 151
Sonnleitner, Johann, 151n34
soprano, 11, 42, 45, 48, 50, 52, 80, 126–27, 139–40, 178–79, 182–83, 188–89, 194, 207
South Pacific, musical, 59
Southland, 44
speech, 60, 177, 182, 186–87, 189, 190, 192–94, 219
Speights & Co., 39
Sphinx, 125n34
Spiel, Hilde, 146
Spielmann, Franziska von, 147
Spike Jones (pseud), 61
Spohr, Louis, 139
    Faust, Singspiel, 139
Spontini, Gasparap, 139, 141, 150
    Die Vestalin (La Vestal), opera, 139, 141
Star, The, newspaper, 45
Stein, Anton, 118n23
Storks, Lydia, 64n20
St Petersburg, 77n13
Stravinsky, Igor, 204, 216
Streicher, Andreas, 147–48
Styx, mythical river, 228
Subotnik, Rose (née Rosengard), 229
suite, 11, 200, 205, 207–8, 210, 213–14, 216, 218–19
Sullivan, Arthur Seymour, 47, 202.
    See also Gilbert, William
sul ponticello playing, 215–16, 218
Sumac, Yma, 61
Sundberg, Johan, 178
Suva, capital of Fiji, 36
symbolism, 10, 124–30, 132, 218

syncopation, 69
Szigeti, Joseph, 52

T
Taane, Tiki, 230–31
Tahiti, 68
    Tahitian language, 68
    Tahitian eroticism, 59
Tahitian Terrace, restaurant, 8, 55, 58, 63
Tait, J. & N., entrepreneurs, 49
Takū, Atoll, 7, 14–33
Talleyrand-Périgord, Charles-Maurice de, Prince of Talleyrand, 137, 148
Tamarapa, Awhina, 224
Tapanui Times, The, newspaper, 50
Tarasti, Eero, 203
Tarchi, Angelo, 76
Taruskin, Richard, 157–60, 216–17
Tasman, 36, 42
Tasman, Abel, 21
Tausig, Karl, 47
Taylor, Diana, 230
Telotte, J. P., 57n5
Te Pou o Mangatāwhiri, group, 230
Te Punga Somerville, Alice, 228
Te Rangi Pai, Princess, 37
Te Reo Māori, language, 7A
Te Tiriti o Waitangi, 233
Te Vaka, group, 68
tenor, 44, 48, 51, 79, 81–82, 133, 139
Tesori, Jeanine, 181–82
    "The Girl in 14G", song, 181
theatricality, 140
Thomas, Allan, 232
Thomson, John Mansfield, 8, 37, 50
Thomson, Virgil, 201–2
Thorne, Rob, 224, 231, 233
Thun und Hohenstein, Maria Wilhelmine von, Countess, 227
Tikao, Ariana, 224
Tiki craze (Tiki fad), 8, 55–63, 65, 67–68
Tikiyaki Orchestra, band, 67
timbre, 77, 103, 171, 188, 212–13, 215
Titon, Jeff Tod, 14–15
Tokelauan language, 68
Tokyo, 57, 59, 63, 65, 69
tonality, 126, 128, 130–32, 203–4, 210
tone, 9, 50, 84, 91, 103, 119, 131–32, 170, 181, 184, 186–89, 216
Tony award, 178, 183, 189
Torricella, Christoph, publisher, 10, 123
tremolo, 215
Triad, The, magazine, 45n24, 50
triad, 208–9, 211–12

trio (terzetto), 79, 82–83, 139, 149
triple meter, 125, 127
tritone, 217
trope, 61, 68n28, 69–70, 91, 106
Troy, Charles E., 77
trumpet, 60, 101, 212, 228
Tuck, Eve, 226, 233–36, 238–39
Tūhea, Nūnua's wife, 25, 27
Tulsa, 179
tuki songs, 18–19, 27
tukumai ritual, 17–20, 25, 29
Turino, Thomas, 14, 16n12
Turkish culture, 70
Turner, John Hastings, 42
Turnovsky, Fred, 35–36
twang, 174, 177, 181, 188–90
type and style, 77, 205, 210–11

U
Uh Oa, goddess of disaster, 62
Ukraine, 227
unison, 18, 126
USA, the, 35, 46, 57–59, 61, 67, 191

V
Vancouver, 36
variation, 55, 69, 77, 89, 103, 140, 146, 177, 218
vaudeville, 45, 48–49, 51
Verdi, Giuseppe, 183
    Macbeth, opera, 183
vibrato (vibration), 180, 187–88, 192, 194
Vick, Brian, 141
Victoria, Queen of the UK, 39–40
Victoria Mary, Princess of Teck, Princess of Wales, 52
Vienna, 9–10, 75–76, 99, 113–18, 122, 131, 136–48, 203, 227
    Congress of Vienna, 136–37, 140, 146
    Gesellschaft der Musikfreunde, 146
    Hofburgtheater, 145–46
    Jews in Vienna, 137, 141, 143
    Musik Kapelle, 118n23
    Nationaltheater, 131
    Society for Private Musical Performances, 203
    Theater an der Wien, 139
    University of Vienna, 117
villanella, 77, 110
Vimeo Video, 17, 32
violin, 46–47, 52, 118n23, 140, 149
violinist, 46–47, 52, 140
virtuoso, 46, 92, 146
vivace, 93

Vivaldi, Antonio, 169–71
vocal quality, 176–79, 181, 186–92, 194–95
vocal safety, 180, 183, 188, 192, 194
vocal technique, 11, 105, 174–76, 178–79, 181, 184, 188–89, 191, 193, 195, 213

W
Wales, 35, 52
Walls, Peter, 164
Walt Disney Company, 8, 55, 56n1. *See also* Disneyland
Walt Disney Studios, 57
    Aladdin, film, 62
    Davy Crockett, film, 57
    Frozen 2, film, 67
    Haunted Mansion, film and attraction, 55, 59
    In Search of the Castaways, film, 67
    Johnny Tsunami, film, 67
    Laughing Place, website, 62n15
    Lion King, film, 62
    Lilo and Stitch, film, 8, 56, 63, 65, 67
    Man in Space, TV program, 57
    Moana, film, 8, 56, 66–68
    Our Friend the Atom, TV program, 57
    Pocahontas, film, 66
    Raya and the Last Dragon, film, 67
    Rip Girls, film, 67
    Snow White and the Seven Dwarfs, film, 57, 61
    Stitch, TV series, 63
    Swiss Family Robinson, film, 67
    True Life Adventures, film series, 57
Walt Disney World, 8, 57, 58n7, 59, 62–70
    Polynesian Revue, show, 58, 63
    Polynesian Village Resort, show, 8, 64
    Spirit of Aloha, show, 64–65
    Stitch Presents Aloha e Komo Mai, show, 63
    Tahitian Terrace, restaurant and show, 8, 55, 58, 63
    Tiki Room, show, 8, 55, 58–67
    Mystic's Tribal Arts Room, show, 69–70
    World Showcase, show, 66
Weber, Carl Maria von, 140
    "Lützows Jagd", chorus, 140
Weber, Constanze, 144
Weigl, Joseph, 76, 139, 141, 145, 149–50
    Die Schweizer Familie, opera, 149
    Flora e Minerva, cantata, 76
    L'Uniforme, opera, 139, 141
    The Orphanage, opera, 145
Weinmüller, Carl, singer, 149

Weißenthurn, Johanna Franul von, 149
Wellington, 42, 46, 49, 51, 53, 137
    Opera House, 42n18, 53
    Te Papa, museum, 38
    Theatre Royal, 49
Wenzel Anton, Prince of Kaunitz-Rietberg, 115
West's Pictures Co., 50
Whittall, Arnold, 205, 207–8, 218
Whyte, Walter, 48
Wild, Franz, 149
Williamson, James Cassius, 8, 36, 42–44, 47, 49–50, 53
Wilson, Charles, 203
Wise, Michael, 143
Woods, Joanna, 45n24, 50
Woolf, Virginia, 200–1, 204
World War II, 59
Wulff, Caecilie, 142

Y
Yang, K. Wayne, 226, 233–35, 238–39
Yoshinaga, Ida, 67n28
You're a Good Man, Charlie Brown, musical, 179
YouTube, 32, 63n, 64n20, 67n27, 174n, 179n27, 181n29, 183n32, 186n34, 188n36, 191n40, 225n9

Z
Zöhrer, Franz, 113

Printed in the USA
CPSIA information can be obtained
at www.ICGtesting.com
JSHW012021200524
63488JS00004B/150